# I'm glad
# I'm not young
# anymore

**Other books by the author:**

*God's Man; the Story of Pastor Niemoeller,* Ives-Washburn, New York, 1959

*When You're A Widow,* Concordia Publishing House, 1968 (Jove Publications, Inc., 1973, 1978; The Patrice Press, 1990)

*Never Underestimate the Little Woman,* Concordia Publishing House, St. Louis, 1969.

*Look Here, Lord,* Augsburg Publishing House, Minneapolis, 1972.

*Webster Groves,* City of Webster Groves, Mo., 1975.

*We Buy Junque, We Sell Antiques,* Hawthorn Publishing Co., St. Louis, 1979.

*Second Song,* Sunrise Publishing Co., St. Louis, 1980.

*The Happy Gardener,* The Patrice Press, St. Louis, 1985.

Cover design by John Ahearn, from a photo by Mack Giblin.

# I'm glad I'm not young anymore

## Clarissa Start

The Patrice Press
St. Louis, Mo.

# Copyright © 1990
# Clarissa Start

No part of this book may be reproduced, stored in a retrieval system, or transmitted in any form or by any means—electronic, mechanical, photocopying, recording, or otherwise—without the prior written consent of the publisher.

## Library of Congress
## Cataloging-in-Publication Data

Start, Clarissa.
     I'm Glad I'm Not Young Anymore /
Clarissa Start.
          p.     cm.
     ISBN 0-935284-80-X   :   $9.95
     1. Start, Clarissa.   2. Women journalists—
United
States—Biography.   3. Aging.     I. Title.
PN4872.S6      1990
     070.92—dc20
[B]                                        90-42802
                                              CIP


The Patrice Press
1701 South Eighth Street
St. Louis MO 63104

Printed in the United States of America

# *Dedication*

*I often gave my son advice on how to be successful and happy in two words: "Make friends." This book is dedicated:*

*To the many friends who have made my life so happy and satisfying and especially to my two best friends, the two men I married, Gary Davidson and Ray Lippert.*

# Contents

# *Prologue*

"**L**OOK, GRANDMA, we've got doughnuts for breakfast!"

My grandson was so excited. I hated to dampen his enthusiasm but I really don't care much for doughnuts. Tactfully, I tried to decline.

"But Grandma, they're really good."

"I know, Brian, but—well, you see, during World War II, I worked as a volunteer at a place called the USO. We served food to soldiers and sailors and marines as they came through St. Louis." You've been in Union Station. It's all shops and restaurants now, but during the war, it was a train station. Most of the military men traveled by train then because there wasn't much plane travel. St. Louis was a big junction so, when they changed trains, they'd come to our third-floor food counter and we'd serve hot-dogs and doughnuts and coffee. I served so many thousand doughnuts that I sort of lost my taste for them."

I thought this was a neat excuse coupled with a short

history lesson. But only one part impressed Brian.

"Grandma—you were *alive* during World War II?"

"Oh honey, I was alive during World War I. I don't remember anything about it because I was born the year the United States entered the war, 1917, and I was still a baby when it was over. But I was alive then."

"And that other war, too, Vietnam?"

"Yes, and Korea. I was alive during all four."

Brian went out to play. In a little while, he came running in, past where I was sitting and on to his room.

He was followed by a little friend who also ran by me but then came to a halt, spun around and leaned over, confronting me with a direct question: "Brian says you've been through four wars. Is that true?"

I told my son and daughter-in-law later that I felt like the last survivor of the regiment, hobbling along in the Civil War parades of my childhood. But I suppose that to the very young generation, those of us who've been "through four wars" seem ancient. Somehow it doesn't seem that long ago to me. I often think of my Aunt Olie, in her late eighties, saying plaintively, "I'm not old, it's just my body."

Even my body doesn't feel old. At times it seems to me that I have far fewer physical complaints than I had in my thirties. True, it's a challenge to "keep the moving parts moving," but, in many ways, there are fewer demands and many more opportunities to relax and have fun. Often I sit back and reflect that this is a great time of life. Even after those four wars!

I'm a part of that fast-growing portion of the population, those who are enjoying modern maturity, the golden years, seniority, or whatever you want to call it.

And I can truthfully say, I'm glad I'm not young anymore.

# 1

## I'm Really Glad

MAURICE CHEVALIER SANG IT in the film, *Gigi*—"I'm Glad I'm Not Young Anymore." In this song, he rationalized that he was much more content now that he was beyond the age of agonizing over romance.

As a happily married, second-time-around wife and a once-upon-a-time widow, I can't say I'm past the age of romantic interest, but I do know I'm glad I'm not young anymore. "Young" meaning a child, a teenager, a young married or a middle-aged person.

I'm glad I'm not young in two ways. Not young right now, facing the economic uncertainties of too much and too little, the inflated scale of today's economics, the threat of nuclear war, the horror of horrible disease that comes on suddenly. In brief, I'm glad I'm not facing future shock.

But I don't want to go back to those much touted "good old days" either. Would I want to go back to being young when I was young, during the 1920s,

1930s? No, no, no, no, no way!

Occasionally, I ask myself if there's a year in my life I'd like to live over. Or a month. Even a week, a day. I don't think so. Oh, there are moments, magical, marvelous moments. The moment when they placed my baby boy in my arms. The wild, hectic night when his father, my first husband, won his first election, as an underdog by the narrowest of margins. There were a few highs in my personal career. A few romantic interludes. Some fun times. The first trip to Europe, the first ride up the Zugspitz, the bus trip around Amalfi.

But those are brief moments.

I wouldn't want to go through climbing up a downhill, trying to find out how to change buses on the way to Amalfi. Or experience the thud of reality following the cloud nine of romance. Or even the 5 A.M. feedings when we took that bundle of joy home from the hospital.

I agree with the comedian who used to say, "You only live once but if you play it right, once is enough."

I've had a wonderful life and some experiences that were simply fantastic. But I don't want to have them again. Even trying to experience the same meal at the same restaurant is usually a flop.

One of the best things about being old is simply not being young. Admittedly growing old isn't enjoyable for everyone. "Old age ain't for sissies," has been said and rightly so. But it's enjoyable for many people and it could be for a great many more with just a few changes in lifestyle.

I feel evangelistic about preaching enjoyment of the last years of our lives. They really are, in a sense, the golden years. There may be limitations but there are great freedoms. Topping the list is the freedom of choice of how you spend those days.

Many years ago, the *St. Louis Post-Dispatch* printed an interview with an Illinois judge, Charles Seidel of Geneva, Ill. It read in part:

> Years ago, I said to myself, "Charles, how can you get the most out of life?"
>
> By the way, I talk to myself a lot; that way I get intelligent questions and fine answers. In any case, I can truthfully say I did pretty well follow the answer I gave.
>
> It was this: "Charles," I said, "work like hell until you're fifty. From fifty to sixty, be more choosy about what kind of law you want to practice. If you live past sixty, do whatever damn well suits you."

A companion remark from the other gender came from my friend, Dorothy Brainerd. When she retired as food editor of the *Post-Dispatch,* a friend who'd retired earlier said to her: "Dottie, some day you'll find yourself sitting in a rocking chair, doing absolutely nothing, and you'll suddenly feel guilty about it. Don't feel guilty. Just say to yourself, 'I have a right to sit here and do nothing. I darn well earned it.' ''

That's the great thing about being retired, from the male or female perspective. You can ''do what you damn well choose'' because ''you darn well earned it.''

It may be such a simple things as sleeping late in the morning. That doesn't happen to be my thing. I still wake up at 6, 6:30, sometimes as early as 5:30 in spring when dawn replaces dark and we haven't confused things with Daylight Savings Time. So sacking in isn't a great treat for me. But sitting at the breakfast table, reading the paper, without the job-slave pressure of, ''Gotta get going. No time to waste.'' That I enjoy. In my early days of retirement, I relished turning on the radio and listening to the traffic-copter tell how snarled up things were at some intersection.

''Tough,'' I'd say, reaching for another cup of coffee.

It took me a while to get used to this new-found freedom. For the first year or two, I found myself thinking, ''If I take two weeks now in February, I'll still have three weeks in the fall . . .'' and suddenly I'd realize, ''Heck, I'm on a permanent vacation.''

I didn't stay that way. I went into another business, got involved in operating an antique shop, in doing antique shows, in house sales which sometimes involve leaving home at six o'clock in the morning. But I choose to do it. No one makes me do it. And that's the difference.

Perhaps that's the real clue to why I relish old age. It wasn't until I was up in years that I was in control of my own life. Before then, someone else was always in control—parents, bosses, husbands, children, the familiar "circumstances beyond our control."

I'm well aware that this happy state of affairs could change at any minute and with shocking suddenness. Accidents, illness, just the aging process itself can make us totally dependent on others. No situation remains static.

But, at the moment, there is a large number of active and involved seniors who are independent. More than seven million of us belong to the American Association for Retired People. Because of the sheer numbers, many stereotypes are giving way. It's no longer headline news when someone our age runs a marathon, dances, skis, pilots a plane, or gets married.

Despite our numerical force, there is still an unbalanced emphasis on youth in our advertising, our television shows, and our fashions. Age is not revered in America as it is in the Orient.

But it is beginning to be recognized. More and more television shows have characters beyond the teenie bopper stage. There are ads for false teeth users. And a few fashions for those of us who can't wear swim suits slit to the armpits. The pendulum, if not swinging, is at least trembling a little.

True, retirement is still dreaded by some for diverse reasons.

''She wants to work forever,'' one woman said of another in her office. ''You can't blame her. She dreads being at home with her boring husband who won't do anything all day.''

But that's a different situation. Retirement isn't the problem; the husband is. Like the situation involving an unmanageable teenager, it should have been dealt with long ago.

Happy retirement is easiest if you plan for it in advance. The time to think about what you want to be when you're old is when you're young. You'll be the same person, only more so. If you're active, interested in people, in life, eagerly seeking new experiences when you're young, you'll continue to be that way when you're old. If you're self-centered, complaining, devoid of interests when young, you'll be a crashing bore when you're old.

I retired when I was fifty-five years old but I'd been thinking about it since I was thirty-eight. At that point I worked at my newspaper job seventeen years and planned to go seventeen more.

Retiring after thirty-four years of a stimulating, interesting job was quite a change. I'd been a feature writer for an important, influential metropolitan daily, the *St. Louis Post-Dispatch*. I'd interviewed most of the big stars of stage, screen, television, top political figures, people in the headlines. I'd been to coffees, teas, and a luncheon at the White House. I had covered Julie Nixon's wedding to David Eisenhower. Often I was treated like the royalty I covered, favorable publicity being so prized.

In addition, for the last part of my career, I'd written a personal column, and it was fun to air my pet peeves, champion my pet causes. My picture appeared with the column and I was a minor celebrity, often recognized.

Even my son was impressed when he was very young. "Mom, is your face a household word?" he once asked.

Believe it, it was heady stuff. And a good way to make a living. Many of my co-workers assured me I'd hate retirement. "You're too young to retire and do nothing," they said.

But I didn't intend to retire and do nothing. I retired to do something, something else. I wasn't sure what I would be. When asked, I would say glibly that I hoped to go to ladies' luncheons, on house tours and watch *As the World Turns* daily. But in my heart, I knew this would never satisfy me.

While I gave up regular newspaper writing, I agreed to do a weekly column on one of my special interests, gardening. I thought I might write a book or two and I have, six of them. One is on antiques, one on gardening and one on second marriage, a state into which I plunged the year I retired.

Undoubtedly I'm not a typical retiree, although many my age are in the antiques business I pursue and many other elders have started new careers and businesses including an old duffer named Colonel Sanders, who went into the chicken-frying business.

I don't think work is essential to happiness but I do think:

- We can avoid being jobless and bored.
- We can't avoid the steady advance of the years.
- Busy or idle, we will get older.
- But we don't have to hate it. We can love it.
- We can be glad we're not young any more.
- Look back, yes. And look forward.

# 2

## Life on the Farm

OFTEN I HEAR people talk about their "happy, carefree, idyllic childhood." They refer to it as the time when they were young "and didn't have a thing to worry about."

I sometimes wonder if they're suffering a memory lapse. We admit, honestly, that old age isn't a happy period for everyone. But not every childhood was carefree.

Part of the reason I enjoy being old is that being young wasn't all that great.

I lived in thirty-two dwellings—houses, apartments, furnished rooms, hall closets—before I was twenty-one years old. That may indicate the lack of stability in my early life.

Sometimes I gloss it over by saying, "My father was a civil engineer and we traveled a lot."

Actually, my father was often an unemployed civil engineer who tried farming, photography, hotel clerking, and intensive and expensive research on a system to beat the odds at the race tracks and bookie parlors. Pastures always looked greener elsewhere. There was a saying in my youth, "It's cheaper to move than pay rent." For us, it often was.

He was a good father in many ways, although it took me until late adulthood to realize it. It was about the time that he became a grandfather, and a superb grandfather, that I began to appreciate my father's own attitude of optimism and faith in the future and an eternal interest in things new that made him akin to all children.

In my younger days, I saw only his inconsistencies, his unreliability, and his bad tempers. In contrast, my mother seemed perfect in every way. Sometimes I meet women who were not compatible with their mothers and I feel sorry for them. A loving mother-daughter relationship is the greatest headstart a woman can have.

My parents were an odd couple, different in temperament and tastes. Only their backgrounds were similar.

They grew up in the same neighborhood in South St. Louis, an area now inner city but regaining respectability because of the re-gentrification of fashionable Lafayette Square home renovations.

They experienced the same city living, public school educations, the great cyclone of 1896, the Louisiana Purchase Exposition (St. Louis World's Fair) of 1904,

*Uncle Len, Ada Huebel (my mother), George Start (my father), Aunt Lil, and friend.*

and band concerts in Lafayette Park where their pick-up acquaintance began.

My father was named George Start after his father and a number of generations of George Starts including the one who came from Start Point, England, in pre-Revolutionary times. His mother, Ellen Theresa Dwyer, was of Irish-Catholic background. There were six children, five of whom survived, four boys and one girl.

My mother, Ada Huebel, was also one of six children, five girls and one boy. Her parents, Adolph and Mary Huebel were children of German Lutheran immigrants who came to this country in the 1840s and settled near Cape Girardeau, Missouri.

Grandpa Huebel was supposed to learn farming from an uncle but, as he told the story, he plowed one furrow, left the plow standing in the field, and took the next train to St. Louis where he got a job clerking in a grocery store and eventually saved enough money to buy his own store and send for his sweetheart, Mary Friederich.

There are lots of myths about the older generations, ours and the ones preceding us. One is that all women were confined to the home and led sheltered lives. On the contrary, both of my grandmothers were working women. Grandma Huebel worked alongside her husband in the grocery, which added a saloon and a livery stable to its operations and furnished employment to numerous young relatives who came up from Cape. A black nursemaid, "Aunt Charles," cared for the children.

Grandma Start was that rarity for nineteenth-century females, a high school graduate and a bookkeeper. While walking to work, she crossed a railroad viaduct, responded to the whistle of a young engineer, and started a beautiful friendship.

When my parents met through the same informal manner, my father was a college student at Washington University. At his mother's suggestion, he was studying engineering although he preferred gardening and caring for injured birds.

Mother's education ended with eighth grade and she was working as a telegraph operator; later she became a power machine operator in a shirt factory. However, eighth grade education in St. Louis schools in those days included Latin and algebra and, like

*My father as a college student.*

*My mother in 1911 at age twenty-six.*

others in her family, she had spent a year in German school, studying the language and religion and learning needlework. An eager student, she never stopped learning.

It was ironic that Mother, who longed for education, had hers curtailed while my father, an indifferent student, went to college. After they met, his grades in English improved. Mother was writing his papers for him.

Both sets of parents opposed the romance on religious grounds. After a heated argument one night,

*Father's home at 1116 S.
18th Street in St. Louis.*

Grandma Huebel announced she was sending mother to California to visit relatives. That night Grandma died in her sleep.

On January 10, 1911, my parents took a train to Carlyle, Illinois where they were married secretly by a justice of the peace, and returned to their respective homes.

Soon Grandpa Huebel married again but his young, fiery-tempered bride alienated his family. She hurled a pitcher at Florence, the thirteen-year-old baby of the family, cutting her head. Mother left, taking Aunt Floss with her.

She and my father ''set up housekeeping'' in sketchy fashion while he worked in Canada, Chicago, and

*"I lived in thirty-two dwellings . . . before I was twenty-one years old."*

*3708 California, where we lived in 1922.*

*My birthplace, 4268A Wyoming.*

*619 Dover Place, our home in 1927-28.*

*3310 Iowa, our home in 1923.*

*We lived at 2831 Miami in 1929-30.*

*116 Bates was our home in 1930-31.*

*In 1931-32 we lived at 4611 South Broadway.*

*We were living at 3608 Iowa in 1934.*

*Our home in 1933 was at 5200 Oleatha.*

*In 1935 we lived at 4919 Winona.*

*We lived at 4744 Alabama in 1936.*

*In 1937-38 we were at 5012 Virginia.*

finally as a highway engineer back in Missouri. I was born in 1917 in a two-family flat I've seen only from the outside. South St. Louis streets are named for states and my birthplace was on Wyoming. We moved to a flat on Wisconsin and subsequently lived on California, Virginia, Alabama, and twice on Iowa Avenue.

When I was two, my father persuaded my mother to try his dream of farming. That farmhouse is the first home I remember. A snapshot shows it as a shabby frame structure. Perhaps because of its simplicity, I remember the interior clearly. There were two rooms, a kitchen with wood cooking stove and potbellied heating stove, table and chairs, and a bedroom with a big bed, a little one, and a chicken incubator in the corner. I remember waking up to the cheep-cheep of chickens breaking through their shells.

*Of course I was a beautiful baby . . . Mama said so.*

*The farm—the first home I remember.*

There was a side porch, a barn for ducklings, a fenced yard for chickens and twenty acres, much of it woods, flooded often by the Meramec River. There was a cherry orchard and a truck garden which, by dint of great effort, almost made expenses.

My father worked on the highways and was home only on weekends. Mother did the farming and household chores but spent most of her time with me. It is an idyllic period in my memory.

On pretty days, it was easy to persuade her to leave her work, pack a picnic lunch and head into the woods to look for wildflowers or sit at the edge of the river. Thoreau would have envied the pristine, untouched scenery and the privacy.

My mother, always a private person, was never lonely, never afraid—or so she assured me in later years. She had her books, her child and soon she was sharing books with me.

She had studied the then-new Montessori method of teaching young children and apparently I responded. I still have a laboriously penciled note, a thank-you to my aunt after a visit, with Mama's proud footnote, "Written when she was only four years old."

On rainy days, I would sit by the potbellied stove with a newspaper and play a game of underlining words. "Find all the 'the's,' " Mama would say. Then the "and's," "who's," and "where's."

Soon I was reading, although I loved for her to read to me. A favorite family story told of my begging her to read to me and a cousin who was spending the night. When the story ended, my cousin was sound asleep and I was still listening, raptly, to a story I'd heard many times before.

Mother was pretty, with dark brown hair and blue eyes, slender, graceful, quick moving, clever with her hands.

"Your mother could do anything," Aunt Olie told me in later years, admiration tinged with envy. "You wanted a hat? She could make it. A chair needed upholstering? She could do it."

She was also patient, gentle, loving, full of laughter. I adored her, followed her like a shadow, emulated her. Even today I find myself absentmindedly singsonging a line from childhood, "Let me see, what comes next . . . Mama says that.''

My father was more remote but he, too, shared mother's interest in my education. By the time I was four, he was taking me on weekly trips to the children's room of the St. Louis Public Library downtown.

It seemed like a long way, although we were only twenty miles out. Papa had a 1918 Model T Ford but when he was away, we were marooned. We had no telephone. To go to St. Louis, we had to walk several miles to the train and wait alongside the tracks. In cold weather, workmen would have a bonfire to warm us. Our nearest neighbor was Mr. Wood-Smith who was building a house he called his castle on a imposing hill. It was never finished.

Life on the farm has a hazy continuity in my mind. The picnics in the woods, shelling lima beans on the porch, picking blackberries as snakes slithered under foot; Mama wasn't afraid so neither was I. Entertaining relatives who cluck-clucked over our isolation but enjoyed our produce. The excitement of a Christmas tree trimmed with popcorn balls and cranberry chains. Many years later, my mother told me my father had forgotten to bring home the store ornaments she'd requested.

In winter there was Thanksgiving at Grandma Start's and trips to see other relatives. But summer was just Mama and me, scrambled eggs and tomatoes for dinner with iced tea from a handpainted pitcher.

And always reading and writing, writing and reading, chatterbox conversation, love and security in the form of someone who thought her child was God's ultimate creation.

When I was five, Mama decided I should go to school—not the nearby Pointe School attended by farm children, but the prestigious St. Louis schools. Aunt Lil lived across the street from Froebel School so I was to live at her house.

Because Aunt Lil and Uncle Howard both worked, I would have lunch and dinner with Aunt Olie and Uncle John. School lunchrooms and latchkey children were unheard of then.

Mama took me to school, fibbed that I was six, not five, and when the principal said it was customary to spend a year in kindergarten, she said, "But she can read," and gave me the morning paper from his desk to prove it.

I read rapidly. Later, in unison classroom reading, I read so rapidly, and loudly, that I was promoted or, I suspect, gotten out of the way and put in a more advanced class.

Mother feared that because I'd led an isolated life with no playmates, I'd be timid and shy. When I came home from school, she and Aunt Olie quizzed me as to how things had gone.

"Fine," I said confidently. "The teacher told me to hang my sweater in the cloak room and another

*Little girl at a picnic in Carondelet Park (me, aged six).*

little girl tried to show me how. But I pushed her away and said I could hang up my own sweater."

"Oh you shouldn't have done that," Mother said. "That little girl won't like you."

"She likes me," I assured her. "She's my best friend. I have lots of friends."

Mother stopped worrying.

The pattern of that year is vivid in memory. Aunt Lil would wake up and sometimes Uncle Howard would sing the World War I song, "Oh how I hate to get up in the morning." Aunt Lil would give me breakfast, dress me, and brush my hair, pulling impatiently at the tangles.

I'd cross the street to school. At noon I walked the three blocks to Aunt Olie's for lunch. After school I'd go back there, sometimes stopping to visit a friend.

The attraction at the friend's house was a wind-up Victrola on which we played our favorite record, "Peggy O'Neill."

Back to Aunt Olie's for dinner, where Uncle John, a milk wagon driver, would be sitting in his rocker, smoking a pipe. Dinner was good substantial food, with lots of milk. After dinner, Uncle Len who was "like a big kid himself," his older sisters said, would play dominoes with me and walk me back to Aunt Lil's. I assumed this was the highlight of his day but later I learned he'd stop off at the saloon for some prohibition brew.

Friday afternoons I'd eagerly await the sign of Papa's Model T, and we'd go the library for the week's supply of books.

Occasionally we'd stop off to visit Grandpa and Grandma Start and sometimes I even was allowed to go see them by myself. Incredible as it seems now, a five-year-old could travel on a streetcar across town without fear.

We lived on the Bellefontaine line (Southsiders pronounced it Bella-fountain), which stopped within a block of Grandma's. I knew when to pull the cord to signal the stop. There was a grocery store on the corner where Grandpa would sometimes have me buy a loaf of bread, instructing me to get only the unwrapped loaf with the union sticker on the crust.

When I stayed overnight, Grandma and I would play in the bedroom called the Blue Room, making a playhouse of blankets.

I remember Grandpa Start as a little man with a big handlebar mustache. Grandma was a big woman and I was always being cautioned, "Don't eat too much; you'll get as fat as Grandma." Fat or not, she was loved by Grandpa who called her, with conscious irony, "Ducky."

Grandma was not a talented cook. Meals were long on wieners and coffeecake and occasionally when she came home late from a euchre card party, there was steak. My mother said snidely that when Grandma's stove got dirty, she bought a new one. I suppose in today's vocabulary, Grandma would be called a club-woman rather than a homemaker. But she was loving and proud of me. Mother told with amusement that Grandma, describing me to a friend, said, ''Of course she's smart; she's got a smart father.'' Then, with a quick look at mother, ''Her mother's smart, too.''

There was subtle animosity between the Irish Catholic and German Lutheran relatives. Asked my name, Grandma would say, ''She doesn't have a name, she's never been christened,'' unaware that I'd been christened in a Lutheran church.

Grandma didn't try to convert me openly but when I stayed on Saturday nights, she'd teasingly say, ''I'd take you to early Mass but you'd never be able to get up on time.'' ''Oh yes, Grandma,'' I'd rise to the bait. ''I can get up early.'' In the morning she'd bang up and down the halls and I'd leap up, crying, ''I'm awake,'' and we would go to Mass at St. Malachy's, where I learned all the ritual the church has now discarded.

All this forms the fabric of that year, 1922-23. Other memorable events include chicken pox at Christmas, measles in May. And my birthday party, a favorite family story for years.

It wasn't intended to be a party. Aunt Olie was in

"frail" health all of her life until she died at age eighty-eight. She couldn't have excitement, so I was told I could invite two little girls for ice cream and cake after school. I did so, but I must have been rather public about it, for others gathered round and asked to come and soon I'd invited the entire class.

At noon I broke the news to Aunt Olie who went into temporary shock but rallied to get in touch with Uncle John, who brought home more ice cream while she made more cakes.

It was a lively affair. One little boy locked himself in the bathroom and Uncle Len had to climb through the window to rescue him. Apparently the children enjoyed it. As I had told Mama, I had lots of friends.

Like Christopher Robin, now I was six, the age Froebel School had thought I was all along.

# 3

## *Touring, '20s Style*

ONE OF THE ADVANTAGES of being of my generation is that we can appreciate the improvements in everyday living which have come about in our lifetime. I'm not talking about television, computers, and microwaves, but about such mundane things as a heater in a car, air conditioning in a car, or, for that matter, just a car.

Much of my youth and early adulthood was spent at the mercy of what was laughingly termed "public service" transportation and many a day I huddled on rainy or icy corners, waiting, waiting. Consequently when I get in my own car, flip a switch for instant heating or cooling and travel on my own schedule, I feel great. When I jet to faraway places overnight, it is still with a sense of awe and wonder.

We traveled when I was very young, and we did have a car, the type known as a "Tin Lizzie." But travel was very different.

Our first junket began on a June day in 1923 when Papa left Mama off at Aunt Olie's house and went on in the Model T with our straw suitcases. We were to meet him on the Mississippi River levee, to board the *Tennessee Belle,* a river packetboat. With our car stowed away below, we would travel to Shiloh, Tennessee, and from there we'd drive to Miami. My father's love affair with Florida had just begun and this was our initial trip.

But first Mama and I would take the Bellefontaine streetcar—not to Grandpa Start's but to my mother's childhood home. I was to meet my Grandfather Huebel for the first and only time. My mother had not seen him since his second marriage had estranged them. Now he was ill and had sent word that he wanted to see her.

Mother, his oldest, had always been his favorite, the one who appreciated gourmet delicacies from the grocery, the one who stood up to him and consequently merited his respect.

He had been the victim of a robbery. At gunpoint, he was told to turn over the contents of the cash register. He had resisted and the men had choked him. He had developed throat cancer and knew he was not going to live long.

All I remember of the meeting was the store interior, a typical grocery with a long counter and curved glass cases. My grandfather was tall, thin, ashen gray and seemed frail. He let me reach into the candy case and select whatever I wanted.

When we left, Mama cried all the way downtown.

"So terribly thin," she explained to me as she wiped her eyes. "And he was such a big man."

I forgot the sadness in the excitement of boarding a riverboat. At dinner the first night, the black waiter asked if I wanted pie, ice cream, or watermelon for dessert.

"What if I want all three?" I asked mischievously. "Then you can have all three." Mama vetoed that idea but it made a big impression. Three kinds of dessert! And you could have all three!

Another vivid impression on that steamboat was of the first night charivari ("shivaree", it was pronounced) for a couple on their honeymoon. Our stateroom overlooked the ballroom and I peered down from my upper berth. Suddenly a woman spied me, and cried, "Look, we have an audience." In embarrassment, I jerked the curtain shut.

We docked at Cape Girardeau and climbed a cobblestone hill to see Mama's cousins. The rest of the trip I remember as a long series of days of sitting on deck, watching the scenery and the magnificent sight of widening rivers merging together.

At Shiloh we disembarked, got into our Model T and Papa took us on a tour of Civil War battlefields.

I'm sorry to say I remember them less than I do the desserts on the *Tennessee Belle.*

It is difficult for today's generation to imagine the primitive conditions of travel in the 1920s. Some models of cars were called "touring cars" and a trip like ours was called "touring." Our car had no window glass but was open to the elements; there were Isinglass curtains to attach when it rained. Ordinary travel was like backwoods camping today, although even our backwoods roads are better than highways then, which often dwindled into lanes.

Papa had bought Mama a pair of tan knickers. She protested they were not ladylike but after a few days of dusty roads and nights of sleeping on the ground, she wore them.

There were no motels, and hotels were only in larger towns. We looked for "touring homes," big frame houses with signs on verandas, discreetly soliciting "Guests." Often we slept in the out-of-doors, I in the car, my parents on a blanket on the ground.

One night we chose a churchyard next to a pasture. Mother recalled for many years, her sensation of waking up to find a cow looking down at her face.

There were few restaurants and we had little money so lunch was often a can of Campbell's pork and beans, purchased at a country store and shared, a spoonful at a time. The pork tidbit was for me.

We traveled through forested areas and often

stopped at lumber camps. Once we were invited to share lunch with the men, who were, I'm sure, sorry for this forlorn trio.

I remember one impressive incident. Because travelers were so few, they were friendly. Often drivers would stop, compare notes and road information and sometimes even traveled in caravan fashion from one town to the next.

We met one such couple traveling through Mississippi. My father had received word, perhaps at one of the lumber camps, that a forested area ahead was to be avoided because of recent heavy rains and impassable muddy roads. He planned to route us around it, although this meant detouring many miles out of the way.

"We'll chance it," the other man said, and his wife laughingly added, "Yes, we're mud turtles."

Some time later we met the "mud turtles" miles from there. They were driving a different car. They'd been forced to abandon theirs in the mud in the midst of the forest and walk to the next town, where, apparently, they were able and affluent enough to buy another car. It made a big impression on me in two ways: 1) Caution sometimes is the better part of valor, and 2) My father was sometimes right, a view not universally shared by either side of the family.

Northern Florida was fascinating. The hanging moss, the gnarled trees, and then the first sight of the

Atlantic Ocean. In those days, the highway skirted
the sea, in and out of little towns, into a grove of palm
trees or other wooded area for a while and then another
breathtaking glimpse of white-crested waves and sandy
beach.

Our destination was Miami Beach, but we ran out
of money before we reached there. We stopped in a
little town—I think it was called Alhambra—and took
a room in a private home. My father wired my grandfather for money, a regular occurrence on later trips.
But it was a Saturday afternoon and the wireless office would be closed on Sunday, so we would have to
wait until Monday morning for an answer.

I can remember sitting on a cot in the room while
my mother opened a box of cookies—were they Lor-
na Doones or fig newtons?—as she carefully explained
that I could have a cookie but I must eat it very slowly and not eat too many at a time as this was all we
would have to eat until Monday morning.

Money arrived and we went on to Miami Beach,
where my father had a job as supervising engineer on
a construction project and we rented a cottage near
the beach.

This was the summer my mother decided I should
acquire religion. Surprisingly, she intended raising me
in my father's Catholic faith, although it had been
many years since he was a churchgoer. She later told
me she thought when one married a Catholic, that was

the way it should be.

On Sunday mornings, she would dress me and send me to Mass with Papa. We would come home and I would show signs of sand in my clothes.

"It was too pretty a day to go to church," Papa would say, "so we went to the beach."

After a few of these tries, Mama reached a decision. There were no Lutheran churches nearby but when we returned to St. Louis, I would go to a Lutheran Sunday School.

We went back at the end of summer. Just why I don't know. Maybe Papa's job ran out, perhaps Mama didn't like Florida (although her opinion didn't carry much weight). More than likely, Florida hadn't lived up to Papa's expectations, although we would return in little over a year.

We drove up the East Coast. Papa's educational tour this time encompassed Washington, D.C. It's a bit puzzling to think that we took an extended trip home when we had little money. In fact, in Georgia or South Carolina, we wired grandpa again.

The return wire also included information for my mother that her father had died.

On we went, driving the Model T past the White House, and then westward. The journey was mountainous; that I remember. Roads had hairpin turns, spiraled upwards, and at many wide spots in the road there'd be cars pulled off to the side, steam shooting up from the radiators. Most of the cars were fancy big ones and Papa was proud as our Model T chugged past them.

Back in St. Louis, we had no place to go so we headed for Grandma and Grandpa's house. Papa's youngest brother summed it up pretty well with his greeting: "Well, I see you're back with your tail between your legs."

# 4

## The Florida Boom

WE STAYED PUT a little over a year, about par
for my restless father. Home was a three room second
floor flat in South St. Louis where the stern owner be-
lieved children "should be seen, not heard," and I
was not permitted to use the front steps; in South St.
Louis tradition, they were scrubbed snowy stony white
each week.

But it wasn't a bad year. I went to a new school,
Garfield, took dancing lessons and learned to toe-heel-
toe-kick to the tune of "The Doll Dance", and received my first big bisque-headed doll from Santa
Claus who came right up the steps to our living room.
Later Mama told me Santa was Uncle Howard. It
must have been an election year for I recall Papa telling a neighbor that "Calvin Coolidge doesn't have
a chance." His political judgment was on a par with

*The fourth grade at Homestead, Florida, 1924. I'm in the middle row, second from left.*

his judgment of horseflesh.

By October 1924 I'd made lots of friends again, had a part in a play at school, and was happily settled down when I came home from school one day to find Mama packing. We were going back to Florida.

This trip was more adventurous than the first. The Model T, the same one, kept breaking down. I recall it sputtering into Pensacola, noisily rattling and clanging as small boys ran alongside making unflattering remarks and I pretended not to see.

When we reached central Florida we encountered

a flood. A bridge at the little town of Fort Bassenger was washed out and we had to spend the night in a private home, along with many other tourists attracted to Florida's booming popularity.

The friendly folk at Fort Bassenger welcomed us warmly and charged us exorbitantly. We could afford to stay only one night, flood or no.

Bravely we drove into the flood the next morning, but when water reached the running board, the car stopped and there we sat, part of a long line of stalled cars. A system of tractors was in force to pull cars, several of them hitched together, but they had reached their capacity when they got to us. A man in one of the cars opened the door and called to my mother and me to get in. My father insisted we do so.

When we reached the next town, simply named Bassenger, we were told we could stay with the people who owned the general store until my father arrived. It was the next day when he was pulled across, having spent the night in the car, and I still remember him walking toward us, trousers rolled above his knees, his hand raised up wagging my favorite toy, a stuffed monkey.

We stayed at Bassenger a week, my father clerking in the store. Unlike the profiteers at Fort Bassenger, the kindly store owner refused to take any payment at all. I'd had my first taste of those basic Southern foods, hominy and grits.

We went on to Miami and thirty miles south to Homestead, Florida, where we rented a six-room frame house which we furnished meagerly. Several of the rooms remained empty the whole year we were there and it made a great place for games of hide and seek with the neighborhood children each night.

To reach the Homestead school, we walked through a stretch of woods skirting the railroad tracks in front of our house.

Most of the children went barefoot, but the pine needles were too stickly for me so I wore shoes. After school we'd play on the boxcars on the railroad siding, climbing over the couplings. It was most exciting when the train started up suddenly.

By this time I was in fourth grade. Mother had placed me there, feeling there was no point dawdling through school. The work was easy and when the teacher read a bit from Jack London or Albert Payson Terhune books, she'd let me take them home to read more.

I remember Valentine's Day in Homestead. Mother, still worried that I was the new kid in town, was afraid I wouldn't get my share of Valentines in the Valentine box so she sent an unsigned one. She needn't have bothered. I received one from every child in class and a few in other rooms. Again I'd made lots of friends. Possibly my strange Northern accent intrigued them.

That summer we moved to Larkin, the next town up the road. Mother obtained fifth grade books and we studied them, memorizing the Sidney Lanier poetry and skipping arithmetic with the result that I've never been able to do fractions. That fall mother enrolled me in sixth grade where I won the school-wide spelling bees.

Florida's boom was in full swing. Real estate was selling everywhere, some of it underwater. When we walked along Flagler street in downtown Miami, entrepreneurs took us by the elbows and guided us into their storefront offices to look at maps.

My parents bought real estate, unfortunately not the part that later sold for the Fontainebleu or even the northside motels, but farmland around Lake Okeechobee. They sold most of it years later without profit, but I still pay taxes on a lot in Highland county in the hope they might strike oil on it someday.

This was also the winter my father discovered another marvelous way to make money—Hialeah race track.

Grandma and Grandpa Start came to spend the winter with us and Grandpa wanted to see a horse race. That was the beginning of the end of financial security in our family. I never knew if my father won and was encouraged or lost and was challenged, but I do know that every spare dollar and many he couldn't spare were gambled for the next fifty years.

Florida was a happy place for a child. We were a long way from Miami Beach, Biscayne Bay, the ocean, and the burgeoning suburb of Coral Gables. Our house in Larkin was four rooms in a square box-shape, smelling of fresh cut lumber. Even the outhouse was new.

Insect life abounded in those pre-DDT days. Vivid in my memory is my mother screaming at flying roaches, and my father's device of a box, hanging from the ceiling by wires and screened in front to store our food.

Some food was expensive. Milk was a dollar a quart and eggs a dollar a dozen, but citrus fruit when ripe was given away at the packing houses. We children would take our wagons to the loading platform and come home with all the grapefruit and oranges we could tow.

The weather was warm and sunny for weeks on end. In September it would rain so hard the schools were closed. We left Florida the spring before one of the major hurricanes. My father had worked on the construction of two major hotels, the Biltmore in downtown Miami and the Roney Plaza on the beach. But early in 1926 the bubble burst. Florida had its depression early.

Again I had put down roots, made friends, and was heartbroken to leave, but my father promised me, as he had before, that he'd build me a playhouse at our next home.

We sold the aged Model T and returned home by train. I recall endless hours of gazing out the train windows at red clay hills in Georgia, which seemed bigger than Russia to me. We arrived in St. Louis on a cold March day. Dirty, slushy snow was on the streets.

Our new home was two furnished rooms, one a bedroom, the other a kitchen with a cot where I slept. Between the two rooms was the bath we shared with other roomers.

There was no room in the backyard for a playhouse.

# 5

## *The Innocent '30s*

"**I** ALWAYS DREAMED of having a little girl so I could dress her in ruffles and ribbons. And here I am, buying her a tomboy skirt."

My mother laughingly quoted the words of another shopper at the downtown Famous-Barr store where she'd gone to buy me a tomboy skirt. I was ten years old, the age at which you must wear what "everyone else" is wearing.

It was the John Held cartoon era of long-limbed, flat-chested, shingle-haired flappers and even little girls wore tight tubes for skirts.

It was 1927, a prosperous year for everyone, even for us. Papa had a job. Our furnished rooms were nothing special but they were in a nice neighborhood and I attended Woodward School, considered a model school in the St. Louis area at that time. Its principal,

Frank L. Eversull, later a nationally known educator, had introduced the "departmental system," whereby children in sixth, seventh, and eighth grade did as high school students did and went from room to room for specialized teaching from different teachers. It was a forerunner to middle school, as they call it now.

In English class we did such innovative things as writing our own plays, acting in them, making the scenery and props. And we made speeches. We did not have spelling bees, nor did we "parse" sentences as Mama had taught me to do.

My sketchy Florida education and the fact that I was too young for my grade level elicited frowns at Woodward. Little did they care that I could recite Sidney Lanier. I couldn't do fractions. I was demoted.

Mama was annoyed but undaunted. That summer she enrolled me in a private school to make up my half-grade. I promptly proved my immaturity by nervously wetting my pants the first day.

But by fall, I was in seventh grade, able to graduate on Mama's timetable and enter high school at age eleven. The newspaper printed a tiny item about my achievement.

The two years were otherwise enriching for me. There were piano lessons at Strassberger's Conservatory and dancing lessons at the Community Center, a big barn-like building on Grand Avenue where thousands of children flocked each Saturday for free

*Woodward School graduate, aged eleven. (I looked forty.)*

lessons. We also went privately and in groups to the Symphony, Art Museum, and Missouri Botanical Garden.

During the summer the public schools had an elaborate program on school playgrounds, from basket weaving to ballet. At the end of the summer, we dancers appeared in a show on the stage of the Municipal Opera in Forest Park.

We had recitals at dancing school, too, and I was selected to take special toe dancing lessons. I wasn't much of a ballerina, but learned to stuff lambswool in pink satin toe shoes and execute a shaky *tour jete* to "The Blue Danube."

I also made friends, many friends. One advantage to our frequent moves was that I never knew a stranger. My very best friend was Mary Felicia Eiermann and we shared giggles over boys and Sunday matinees at the nearby Virginia Theater. How I envied little Mary Dunphy who won all the amateur contests doing the Charleston to "Ain't She Sweet?"

I also became better acquainted with my St. Louis cousins. There was Aunt Esther and Uncle Ben's three: Bernadette, Joe, and Mary; Uncle Dwyer and Aunt Adele's boy, Hartwell; and on Papa's side, Uncle Charlie's baby girl, Jacqueline. Grandpa and Grandma Start lived with Uncle Ben and Aunt Esther by that time, having sold the big house downtown.

On Mama's side of the family, her baby sister

*George and Ada Start in 1929.*

Florence was married to Uncle Jule; their son was born a few months after Hartwell Start. Aunt Floss liked the name so I had two cousins named Hartwell. Aunt Hattie and Uncle Fred had three children: Grace, Florence, and Freddy. My bachelor uncle Len finally married pretty, dark-haired Aunt Marie, and they had a baby girl, Rosemary.

Mama's family all assembled each August at Aunt Florence and Uncle Jule's home in O'Fallon, Illinois, just across the river for a homecoming weekend, a noisy, marvelous affair for the children. It was there that we saw our first airplane.

Two years is a long time in a child's life. It seemed as if we'd always gone to homecoming, always lived on Dover Place, that Mary Felicia and Virginia and Ardella had always been friends.

But this came to a screeching halt on eighth-grade graduation when Papa announced we were moving back to Florida. I cried and pleaded and pouted but it didn't matter. Mama and I took the train to Miami to find a place to live until Papa could come down.

We moved into an apartment, by far the nicest place we'd ever had. It had a courtyard with a fishpond, where I sat and wrote poetry and wept.

But of course I made friends and soon I was in an auction bridge club. I remember the name of only one of the girls. It was a memorable name— Mary Wortley Montague Quisenberry.

But nothing took the place of my St. Louis ties and I begged and badgered poor Mama until she wrote Papa that we were coming back.

Somewhere in our family trunk is a telegram from Papa telling us to "stay until I arrive" and ending with the plaintive query, "Can't you do anything with Clarissa?"

Mama couldn't. We took the train back to St. Louis and Papa was furious. Uncle Dwyer, who had an automobile, took us house hunting. When we found a furnished flat on Miami Avenue, just within the district of Cleveland High School, which my Woodward School friends would be attending, I pointed out its virtues.

"It's not far from school and church," I expounded. "The rent is only $50 a month and we'd save money because we wouldn't have to buy furniture, and—"

Papa turned on me in a rage and shouted, "You don't have anything to say about it. You're just a little girl!"

I was very hurt. I was a rather big little girl, eleven years old, five feet two and ninety-eight pounds, and very mature. I retreated into my shell, but we rented the flat because it was right for us for all the reasons I'd outlined.

It was the fall of 1928 and good times still held forth. Papa worked for a brick contractor, bringing home long rolls of blueprints and working on estimates into the night so he could free his days to pursue his hobby of betting on horses.

We saved no money but there was enough for necessities. The summer I was twelve, I got a job at a newly opened Neisner's Dollar Store on Cherokee Street. I put in my first application on a rainy Friday afternoon. I was wearing old clothes and a raincoat. Asked my age, I said I was sixteen.

"Sorry, we're only taking seventeen year olds," the manager said.

On Monday afternoon, the sun was shining. I dressed in my best clothes, did my hair differently, wore a hat, and applied again. Asked my age, I smilingly said, "Seventeen." The manager looked a bit suspicious but I was hired.

I worked each Saturday, from 1 P.M. to 9 P.M. with a half-hour off for dinner. When I exited via the alley I was given a crisp one dollar bill in an envelope. Since I was not too good at my job, wrapping pots and pans, it was about what I was worth.

In high school I made a new "best friend," Ruperta Woodcock, Pert for short. Soon we had formed a group, Pert, Mary Felicia, and I and two other girls, Dorothy Diederichsen and Viola Kuhnhenn. We were sports enthusiasts and loyally attended all the games, not just football, which everyone supported, but also basketball, baseball, and even track meets. The attraction was obvious. It was the place to meet boys.

My diary is filled with references to them—boys from Cleveland, boys from Roosevelt, Soldan, Beaumont, Central. We met most of them at basketball play-offs at the Washington University field house, which we reached via a rickety-rackety streetcar filled with screaming teenagers. Double-deck buses were popular transportation then, too.

I thought there were five city high schools at that time. Our school song began with the verse, "Oh this town has five great high schools. . . ." Years later, a black friend in Webster Groves corrected me gently when I quoted this song. The town had seven high schools, including Sumner and Vashon, which were for blacks. We simply didn't know they existed.

As in Florida, we had no feelings against blacks that I can recall. They lived in another part of town and were invisible to us.

St. Louis was not an urban center, just a friendly old-fashioned city. We teenagers went to the big movie houses downtown and on Grand Avenue in midtown.

We roamed the department stores, trying on hats and squirting each other with the perfume atomizers on cosmetics counters.

Our favorite movies were drawing-room comedies with Norma Shearer and Robert Montgomery, or comedies with Bert Wheeler and Robert Woolsey. Radio was everyone's home entertainment and we stayed up late to listen to Rudy Vallee, the "crooner." We succumbed to radio fever in 1929 so we no longer had to go to Uncle Dwyer's to hear "Amos and Andy" or the Cardinals and Browns baseball games.

Church was a part of our life, too. Mother and I had joined Holy Cross Lutheran Church, which was within walking distance of our flat, and mother enrolled me in special confirmation classes for students who did not attend the parochial school. Our teacher was Pastor Paul Koenig, who, perhaps because he was prematurely bald, seemed very old to me. He lived to attend the fiftieth reunion of our class.

In our third year of high school, Pert's parents moved to the West End and she transferred to Soldan High, a blow to us. But we kept up our friendship via telephone and letters. "I am sitting in study hall thinking about last Saturday's game," a typical letter began. "Do you think we'll ever see them again?"

Fraternities and sororities were not encouraged but were condoned. We formed one of our own, Pi Rho Sigma. Some of the girls we didn't invite to join cattily pointed out the similarity of the name to Py-Ro-Sana, a popular toothpaste.

Pert's new school was in a largely Jewish neighborhood, so we invited one of her new friends, Sylvia Edelstein, to join our sorority, proving, I suppose, that we had no prejudices. Actually prejudice simply never occurred to us.

My parents and I moved that year to an apartment at 1116 Bates Street, an address numerically identical to my grandparents' house at 1116 South Eighteenth. Ours was in a new building, "very snazzy," I wrote in my diary. It was above stores, but they were nice shops like the beauty shop where I had my frizzy croquignole permanent set each week.

The apartment itself was a marvel of efficiency. It consisted of one room, a living room, with tables and benches which folded down from the wall. The bed folded down from a closet. The kitchen was a closet. It was called a Pullman kitchen and had a built-in stove, undercounter refrigerator, and overhead cabinet space.

The living room was furnished with a brown satin studio couch on which I slept, one chair, and, our pride and joy, a new radio, the Majestic "Mighty Monarch of the Air."

Aside from our intramural acquaintances, we had no dates at our age. Occasionally a boy brought me home from a school dance or Walther League at church, but he had to leave me at the door because my parents were asleep in the living room.

My father was thinking of college for me. He sent away for catalogs—from Tufts College, which Start family members had attended, Northwestern, and Columbia. I had shown a small writing talent and had had pieces published in the interschool newspaper, so he thought I might study journalism. I didn't care as long as I could be Betty Coed and go to football games like those in the Joe E. Brown movies.

Schoolwork? Oh yes, there was that. We were graded EGMPF. I received E's in English, Latin, and French; G or M in those other things—math, history, science. In physics class, my girl partner and I looked at each other in dismay when we were assigned to hook up a doorbell. Finally a boy did it for us. (The last time I moved, my husband connected the doorbell.)

It never occurred to me that I could work harder and do better in difficult subjects. I was not good at athletic games so I didn't go out for them. I was good in dancing so I joined "Pipes O'Pan," the dance club. There were many other activities after school and at an early age, I was a joiner. There were no school buses then. We all walked home whenever our school activities were over. Sometimes we took buses or streetcars to skating rinks or swimming pools in other parts of town.

Such was the innocent pattern of high school life

in the early 1930s. The living was easy but it was about to change.

We were to start down a long dark corridor, a tunnel which seemingly had no light at the end. We were about to enter the Great Depression and we would not emerge for ten years.

# 6

## *Bachelor Girls*

THE HISTORY BOOKS date the Great Depression as beginning with the stock market crash of October 1929. Those of my generation, not quite teenagers at the time, weren't aware that there was a stock market crash. The depression didn't begin immediately. It wasn't until President Herbert Hoover cautiously stated that "we appear to be in a depression." By then, we were.

We found out gradually and individually. We found out when firms announced full-scale layoffs of employees, or salary cuts. For each of us, it began when the pinch squeezed our own family. In our case, it was the summer of 1931.

My father was still working as an estimator for a brick contractor. When building slowed down, there were no blueprints, no need for bricks, no need for a brick estimator.

At the end of the school year, my parents went to Chicago, ostensibly so my father could follow a job lead, but actually so he could try his luck at Arlington Park Race Track.

Pert's mother, in my eyes a glamorous creature, was a divorcee in her early thirties. She had been seventeen when Pert was born. Now married again, she took a month-long honeymoon with her twenty-nine-year-old bridegroom. Our parents consented to the two of us, Pert and me, staying in their apartment.

My parents, I'm sure, were under the impression that I was staying with Pert's mother. She, in turn, was under the impression that her new husband's parents, who had recently moved up from the South, were staying with us.

But they had another child, a daughter, and stayed with her instead, looking in on us only occasionally. They apparently were under the same impression as the mother of Tess of the D'Urbervilles (which I'd read)—''anything that happened would be God's will.''

Actually nothing untoward happened as our conduct was beyond reproach—amazingly so, considering our giddiness.

We didn't smoke—only ''fast'' girls did that in high school—and while we giggled a lot about ''taking a snifter'' and ''going on a bender,'' (alcohol being an

*Best of friends—Pert Woodcock, Mary Felicia Eiermann, and me in 1931.*

amusing joke then), the closest we'd come to liquor in those prohibition days was a glass of Christmas wine for Pert and a strangling swallow of that South St. Louis brew called Heimgemacht for me.

We really craved to taste pink champagne but none was offered us. As for the third evil, sex, it never reared its head further than the concrete steps in front of the building where we sometimes entertained callers.

This may have been because we lived three flights up. The apartment was an impressive building with one of those fanciful names of the thirties like Le Chateau or El Mirador—names which went with the craftex walls and wrought iron lighting fixtures.

Ours was the last cubbyhole on the third floor and as we puffed up the stairs, we often sang a popular tune, "Love for Sale", which went, "If you want to buy our wares, follow us and climb the stairs." Fortunately this innocently given invitation never reached receptive ears.

Like all "bachelor girls" (our name for ourselves)

our life was built around culture: theater and the Municipal Opera in nearby Forest Park; eating places, such as the ice cream parlor on Delmar and the watermelon stand on DeBaliviere; home entertaining, the aforementioned front steps; sports, such as swimming at Forest Park Highlands amusement park; and a minimum of education—Pert had flunked typing and was attending summer school.

Our housekeeping was sketchy. Pert's mother was appalled to find the kitchen floor had not been washed in her absence. We used the folding davenport rather than the "in-a-dor" bed because it was simpler to stuff the bedding in it. Occasionally we changed sheets.

The endless hours between duty and pleasure were given over to polishing our fatal beauty and discussing "men" (really boys), always to the accompaniment of appropriate mood music on the radio. Pert was a Bing Crosby fan while I was a Russ Columbo devotee. There was something in the way Columbo crooned, "You call it madness—ah, but I call it love," and Bing pleaded for, "Just one more chance", that caused us to shriek like the latter-day Beatles fans.

Discussion of boys was lively because there were quite a few of them in our lives, or to be strictly accurate, there were quite a few in Pert's life and they spilled over into mine.

We had had our first dates a year before. My father strictly forbade me to go out with boys, so I had "sneaked out" by spending the night at Pert's house; her mother and mine, too, indulgently went along with the conspiracy. The dates were with Emory and Marvin. Emory was a good looking boy (Pert's naturally), and Marvin was short, plump, inarticulate, and in addition had trouble pronouncing my name. Pert, choking with laughter, insisted he called me "Crassa."

We both disliked our names and were forever searching for nicknames. "Don't call me Curly any more," Pert urged in one of our interschool letters. "What do you think of Sally or Ginger?"

I preferred "Kit" for myself or even Kitty, and for a while we passed ourselves off as Bobbie (Pert) and Billie (me), even to embroidering the names on our swimsuits.

Eventually we tired of Marvin and Emory and tried to brush them off when we met at the watermelon stand, with what Pert termed "carefully chosen words of poison." By this time we were more interested in Arnold and Dick, whom we'd met at the Highlands pool. Arnold was Pert's beau, a handsome blond boy, and Dick was his friend, not good looking but "loads of fun."

Then there were Burleigh and Bud. Burleigh was the good looking boy who lived next door and Bud was his friend, a shy inarticulate one. I yearned for Burleigh who yearned for Pert.

At fourteen, I had already resigned myself without

bitterness to the fact that the leading romantic role was not for me. I was always to get the shy boy or the one who was "loads of fun." I even suspected that blind dates described me as "not much to look at but loads of fun."

As the summer went on, the popular open-air Municipal Opera in Forest Park became the hub of our social life. We attended every night, knew every line and song of the principals: Guy Robertson, the handsome lead; Leonard Ceeley, the dashing villain; and Jack Sheehan, the comedian.

One night, right in the middle of "Nina Rosa", a blond boy in an usher's uniform approached Pert and asked if we'd like to come down to the fifty cent section where there were some unsold seats. We moved down quickly. It was only the first step.

From the fifty cent seats, Pert worked us into the $1.00, then the $1.50 and finally, near the end of the season, to the box seats.

In the box seats, I, too, acquired an usher. Pert's was a handsome boy named Jack, mine a shy inarticulate one, Bob. They attended McBride High School, and amid giggles, we learned that they knew two of our other friends, another good looking Jack and his friend, Eddie, who was "loads of fun." We had met them in a more cultural way at a display of French prints at the Art Museum one Sunday.

Our parents might have frowned on these unorthodox meetings but to us they were perfectly normal. Pert always said that every boy she'd met through an introduction turned out to be a flop.

But all these real conquests were nothing compared to our "dream men." These were the results of the afternoons we didn't go swimming but sat in the apartment talking about Life. We decided a man's name was very important as you would be changing yours to it and to that purpose, we perused the telephone books picking out favorite names.

We picked only the better addresses—Washington Terrace, Portland Place—and when we found a likely name, we'd make up a likely young man. Pert's favorite was Martin Carroll; mine was Roger Trevor. We never walked by the homes of the Carrolls and the Trevors; courting disillusionment was not part of our plan. But we dreamed, discussed, and named our first three children.

As part of our plan for the future, we also made a sacrifice on the altar of beauty and went on the Hollywood eighteen-day diet. I was overweight, a bulging 128 which I longed to reduce to 118. Pert weighed only ninety-eight, but felt she'd be shapelier at ninety-two.

Together we embarked on the regime of "lamb chop, three radishes, two olives, half a grapefruit, and black coffee."

We followed it to the letter. If dinner required one

lamb chop and one strip of bacon, we purchased these quantities from the patient butcher at the local market. If salad required one-half a cucumber, we threw the other half away.

Each evening we tortured ourselves discussing our suppressed desires, for Pert a hot fudge sundae; for me, a strawberry ice cream soda. Before going to bed, when hunger assailed us, we'd get out a jar of peanut butter, half-full, look at it longingly, and heroically put it back on the shelf.

We stuck it out until the thirteenth day. By this time, Pert had reached her desired ninety-two and I was willing to settle for 123. In the twilight of a dull rainy evening, which meant no open-air opera, we listened to Bing Crosby, and I yearned routinely for a strawberry soda. Instead of sighing, Pert stood up.

''I'm going to get a hot fudge sundae,'' she said.

I was aghast. It had never occurred to me that, once committed, you could get off the diet. As the realization of freedom came over me, I leaped up, adjusted my fuzzy angora beret in the Norma Shearer angle and said, ''Let's go.''

At the ice cream parlor on Delmar, Pert had her sundae and I, my ice cream soda. Then we each bought a double-dip ice cream cone which we ate on the way home. Before bed, we got out the loaf of bread reserved for dry toast and cleaned out the jar of peanut butter. Then we sprawled on our unmade bed and dreamed of Martin Carroll and Roger Trevor.

This idyll of the bachelor girls ended when Pert's parents came home from California. Mine were still in Chicago.

For my father the attraction was Arlington Park Race Track but mother had another reason for going to Chicago. My Aunt Lil was dying of cancer in a small town just outside Chicago and Mother wanted to see her sister one more time.

They set a date for the visit but the night before, Mother had a vivid dream. In her dream, Uncle Len was pounding on our apartment door in St. Louis, calling Mother by name. When she answered the door (in her dream), he told her Lil had died.

"We must go to see her today," she told my father.

But before they could leave, a call reached them that Lil had died the night before. Later they learned that Uncle Len had been knocking on their apartment door that night!

They stayed on in Chicago and made arrangements for me to stay with Aunt Hattie and her family. I spent a week there and then stayed a week with my father's brother, Uncle Dwyer and Aunt Adele. I'm often amazed when I think of the casual way in which my parents allowed me to travel from place to place without fear or concern. But it was a much safer world then. It was assumed that all adults would be kind to all children.

When my parents returned, our happy reunion soon turned to sadness, when we did a frank financial appraisal. We could no longer afford to keep the ''snazzy'' apartment. Once again we would have to move. Papa shopped around and found a place.

Pert, Mary Felicia, and I had looked with pity on one of our friends who lived on South Broadway. There was nothing really wrong with South Broadway. There were even a few stately homes overlooking the Mississippi River. But much of the street was second-hand stores and shabby housing.

Father's new home for us was a duplex bungalow. Our address: 4611 South Broadway.

# 7

## California Summer

IF THE SUMMER OF 1931 was mostly fun, the winter of 1931-32 was mostly grim. The economic situation became worse. We had cut expenses by lowering our rent from the $52.50 of the apartment to $30 a month, but soon we realized that we couldn't even pay that.

How we subsisted I do not know. Perhaps my grandfather came to the rescue again, perhaps my father had occasional work or caught a winner at the bookie parlor. I recall my mother becoming hysterical on one occasion and how it distressed me.

Mostly I was humiliated over my own descent in the social scale. In addition, Pert's mother and step-father had liked California so much that they moved there and Pert was attending high school in Beverly Hills. We lamented our woes in six-page single-spaced typewritten letters exchanged once a week.

Not many years ago I attended a high school re-union with a classmate whom I'd known only slightly in school but had come to know better when we found ourselves near neighbors. I was surprised and a little envious to hear her reminisce with others of "the fun we had" at "all the parties." Her father had been a baker, theirs was a large family, and apparently her senior year had been a happy time.

I remember going to only one party in my senior year. It was a Halloween party and I remember it chiefly because I got lost, arrived late, made a funny story of my mishaps, and was amazed to find myself at the center of a group, listening and laughing. It was my first performance as a humorist and it was a heady sensation. But it was an isolated incident.

Gone were the days of matinees and shopping excursions. Occasionally my parents and I went to a movie at the neighborhood Virginia Theater, where the management gave away dishes, probably the depression ware we sell in antique shops today.

Other than that, our entertainment was the radio, a powerful force in those days as Fred Allen and Jack Benny made people laugh in spite of their woes.

There was not much money for food but my parents gave me ten cents a day for lunch. We bought lunch checks at five cents each. For one lunch check, you could purchase a plate of beef stew or even roast beef, mashed potatoes and gravy, and for another lunch check, a salad, a bowl of soup, or a dish of ice cream.

I stopped spending my lunch money in mid-

*Pert and I en route to Catalina Island in the summer of 1932.*

semester when Miss Edith Babbitt, my French teacher, asked me to tutor a freshman who was not doing well. The pay was ten cents an hour and the time set was my lunch hour. I was happy to do it. I not only earned fifty cents a week but saved the fifty cents I didn't spend. By the end of the year I had a nest egg—and a goal.

In our voluminous correspondence, Pert and I gradually evolved the idea that I must spend the next summer in California. Her mother had a job as sales representative for a hair dye company, her stepfather also worked as a salesman, and they had an apartment in a lovely area. It was tempting. My father said it might be possible for my grandfather to get me a railroad pass. He was a retired Terminal Railroad employee who had been a locomotive engineer for fifty years.

Graduation was not much of a highlight for any of us in 1932. In previous times, girl graduates had dressed in long, fancy formals, carried flowers and gone out with boys in rented tuxedos to dance at some elegant place like the Hotel Jefferson downtown or the roof garden of the Chase Hotel on Kingshighway.

In our year it was decided that because some girls could not afford formals, we would all wear simple daytime dresses, secured for us at the reasonable price of $4.00

It was probably the ugliest dress I ever owned. In our class colors of brown and tan, it consisted of a sleeveless sheath of cream colored crinkle crepe with a cheaply made brown bolero jacket. Even the prettiest girls didn't look pretty in them. We wore them for Class Day, a kind of glorified amateur performance of singers and dancers, and for graduation. I rarely wore mine after that.

I do remember Class Day for the act we didn't perform.

Our dean of women, Edna Fisse, was a strict enforcer of regulation. During my sophomore year a fad called "whoopee socks" (ankle-high socks) became popular, and she decreed that we could not wear them to school but must wear stockings. Some of us defied the edict and wore socks one day. I was sent home to change, walking thirteen blocks each way to do so.

Years later I became an honorary member of Delta Kappa Gamma, educational sorority and one of my sorority sisters was Miss Fisse. I told the story once too often and she protested, "Clarissa, don't you remember anything else about me?"

Well, yes, I remember that she censored our Class Day act. A girl named Eleanor with a good bluesy voice, decided to sing Cab Calloway's "Minnie the Moocher," and enlisted some of us as her background chorus. Miss Fisse listened to one rehearsal:

"Folks, hear the story 'bout Minnie the Moocher . . . she was a low-down hootchie cootcher . . ."

When our chorus began our "Hi-di-hi-di-hi— Ho-di-ho-di-ho" complete with undulating hip grinds, Miss Fisse cried, "No," and stopped the performance. I can't help but feel she was entirely right.

Graduation night was a quiet occasion. I'm sure there were parties and some of the fortunate few had dates, but I visited in the gymnasium with my parents, aunts, and cousins, and then walked home.

Like most things in my life, my graduation status was satisfactory but not outstanding. I ranked thirty-two in a class of 320. Just before graduation, my adviser completely confounded me by saying, "I'm disappointed in your grades. You know, you have the highest IQ of anyone in this school."

I was stunned. Nobody had ever indicated to me that I had any potential. A few of my English teachers, like Dena Lange, had encouraged me in writing, but I thought they were just being kind. I thought languages were easy and other subjects were hard and was so convinced I could never master higher math that I dropped the course and took shorthand and typing instead, a decision which was wise in view of life's later requirements.

In recent years I've met fellow students who say, "Oh I remember you; you were a real brain," but this I considered a judgment after the fact. In my memory I was an absolute nonentity in high school.

A week after graduation I had a date, a blind date arranged by Mary Felicia and her boyfriend, Ollie, who had a car. We drove to a country swimming hole on a river. On the way home, Ollie turned his head to joke with us in the backseat, the car went out of control on a sharp bend in the road and we overturned, twice.

I can still remember the sensation of bracing my

hands against the ceiling as the car turned upside down but I was wedged between two boys and we were unhurt, just shaken up. I said nothing to my mother, and it wasn't until later that summer that she met up with Mary F.'s mother who said, ''Weren't the children lucky?''

Mary F. and my new friends planned to take me to the train. A train trip was a big occasion then, calling for a bon voyage party. But my father insisted I visit my grandfather to thank him for getting the railroad pass which would allow me to travel to California to be with Pert. I was disgruntled and my grandfather quickly caught the vibrations and found out why. With a twinkle in his eye, he said, ''You'd better not be too strict with her. You know, her great-grandmother ran off and got married at sixteen.''

I was only fifteen and the trip to California itself was delirious excitement enough for me. I remember my seatmate, a young woman from Virginia going to California to be married, and how we both bemoaned the lack of trees in the barren stretches we crossed. I also remember the romance of the names of towns as we neared Los Angeles—Santa Ana, San Bernardino—and the big station where I alighted, just like the movie stars I'd seen in the newsreels.

And then the apartment, in Beverly Hills. Really swanky! Across the hall lived a real movie starlet who was visited by a real movie director. Pert and I would hide in the shrubbery to watch them get into the (rented, I'm sure) limousine.

1932 was the summer of the Olympics in Los Angeles, and Pert's stepfather had managed to get us tickets to the swimming meet. The seats were high, high in the bleachers, but who cared? We were seeing the Olympics! We also went to a premiere at Graumann's Chinese Theater and saw stars' footprints in the sidewalk.

Mac and Trudy, Pert's parents, partied a lot and were most permissive with us. We spent many evenings at the dance halls on the pier at Santa Monica, mecca for teenagers, and soon Pert's red hair attracted a cute boy who had a shy friend and soon we were going to wiener roasts at the beach, and being kissed enthusiastically—but only that. In those days, teenagers, at least of our type, were not sexually active as the phrase goes today. Girls who became pregnant "had to" get married and that meant the end of everything.

Another big event literally colored my summer. Pert's mom was a hair dye representative and gave demonstrations in beauty salons. One day she needed a model. Speculatively she looked at me. "Kitty" (my newest nickname), "how would you like to be a redhead." A redhead? Like Pert? Like Jean Harlowe, normally a platinum blonde, in her latest movie? It was a dream come true.

When I went home at the end of my marvelous summer, russet-haired, bronze-skinned, wearing the white suit mama had made for me, I felt proudly important, especially as I explained to people on the train that I was going home "to college." My father had written that he'd made plans to enroll me at the University of Missouri in Columbia, and I was to go directly there. I did not question how this had been arranged financially.

I remember the surge of joy as we crossed over the state line from Kansas into Missouri, and it seemed we were immediately in the midst of hilly landscapes, and leafy trees along a river's edge. I was going home and it was beautiful.

My parents met me at the railroad station and told me that Columbia would be home for all of us. They had moved there, too.

I had never been to Columbia, but I sensed instantly that we were living in the wrong part of town. We had two rooms above a grocery store, one a living room with the brown studio couch (my bed), the chair and Majestic radio, the other a room with a double cot for my parents, a table and chair, and my mother's cherished walnut sewing machine. There were no kitchen facilities so the sewing machine top held the dishpan. Already there was a white ring on the finish.

If South Broadway had been a comedown, this was the bottom. The rent was $15 a month. We didn't have it, but my father was sure he'd have a job soon. There was no money for tuition either, but mother had written Uncle John and he had agreed to advance $40 for the first semester's fees. Mother would repay him as soon as she got a loan on her insurance.

That night, after my parents had gone to bed, I sank down on the studio couch and sobbed. My dreamy, impractical parents, meaning the best for me, naively assuming everything would work out. Couldn't they see that this was an impossible situation?

Not for the first time, I felt as if I were the parent and my parents the children to be guided and protected. Never could I let them know my deep disappointment. But what was I to do?

About midnight, I sat up in bed, dried my eyes, took a deep breath, and made my decision. I would go to college. I would make good. Some day I would be Somebody. I would not let them down.

# *8*
## *Old Mizzou*

"**N**ON IN SPECULARUM sed in studium."

This was—still is—the motto carved in stone at the entrance to the University of Missouri campus, the "red" campus, so designated because the buildings are of red brick in contrast to the "white" campus with its buildings of white stone. The main building on the red campus was Jesse Hall, the administration building which faced a grassy green quadrangle in the center of which were the much revered "columns, vestiges of an earlier building which had been destroyed by fire.

Not many people entered by way of this north gate because the fraternity and sorority houses and most of the boarding houses were south of Jesse. We lived north of Broadway, the dividing line between what used to be called "town and gown," the native residents divided from the college. I had rightly surmised that, as far as campus life was concerned, we were at the wrong end of town.

But no matter. I was in college and it was too good to be true. I submerged myself in all the traditions, learned all the lore. There were the two stone lions in front of the journalism building and upperclassmen would tell you that whenever a virgin walked by, the lions roared, but that they "hadn't roared in twenty years." Actually, there probably were quite a few virgins on campus in my day but none of us would admit it.

My father and I went to the registrar's office, paid Uncle John's $40 for what was called a "library, hospital and incidentals fee," in lieu of tuition, and I was assigned to an advisor to select the classes I wanted to take.

I cautiously chose the ones I knew I could handle: English, Latin, French. My advisor added ancient history, a requirement. Physical education also was a requirement, with the option of choosing a different type each semester. I chose interpretive dancing, followed it the next semester with horseback riding and then alternated with more dancing and more horseback riding. I proudly considered myself a non-athletic intellectual.

My teachers were Stanley Johnson, English; Dr.

William Gwatkin, Latin; Dr. Jesse Wrench, history; and Mme. Germaine Sansot Hudson, French. Mme. Hudson, a product of Le Sorbonne in Paris, had married Dr. Jay Hudson, an MU philosophy professor.

In retrospect, I realize how fortunate I was to have such fine teachers. Professor Wrench was a "character," on campus, with shoulder-length hair which he tucked into a hair net, and a Van Dyke beard. He rode a bicycle in a day when only little boys rode bicycles. He was also a brilliant teacher, a friend to students, and he stayed around long enough that I was privileged to interview him in my newspaper years.

Like many freshman classes, his was a big one, rows on rows of students in an auditorium. History didn't interest me much but he kept it lively.

Mme. Hudson terrified me at first. I had studied French for four years, but it was reading and writing French. Now I was in a conversational class where even "Open the window," became "*Ouvrez le fenetre,*" and I felt over my head. But Mme. was kind to terrified students and I survived.

Stanley Johnson was tall, slender, bespectacled, and, I later realized, very young and wonderful to me, perhaps because I already knew everything he was trying to teach the less academically fortunate.

My favorite class was Latin. It was a small class, one other girl—I believe her name was Ruth. I remember the boys better—Lazar, a thin, bright boy from New York; Bud, a handsome youth from Southern Missouri; and Joe, who had graduated from our rival school, Roosevelt High, in St. Louis.

During our second week, Dr. Gwatkin invited us to a wiener roast at his home, with students from other classes. I walked there and Bud offered to drive me home. He drove out to the Hinkson Creek and tried to kiss me. I resisted with righteous indignation. Amused, he took me home, and that was the end of my first encounter with college boys.

It didn't matter because I was already attracted to Joe. Black hair, brown eyes, goldrimmed glasses and a shy sweet smile.

In late October, I managed to scrounge $3 for a round-trip train ride to St. Louis to spend a weekend with Mary Felicia. Joe just happened to be on the same train. On the way home, the train stopped—I believe it hit a cow—and when most of the students got off to investigate, Joe kissed me.

This was the beginning of my first great romance. It lasted only four months but it was intense.

We walked the hallways of Jesse Hall, holding hands and gazed into each others eyes at Jimmy's College Inn. We went to see Bing Crosby in *The Big Broadcast of 1932* and "Please" became "our song."

We went to the bonfire and pep rally the night before the homecoming game, and it was even better

than the Joe E. Brown movies. I discovered Sara
Teasdale poetry and read it dreamily. We had a brief
lovers' quarrel—his family were rock-ribbed
Republicans and I was a Franklin Roosevelt fan—
but after the election we made up.

I was even rushed by a sorority, Alpha Phi (they
pronounce it "Fee"), and although my chances of
joining were nil because it cost $25, I was thrilled to
be told I was "the cutest girl we've had at the house,"
though I was worldly enough to know they told this
to all the girls.

In preparation for this book, I went through my
diary of that year and read of my sorority experience.
I mentioned several girls: Betty Belle Estes, Ida Lee
Cannon, and—to my surprise—Alice Virginia
Shoemaker, who became my present husband's first
wife in 1941. In discussing Alpha Phi and college days,
he and I had often wondered if Alice Virginia and I
had met and now I knew.

Our family finances were still shaky. Mother and
I had only one winter coat for the two of us, her
Shagmoor, bought in more prosperous days. She was
a size larger than I, but I wore it. We dyed my white
California skirt brown; it turned into a muddy
chocolate color and gave me a permanent aversion to
brown.

There was speculation as to how we would raise the
money for my LHI fee the second semester, as my

father was still unemployed. But then my grandfather Start, always the kindest and most considerate of men, did the kindest and most considerate thing he could have done. He died. The resultant inheritance, a few hundred dollars, saved the day. Grandmother Start had died of a stroke four years before. I was sorry in each case but did not grieve. After all, they were both very old, in their sixties.

The next death in the family shook me much more. Just before Christmas, my boyish, laughing Uncle Len, thirty-nine years old, not long married with a three-year-old daughter, died. He was playing dominoes with a neighbor girl, much as he had done with me years ago, when he slumped over the table. The little girl pummeled him, thinking he was playing, but he was dead.

Grandfather Start's inheritance covered my fees and also books, which in those days totaled perhaps $5 a semester and were purchased at one of two used book stores, the Missouri Store or the Co-op. One bought a Latin book for forty-five cents in September and sold it back at thirty cents in January. I always wished I could keep my favorite books but such extravagance was impossible.

The money also covered some clothes, and just in time. Mother's Shagmoor was beginning to go. It was a good time to shop because my personal world had fallen apart. I never quite knew what happened. I suspect that Joe's parents were alarmed at the serious relationship that had developed between their eighteen-year-old son and this precocious fifteen-year-old girl, although our talk of marriage was a dream of many years hence.

At our one stilted meeting in a cafe in Columbia, his father had smiled genially, but his mother seemed wary. When Joe told me he thought we should "start seeing other people" and that he already had, I knew it was over and my heart broke.

But the new gray suit, the blue dress with checked taffeta puffed sleeves, and jodhpurs and riding boots and green suede jacket for my "equitation" class helped my spirits.

Also my father had been hired by a St. Louis firm, Boaz and Kiel, to help supervise the building of a big project, Kiel Auditorium on Market Street in St. Louis. As a civil engineer with a rather responsible job, his salary was $18 a week. He told us ruefully that bricklayers and hod carriers were paid more than he. I had my first lesson in the power of unions over the unorganized.

It was decided that mother would move back to St. Louis. They rented a "darling" apartment at 5200 Oleatha. And I moved into a boarding house at 607 Maryland Avenue in Columbia.

It was operated by "Ma" Casebolt and it was a first-rate establishment. For $22.50 a month I received room and board and three marvelous meals a day. Mr. Casebolt was a grocer, food was plentiful, and Mrs. Casebolt had an excellent cook. Breakfast would be fruit, bacon and eggs, and hot biscuits. Lunch was a big hot meal with more biscuits. Dinner the same. On one's birthday one was allowed to choose favorite foods. There were even snacks. Mrs. Casebolt thriftily saved the orange and and grapefruit rinds from breakfast, candied them, and brought them around and sold them to us at night.

I gained weight that winter but bouncing along in equitation class helped keep me somewhat in shape.

My room, the only one available, was little more than a hall closet. It was on the third floor with only two other rooms. At the far end of the hall was a room for the two boys who fired the furnace and did odd jobs. Their names were Watson and Holmes, just like the detective stories. Phil Watson was a big good natured boy, not much older than I. He would boom, ''Man coming up,'' as he mounted the stairs.

The others all had to walk through my room but there was no impropriety in this, for the other room was occupied by two women graduate students, one married and one divorced.

The other single girls were all pretty and fun and they took a big sisterly, protective interest in me, cautioning me against dating certain boys which, of course, only heightened my interest. They also found dates for me and my social life was lively.

I danced at fraternity houses and went on "jelly" dates—the campus term for coke and conversation at the south campus "in" spot, Gaebler's, where there was live music every afternoon and evening and an ambience no Paris or London cafe could top.

I still saw Joe in Lura Lewis's English class, but I also dated another boy in class, Jim, a talented writer. In May he took me to a formal dance, and I wore a yellow sheer ankle-length dress with white organdy flowers around the neckline and silver slippers.

This relationship was off to a good beginning when another one began. One evening, the phone on the stair landing rang. It was Gary, a boy I'd met in fall freshman English. He, too, had graduated from Roosevelt High and often teased me about Joe.

Now he was calling to ask me for a date. A friend of his wanted a date with Marge, one of our girls, and he suggested we "double." I went hunting Marge, only to find her on the porch swing in the midst of a sobbing emotional quarrel with her more-or-less steady, and when I interrupted her to convey my message, she screamed something about never wanting to see another man as long as she lived.

I explained to Gary that Marge couldn't make it. Well perhaps we could go out anyway, he said. Peachy keen, I replied.

So we did. I thought our first date was pretty dull. He talked a lot about baseball and I hadn't been much of a fan since my days at Uncle Dwyer's first radio. But he was nice and he took me to his fraternity house, Phi Kappa Psi, to dance.

He made a date for the last night of school. Jim also called for that night and I suggested we could have a "late date," at 10:30, which was the custom for those girls lucky enough to be asked by two boys for the same night. But Jim thought not, and I wasn't surprised. He wasn't one to take second place.

I've often speculated on what might have happened had the situation been reversed. Jim didn't return to school the next year and neither did I. We didn't meet again for many years.

Jim, who was Jim Griffing Lucas, went on to become a newspaper reporter in Oklahoma, and a marine in World War II. He wrote *Combat Correspondent,* which included a first-hand report of the marine landing at Tarawa. That book won much acclaim.

Gary, who was E. Gary Davidson, went on to become a lawyer, a state senator, and my husband for twenty-nine years.

But none of us knew any of that was going to happen at the time.

# 9

## A Long Dark Road

IF WE COULD LOOK into the future, have just a brief, flashing glimpse of ourselves ten or twenty years hence, I wonder if we'd want it. Certainly not at my age. Perhaps not at any age. And yet, there are times in our lives when it would be consoling to be able to look ahead through the clouds to the sunshine.

For instance, it would have been cheering for George Washington to have been able to say to the men at Valley Forge: "Stick it out, fellows. We're making history and besides that, everything is going to come out all right in the end. No fair peeking at the last page."

For my generation, Valley Forge was the winter of 1933, the year when the depression hit just about everyone. The year when, "Brother, Can You Spare a Dime?" was a top pop tune. When people who had once held responsible jobs stood in line at soup kitchens and relief offices or tried to sell apples on street corners.

I had planned to be back in college that year. In fact, my rosiest early plans after my freshman year were to stay on in Columbia and attend summer school. I sensed that it might be wise to speed up my education, doing four years in three. If it were possible after that, maybe graduate school. I'd read of others getting a Ph.D. degree at age twenty-one. Why couldn't I?

One of the girls at Ma Casebolt's was a Phi Mu and she had sounded me out on the possibility of joining in the fall. Meanwhile, the Phi Mu house was renting rooms over the summer at $3 a month. Was I interested? Sure.

The Phi Mu house was, in my eyes, absolutely gorgeous, even prettier than the Alpha Phi house, a white colonial structure with dormer windows on the third floor, situated on the last street in town, fronting the green sweep of the golf course.

I rented a third-floor cubicle; it was rather sparsely furnished but I moved in all my possessions, including my wardrobe trunk. (We traveled with wardrobe trunks in those days and it still amazes me to think of the ease with which we had them transported by the express company for a fee of something like seventy-five cents. With dresses and coats hanging on one side, drawers on the other, they served as furniture.)

Back home for what I thought would be a brief vacation, I was brought down to earth with a thud. My parents were moving out of the pretty apartment on Oleatha Avenue. My father was in Chicago, where he hoped to parlay the remainder of his small inheritance into more, at the racetrack. Instead, he lost it all, and while he slept on a park bench there, mother and I moved in with Aunt Olie and Uncle John.

It was a sad day when Mary Felicia, her kind boyfriend, Ollie, and I drove down to Columbia and Ollie hoisted my wardrobe trunk and books into his truck and out of the Phi Mu house forever.

My aunt and uncle had moved from the bungalow where I'd lived with them ten years before and into a two-family flat on Wilcox in the Bevo Mill area of South St. Louis. Uncle John was out of a job; the dairy for which he worked had folded. He had some savings and rent from the first-floor flat but his enthusiasm for two extra mouths to feed was understandably weak.

One of those sharp fragments of memory still remains. Mother told me after dinner one night that she had started to reach for a second piece of bread, felt Uncle John's eyes follow her hand, and withdrew it. Perhaps it was her imagination. He was not an unkind man, far from it. Just frightened, like everyone.

"Anybody can get work if they want it," was a popular phrase, usually voiced by those who had a job. It was untrue.

I read the short columns of help-wanted ads daily, answered ads, and followed leads. The Granada Theater, a neighborhood movie and vaudeville house, was hiring ushers. I joined the hundreds of teenagers who crowded outside the building, but I was not one of those hired. At employment agencies, it was always the same, a gentle, "You're too young, dear. Let your parents look after you."

Every day I went out, looked for work, came home, helped with the laundry and other chores, had dinner, went to bed. We did not sleep well. It was a blisteringly hot summer. There was no air-conditioning in those days and we four sat on the tiny, screened-in back porch, or lay on the floor in the hall where an occasional stray breeze stole up the stairs.

Newspapers carried stories of people sleeping in the parks, on their lawns, anywhere to escape the oppressive heat indoors. It is next to impossible for this generation to imagine it.

In August my father came back penniless. We applied for relief and were given enough to rent a furnished room for $7 a week and buy a little food. My father was put on the waiting list for a WPA job.

Our furnished room was on Iowa Avenue, a few blocks south of the flat where we'd lived when I was younger. Our room was the center one on the second floor. It was furnished with a table and four chairs, a sink in one corner, twin beds and a wardrobe for a closet. My father slept in one bed, I in the other and mother took turns with us.

The room was divided by glass doors from the front room where a young couple lived, fought, and made love, all rather noisily. We shared a bathroom, kept clean by a very young girl who did the housework for the building for $3 a month. ''More for home than wages'' was the job description.

Toward the end of summer, good fortune smiled. Mother got a job at the only thing she was trained to do, operating a power machine at the Angelica Jacket Company on Olive Street in downtown St. Louis. The pay was on a piecework basis. Mother was one of the fastest workers in the shop. Sometimes she made as much as $5 a week. Many of the girls averaged only $1.50 or $2.

This may explain why garment workers across the country began going on strike. For many of them, no wages were better than exploitation. Soon Angelica was on strike.

Mother wasn't a striker by nature and we needed the money so, despite my father's objections to crossing a picket line (remember Grandpa Start and his insistence on the union sticker on bread), Mother stayed on awhile.

Pressure was strong on the nonstrikers to go out.

"It worries me," Mother confided. "Those organizers sound like Communists to me. Today one of them had a newspaper society section with the pictures of the girls who are maids at the Veiled Prophet Ball next month. He said, 'Look how the rich live while you starve. Is it time to put an end to capitalism or not?' "

Soon the behavior got rough. There were eggs and rocks thrown at the women arriving for work. The company hired a bus with bars on the windows and an armed guard. My father raised his voice and mother gave in and quit her job.

A short time later, she saw an ad by the Alligator Raincoat Company, answered it, and worked there briefly. But word got out that some of the new employees had gone on strike against other companies and they were summarily fired.

Eventually the strikes were settled. A minimum wage came into being, and power machine workers were paid $13 a week.

I had dreamed of going back to college, maybe on a student loan since they were available, but when I wrote to inquire, I received the reply that the maximum loan available was $75 and they could not guarantee a job for my room and food.

Early in September I heard that the National Candy Factory, on Gravois near Chippewa, hired people seasonally. Every day I walked the thirty-two blocks to join the others who had heard the same rumor. The first day there were a handful of us at the employment office entrance. A tall, thin, rather elegant looking young man walked by. At the door, he turned and said, "Nothing today."

We dispersed and I walked slowly home. There was nothing to do so I sat for a while on a bench in Gravois Park. A sixteen-year-old girl could sit on a park bench in those days, safely.

I had never heard the terms "child molester" or "pervert" at that time. In fact, I was in my senior year of college before I knew that a "fairy" referred to anything but the mythical little people at the bottom of the garden, or a "pansy" was anything but a flower. "Gay" meant "happy."

When I learned from a student in psychology that there were people called "homosexuals" I couldn't believe it. To think that men would—with other men —and women—with other women—incredible! Later I learned that a well-liked professor whom we'd thought of as a "sissy type" was "one of them." Many years later he lost his job.

For all its economic dangers, our world was socially safer then. In that golden autumn, you could sit in the park and ignore the many others sitting there. No one spoke to you or even to each other. There was nothing to say.

The second day I walked to the candy factory there

were a few more people there. The crazy thought occurred to me that if I persisted and kept coming back
day after day, the tall, elegant young man would notice
and reward such persistence.

But he never noticed because daily the crowd increased. More men, more women, more teenage boys
and girls, a restless, milling crowd. When the car
stopped and the young man got out, we would step
back and make a path for him to walk to the employment office and each day as he reached the door, he
would turn, face us, and say, "Nothing today."

I went to the plant daily for thirty days. The crowds
grew larger and more restless. Occasionally, someone
bold enough would step out of line into the man's path
but I never did.

And then one day, something curious happened.
As the young man turned around to give us his usual
message, the crowd surged forward and for half a second it became a mob. And as the young man said
the familiar words, "Nothing today," I watched his
eyes and the expression on his face.

"Why, he's afraid," I thought. "He's afraid of us."
The thought struck me as monstrous, as obscene, and
yet I knew it was true.

I never went back because I realized how hopeless
it was. There was nothing he could do. It wasn't his
fault. He could only act as the middleman and give
us the message of that autumn of 1933: "Nothing to-

day.''

But life wasn't entirely hopeless for a sixteen-year-old girl. I enrolled in a class in German at Roosevelt High School night school, which was crowded with students. I'm sorry I stayed only one term. I'd like to know more German today.

Some days I walked downtown, a very long walk but it broke the monotony and I enjoyed looking at clothes even if I couldn't buy any. Eventually my shoes wore out. You could buy new shoes for as little as $1.95 but even that was out of reach for me. Shoe repair shops where you sat and waited for heels or soles to be replaced, did a thriving business then but many of us could not afford that either. Standard procedure for a hole in the sole was a sturdy piece of cardboard inserted inside the shoe. It lasted pretty well until the first heavy rain.

By October I'd found a more productive use for my days. Aunt Marie, Uncle Len's widow, had remarried, a kindly man who became Uncle Fred. He said quite frankly that he realized Aunt Marie did not love him romantically but he wanted to take care of her and her little girl. She had always wanted to operate a delicatessen so he financed her to a small shop on Arsenal Street, a sort of glorified general grocery store which served noon meals to the men from the packing house nearby.

I started dropping in, helping wait on tables and

clerk in the store. Aunt Marie couldn't pay me but gave me groceries to take home.

One day a young man customer asked if I'd like a job. He and a friend were opening a cleaning shop next door and needed someone to answer phones and wait on customers while they were out. The salary was $3 a week. Of course I accepted eagerly.

Sad to say, the job lasted only a couple of weeks. On a Saturday, the day the young men, Mac and Bayne closed up, they mixed me a Manhattan cocktail and we drank to better times ahead. They were a long way ahead.

# 10

## *A Very Important Year*

I WAS A DEDICATED diary keeper all through my youth and these notebooks with lined paper, torn covers and often indecipherable entries survived. Some day I may work up the courage to burn them. They are pretty silly and nothing to pass down to posterity, but they are interesting, not so much for what they contain as for what they omit.

The 1933 volume was titled "A very Important Year," which it certainly was. But the "very important year" chiefly chronicled how much I missed college life, how much I missed Joe and Jim and others (all boys) plus an ongoing recital of my social life.

Here and there are references to the outer world. I wrote of my mother's participation in the clothing strike but in a casual way, only as it affected our life at home and not from a broad social picture.

This was the year of the bank holiday. It was the

year the United States went off the gold standard. It included the beginning of Franklin Delano Roosevelt's social welfare measures, the NRA, the CWA, WPA, PWA. Prohibition was repealed. Hitler was beginning to rise to power. But little of this found its way into my diary.

The song of the year was Duke Ellington's "Sophisticated Lady," and it was my theme song. I felt its sad lyrics accurately described my life: "They say into your early life romance came. . . ." My early life was over at sixteen and romance was gone.

But ever the optimist, I took steps to enliven my social life, attending high school alumni meetings where we of the class of '32 commiserated with one another over our lack of jobs.

I spent a lot of time at the public library, this in the interest of continuing my education. Looking back, I may have learned more that year than in any year in college, as I read the English classics—Dickens, Thackeray, the Brontes, Jane Austen, and every modern writer I could get my hands on. From *Cranford* to *The Forsyte Saga,* I devoured them all.

From time to time I wrote a short story, sent it away, and received a rejection slip. In one diary note I wondered despairingly "if I would ever be a writer."

My diary contains a great deal about a boy named Kermit. He worked at the packing house and came to Aunt Marie's deli for lunch. On our first date he took me to the Ambassador Theater downtown where we saw a stage show and heard a "keen" new song, "Did You Ever See A Dream Walking?"

We also went to wrestling matches and to the walkathon, a phenomenon of the period. This was a spectacle somewhat like the sacrifices of the Christians to the lions in the Roman Coliseum in that people came to watch other people suffer.

The dancers in the walkathons, or dance marathon, signed up to dance until they dropped, dancing continuously with only brief rest periods, for days, sometimes weeks. Eventually the competition would be down to two or three couples, hanging to each other, falling to their knees and finally to the floor. When only one pair remained, they won the prize— was it $50? Much as I loved dancing, I never considered it.

My father, back from the south and jobless still, didn't like my packing house boyfriend, considering him beneath us. I remember my mother sarcastically saying, "Well, who do you expect to come to a dump like this to see her, the Prince of Wales?"

Papa needn't have worried. The new romance had a big setback New Year's Eve when I wore a new dress—how we found the money to buy a few dollars worth of material I don't recall but I remember the dress in detail. It was purple silk crepe with slits from the shoulder several inches to the bustline with rhinestone clips at the top of the slits.

This elegant dress went to a party in a rooming house third-floor apartment where my boyfriend got so drunk that I left him and went home by myself. It seemed a long way from the fraternity crowd in Columbia where they also got drunk but with more class. He apologized, we made up, but the romance was in the cooldown stage.

Since I didn't record such unimportant things, I'm not sure when my father found work, but dim recollection is that he was hired for a PWA job in Mississippi. It didn't last. Father, ever hot-tempered, got into a fight with his supervisor and quit. He later was hired for a CWA job.

Somehow we managed to muddle through and to leave the furnished room and rent a more respectable apartment on Winona Avenue just west of Kingshighway and south of Chippewa and the area I considered so prestigious—Southampton, it was called. The apartment was built on a peculiar slant and our living room was, well, crooked is the only word for it. But we turned under a corner of the 9 x 12 rug and it looked fine with the brown studio couch, chair and the familiar Majestic radio.

How had we managed to pay storage on them? No word in the diary about that.

My social life was sparse until one spring night when I attended a political organization's dance (I don't even recall which party) with friends I'd known from confirmation class. There I renewed acquaintance with Norman, a high school friend.

A few weeks later, the same crowd of girls went to a dance at Forest Park Highlands amusement park where I picked up with my usual type, a shy boy who appreciated my outgoing nature. His name was Ted.

Ted took me to a very special event, a sunrise dance at the Century Boat Club on South Broadway (the nicer part of South Broadway, far from our duplex, near the big homes.) Sunrise dances began at three o'clock in the morning so my date and I went somewhere else first. With another couple, we visited several roadhouses and by 3 A.M. I'd spent as much time as I'd wanted with my date but the dance was still to come. As luck had it, Norman was there and it was great fun.

There were two orchestras on two floors, a view of sunrise over the Mississippi and, when morning came, a big breakfast.

I had more dates with Ted, but the big news was that I had plans to go to summer school and try to catch up on the year I'd missed. There was one problem. With all my savings all year, from allowances from my parents, an occasional job or tips at Aunt Marie's, I was still $10 short of the $36.25 tuition.

With only a week to go, it didn't look bright but I answered another of the ads headed, "Girls

Wanted." This one was for girls to enter a bathing beauty contest, the prize a trip to the Chicago World's Fair.

There was no danger of my winning the contest. I was one of the least-endowed of the twenty selected. And anyway, the promoter's girlfriend was already slated to win the contest.

The rest of us were assigned to advertise the sponsors, parading before the judges on the night of the show and for three days beforehand, riding around town. We would be paid $10!

I was Miss Eighteenth Street Tavern.

There were some hitches to the entire affair. We were provided bathing suits, but they were something new, all rubber and not too comfortable or well-fitting. When we arrived at the auditorium, the same one my father had helped to build, we found we would not be on a stage, but in a boxing ring.

The floor of a boxing ring has a lot of give to it and is not made for high heels. We lurched rather than glided regally as we'd been rehearsed to do.

The final hitch was that the boys at the Eighteenth Street Tavern had issued a command performance request that their representative come over and have a drink and mingle after the contest. My father, when he heard of it, said absolutely flatly "no." When I wrung my hands and explained the promoter told me I wouldn't be paid if I didn't go, he said we'd see about that and he went to the auditorium with me.

The upshot was that I didn't visit the boys in the tavern and I did get my $10, plus a compact and the suit. If the whole idea didn't hold water, that suit did. I wore it only a few times but found it had a tendency to fill up and fall off of its own weight when you climbed out of the pool.

The grand finale was Sunday night. Monday morning I enrolled in logic and epistemology and sociology at Saint Louis University, and in a few days my new role had taken over.

In contrast to riding around the city in an open car, wearing a swimsuit, my banner, and waving at the crowds, I wore my summer cotton dress, caught the Chippewa bus to Grand and the Grand streetcar to the college.

Usually arriving with split-second timing, books under my arm, I would race across the street, run up the steps and as the bell was tolling in the college church, would race into class, drop to my knees, cross myself, and begin the first Hail Mary.

All classes started and ended with prayer in those days. Grandma Start's training stood me in good stead and I could keep up with the best of them, an achievement since the logic class was made up almost entirely of nuns and priests with only a few of us "civilians." Among them, my diary records "a cute boy—I think his name is Jimmy."

Further, my diary relates that I was starting to write a novel, titled "Spotlight," that my social life was dull and that, on reflection, I'd realized I'd fallen in love in October, January, and April, but never in June or July.

I didn't remedy the situation that year, but I have a feeling that I did later on, somewhere along the way.

I enjoyed my classes—Father Husslein in sociology, Father Hendrix in logic—and was pleasantly surprised by my grades, both A's, a ninety-two average in sociology, and a ninety-seven, highest in the class, in logic. Years later, I lorded this over my lawyer husband, who had just squeaked through logic at Missouri U—"a much tougher course," he'd insisted.

Summer was nearing an end and I was making plans to go back to Mizzou on a student loan for the $75 which had seemed so inadequate the year before. But this time my father had a job and I would try to get work at school.

I made arrangements by mail to rent a room at 1000 University Avenue for $7 a month. Mother made a suit and a dress for me. My purple New Year's Eve dress would do for "best." I had two sweaters, three blouses, and I got a permanent wave for $1.95.

I took the Wabash train to Columbia and made a new friend, a girl from Michigan who was being sent to college by her parents to recover from a marriage annulment, a real shocker in those days. I arrived at the rooming house and met my roommate, a friendly wholesome physical education major, Virginia Lee Watts—"Watty." After agonizing over whether or not my loan would be approved, it was indeed and I was a college student once again.

I went to the young peoples' meeting at church and all the boys I remembered were there.

I ended the diary of that Most Important Year with a promise to myself to do well in school, to try to become a writer some day, and with the hope that my ability to be one had improved with all the reading and writing I'd done in my year away from college.

"So perhaps, as the Bible says, things do work together for good," I wrote. "It may turn out that this past dull, sordid, painful year was the best thing that could have happened to me."

And perhaps it was.

# 11

## Student of Economics

THERE WAS A SHORT STORY, titled "A Student of Economics," in one of the freshman English textbooks when I was in college. It told the poignant tale of a student who was working his way through college, stoking the furnace in his rooming house, waiting tables at a hashhouse, and squeezing in a variety of odd jobs. He spent so much time earning a living that he failed his major class—in, of all things, economics.

I was no longer a freshman when I read the story in another student's textbook, probably that of someone I was tutoring. But I certainly identified with it, and recalled feeling lucky to be a survivor. My grades set no records but they were passing, although at one point in my college days, I worked at four jobs between classes.

My grades actually were enough above average that I accumulated extra credit hours and completed my four years in three, plus the summer at Saint Louis U. and an extended period of summer and intersession in the summer of 1935.

All that was still in the future. In the fall of 1934 it was enough to be back on campus, my tuition paid for one semester, with sufficient money from home to pay my $7 monthly room rent and buy an occasional meal at the Ever Eat Cafe across the street, supplementing it with cheese, crackers, and apples.

Our boardinghouse was vintage small town, white frame with a front porch, small parlor, an L-shaped staircase that led to four bedrooms and one bath upstairs. Downstairs behind the parlor was our landlady's quarters, entered only on rent day.

We had a full house. Dorothy (nickname "Danny") and Helen were graduate students who shared a room. "Watty" and I shared a room. And there were two single rooms occupied by two singular people, Mary, whom we called "Garbo," for reasons too involved to relate, and Edith, who was called "Cas," again from an inside joke.

Garbo came from a small town in Illinois. Outwardly loud and brash, she was inwardly shy and sensitive, an adopted girl who spent much of her time writing letters trying to find her "real parents."

Cas was older than the rest of us, a divorcee in her late twenties with a handsome wardrobe of tailored clothes and a mannish haircut, but a very feminine attitude and an ambition to be a writer. We sensed an instant rapport, perhaps because the others were Phys. Ed. majors and we were "artists."

We all went our separate ways but congregated at night to talk and think up mischief, or at least Garbo, Cas, and I did. Watty eventually moved to the dormitory, Read Hall, because it was closer to her part-time job at the women's gymnasium.

When I look back on my meager finances and meager meals, I am appalled, but at the time, hunger was a normal state of affairs. The food at the Ever Eat, which we soon named the Never Eat, was nothing for a gourmet but it was cheap. I seem to recall that Cas provided many of my supplemental snacks.

Later that year a new restaurant, the Topic Cafe, opened on the street with Gaebler's Black and Gold Inn and Jack's Shack, the popular student hangouts. This became my regular dining place because the food was both cheap and good.

A full dinner—meat, potatoes, vegetable, salad, (dessert? I'm not sure) cost thirty cents, and for a dollar you could buy a meal ticket good for six meals a week.

On the seventh day I went to the young people's social at the Lutheran Church which mother and I had

joined, and often there was food there. Sometimes a
boy would even ask me out to eat but not very often.
Few could afford to feed two.

Eating was only incidental but drinking was a major part of the curriculum. I've heard apologists for
marijuana dismiss the habit as equivalent to alcohol
for young people in previous generations.

I don't know what effect marijuana has on the body
and since it's illegal, I don't condone it, but I must
admit there was a lot of drinking in our days, no doubt
some of it harmful.

Most of us soon learned how much we could drink,
which, in my case, was not much. And drinking did
not lead to many car accidents because there were so
few cars.

I knew only one student who owned a car, a St.
Louis boy who defrayed the cost of his education by
taking students to St. Louis on weekends, charging
$2 a round trip, or $1.50 if you sat in the open rum-
ble seat, thus undercutting the rail and bus transportation which charged $3 to $4 a round trip.

Mostly, we walked around Columbia on our dates
and if we went to the student attractions on the
highway, the Coronado or Springdale, we took a taxi.
In one diary entry, I noted with hilarity that five of
us had piled in the backseat, and then "Mississippi,"
a student from that state, had dived in and sprawled
across the rest of us. Within the city limits, cab fares

were fifteen cents. Out of town, we'd split the thirty-five or forty cents fare.

All student residences, dormitories, and private homes alike were supposed to observe hours—a deadline of 10:30 P.M. on weeknights, 12:30 on Saturday night. As a result, for many of us, there was little going on after hours.

But rules are made to be broken and we did our best. On one occasion Ruby, our landlady, went out of town for the weekend and we all stayed out after hours. She heard of it and I made my first acquaintance with Dean Mary Rose McKee. She gave us a stern reprimand and said not to let it happen again. It happened many more times, but either we became more careful or Ruby became more tolerant.

Liquor had been the bootleg product in our freshman year but now drinking was legal, prohibition having been repealed. I was not in school that year but was told that the day beer became legal, a line many blocks long formed in front of Jack's Shack.

Sometimes we drank beer, but more often there were more exotic concoctions. We didn't know about such fine distinctions as bourbon versus scotch, and rye was unknown in the Midwest. We merely bought a half pint of booze (I imagine it was bourbon) at a drugstore, for thirty-nine cents and sometimes, even twenty-nine cents. We bought it by the brand name—''Two Naturals'' was one.

More serious drinkers consumed straight alcohol, colorless and available in half-gallon bottles. This would be mixed with grape juice for a drink called Purple Passion. Some simply drank alky straight with a beer chaser.

Quite often, everyone got tipsy and part of the fun was rehashing it all the next day, screaming, "You don't remember doing that? And that's only the beginning . . ."

The light approach to alcohol was not invented by college students. We were copying our role models in movies where there was often a lovable drunk or a hilarious drinking scene. Getting "blotto," "squiffed," "pie-eyed" was humorous. And not a bad way to forget the depression.

For me it was party-party all that fall of 1934. One memorable night was the eve before the big homecoming game. By this time I was dating a journalism student, Al, who had transferred from Stanford. I resisted going steady however.

For one thing, I was still persuaded my heart had been broken and I would never trust a man again, and also I had read that there were seven men students to every woman enrolled that year and I announced that I was out to get "my seven."

Usually, Cas, and Garbo and I went out on group dates, our crowd growing larger at every stop. By the time we reached Dixie Cafe, which was uptown next to the Tiger Hotel, there were eight to ten of us around a big table, filled with school spirit and other spirits.

At someone's urging, I climbed atop the table, led some cheers and then asked the immortal homecoming eve question: ''Are we going to beat Kansas?'' As the answering roar, ''Hell, yes,'' floated back, I leaped from the table and was caught by two boys, one with an amused and familiar face. It was Gary Davidson, whom I'd dated my freshman year.

''You've had too much to drink,'' he said. ''I'm going to take you for a walk around the block.''

In later years I would tell that his idea was sound, but it would have been better if he'd suggested I wear a coat. The weather was freezing and by the time we'd sloshed through the misty rain the next day at the big game (which Kansas won) I had a sore throat. On the following night when I had an official date with Gary, I couldn't speak above a whisper.

It didn't matter. We didn't go anyplace, but had a ''parlor date.'' His first words to me were prophetic: ''I'm a little short of money so I can't take you anyplace.'' He rarely could.

Soon we were dating regularly but not steadily as I still had my sights on those seven swains. Eventually I had at least half-a-dozen regulars and occasionally seven dates in a week.

They're hazy now in memory. One was a friend of Gary's, who lived at the same rooming house. They were given to nicknames, too. There was Gary's roommate, Wimpy. Gary was "the Judge." A sweet, fresh-faced freshman was "the Saint." We dated on Tuesdays. Al was for Monday and Friday, Gary for Thursday and Saturday, Carl (from church) for Sunday, and Wednesday was for the boy Gary called "Fred the Fish."

Freddy was a drinker, a kind of W. C. Fields type, but he was a nice boy and one of the few dates who could afford to buy me a hamburger. On my eighteenth birthday, he sent me eighteen red roses, an extravagance unheard of then. This was March 28, 1935, and I was taking equitation lessons again and had been thrown from my horse that day. Bumps and bouquets.

We went home for the Christmas holidays, in the $1.50 rumble seat, and since California was too far for Al to go home, he also came to St. Louis to visit cousins. I threw a party at our apartment. My father obligingly took up the bed and stored it in the bathtub, so we had room to dance.

On New Year's Eve I went out with Al and his cousins—Gary was still dating his old St. Louis girlfriends and we weren't as yet "serious" steadies. One of the cousins was a charmer and soon I was coming to St. Louis on weekends to have a rendezvous in a booth designated "Sigma Chi," at one of the Washington U. hangouts.

This was expensive diversion as I had to take the

train, but I also had a Saturday job in St. Louis. One of the ads I'd answered a year before had led to work as a photographer's model.

I posed for hosiery ads and my legs were in the *St. Louis Post-Dispatch* before my byline ever was. It was profitable work, $2 an hour, but arduous. You had to hold the pose, legs crossed at the knee but not resting (so there was no bulging calf) and stay that way fifteen to twenty minutes.

My employer also sold photographs to artists who could not afford models, so now and then I had an assignment to lie on the floor as a dead body (detective magazine illustration) or stand in the doorway in a negligee looking sultry (love stories). He sold other types of photographs too, and when he became too insistent about my taking my clothes off, I regretfully gave up my modeling career.

By this time the St. Louis romance had cooled and at the same time, the romantic spring had made Columbia a lilac-scented setting and I was ready to give up my multiple datings and settle down to Gary.

Summertime arrived, he went home, and I stayed on to make up for lost time that summer and during the intersession, the five-week period before fall, Cas moved to a basement apartment by herself and Garbo and I found another rooming house. Two weeks later I became better acquainted with the dean for a ridiculous escapade.

We weren't too happy with our new home. The residents were all older, graduate students, mostly school teachers and the house parents seemed a stuffy pair. They were equally disapproving of us and our youthful silliness.

One afternoon Garbo and I went out for a quiet walk with one of her boyfriends. We ended up at the Dixie, where he had a beer and the two of us, much to his disgust, ordered soft drinks. I was on one of my regular reducing diets. Despite starvation rations, I always had a weight problem.

He walked us back to our house and called out, "Don't drink so much next time." We giggled, ran up the steps and Garbo (who had her nickname partly because of the size of her feet) tripped on the top step. Several of the teachers sitting on the porch, looked disapproving or so we thought, so I said, "You've had too much to drink. I'd better put you in a cold shower."

We ran on up the stairs, swinging from side to side on the bannisters. I did get Garbo as far as the shower when we gave up our charade and settled down and thought no more of it. Until we received a note from our landlord that due to our "unbecoming behavior" we were asked to move at the end of the week.

This was no great blow until we learned there would be no refund on our one month's rent paid in advance.

"If you have any objection, you can take it up with

the dean of women,'' he said smartly.

He reckoned without my Irish ancestry. Also my desperate need for money. I went straight to Dean McKee's office, figuring I couldn't be any lower in her estimation than I already was. I told her the whole story, admitted it had been a silly stunt but that ''we were not drunk or even drinking.''

She tsked-tsked a great deal and I suspect had a hard time keeping a straight face, but said she'd look into it.

The next day she called me in again. In an envelope was our rent refund. There also was our new room assignment, at Read Hall, the girls' dormitory. ''Where I'll be able to keep an eye on you,'' she warned us.

We groaned as we moved. Read Hall and even Hendrix Hall, the other fancier dormitory, were known for strict rules enforcement and we feared we'd lost our freedom forever. But, at least the price was right. Room rent was $3 a month.

And there turned out to be a much brighter side. My financial picture was even bleaker than it had been the year before and I admitted this to the dean in my confession. I did have a part-time job, at Forney's Typing Bureau, owned by the husband of one of the graduate students at Ma Casebolt's. An excellent speed typist, I was able to turn out a large amount of work and because of my journalism school schedule of only morning classes, I could work all afternoon and into the evening. But typing rates were low—five or six cents a page of which the typist received two cents—and so my top income was $7 a week.

The social worker who had helped my parents for awhile had obtained a special grant to pay my intersession tuition and also had suggested I apply for a student NYA job. And, after our moving episode, Dean McKee came up with another source of help, a kitchen job at Read Hall.

I was a successful student of economics at last.

# 12

## Graduation At Last

THE UNIVERSITY OF MISSOURI School of Journalism has an excellent way of preparing students to
work on a newspaper, radio, or television station. The
school operates a newspaper, and both radio and TV
stations, and staffs them with students, under faculty
supervision.

With the exception of television (not in existence
then), it was that way when I was a student in the
1930s. During the summer of 1935 I worked on the
Columbia Missourian as society editor, a title which
filled my disrespectful friends with mirth.

One learned from this apprenticeship what could
and couldn't be done. I soon learned I had no interest

in society. I did not want to sell classified advertising either, but I had to do it.

Classified ad soliciting was done by phone. You called an advertiser and asked, "Have you found your dog yet?" "No, no, do you have word?" they'd ask eagerly. When you said, "No, but I wondered if you'd like to continue your ad," they hung up.

I did better at selling display advertising. This was done by making personal calls and I had fair success, not at selling big half-page ads but little one-inch ones. One of my accounts, a beauty parlor, advertised, "If your hair isn't becoming to you, you should be coming to us." Another, a small restaurant, was always good for "Chicken every Sunday, all you can eat. 50ᶜ."

"Hey, someone actually came in and asked for chicken last Sunday," the owner greeted me one week.

"See, it pays to advertise."

"Yeah, but we didn't have no chicken last Sunday."

There was no Sunday chicken dinner in my life. Chicken, now considered an economy meal, was pretty much a luxury then. My diet that summer of 1935 consisted largely of lettuce sandwiches.

I could buy a loaf of bread for five cents, a head of lettuce for the same, and have lunch and dinner for four or five days. Half a watermelon costing five cents, was filling, too. And occasionally we took night strolls through the university Ag School garden and brought home a head of cabbage, which we boiled. Apples from the university orchard were another staple.

A Read Hall classmate, Dee Evans, now a near neighbor of mine, remembers our apple-filching escapades.

"One night we went out with a pillow case," she recalled. "We were filling it and backing up across the orchard when we backed into someone else. We panicked until we found it was another student doing the same thing."

Dee also remembers the weekend she and Garbo obtained permission to stay over a holiday when everyone else went home.

"We had no money and no food," she said, "so we decided we'd live on water. The first day we had nothing but water but then Mary (Garbo to me) got a box from home of cookies and nuts. She divided it evenly—one for her, one for me. It was wonderful.

"I wouldn't live through that again," she said, echoing my sentiments about college days. "I wouldn't have the nerve to do what I did then, to go off to college with all my belongings in a suitcase, no money and no plans, just the optimistic thought, 'I'll get a job somehow.' "

To repeat my theme: I'm glad I'm not young any more.

*Gary, me, and classmates Polly Gum and Elinor Roth at Read Hall in 1936.*

And yet we had fun, as young people do despite handicaps. I was still dating others. Platonic dates, I assured Gary. Cas had a friend who had a friend and we went out as a foursome. They not only had spending money, but one had a car and we went to such faraway places as dances in Jefferson City and Boonville. Often they bought us hamburgers, a real treat.

My date and I had an early agreement. "I'll have

to tell you, I'm not the marrying kind," he said.

"Never mind," I said airily. "I'm not the marrying kind either."

That was not true. My future plans included being Mrs. E. Gary Davidson, wife, mother, and writer. One day, Cas suggested that after graduation, she and I might go to South America. I explained my plans and she laughed, "Oh, that little affair will be all over by then."

But it wasn't. All that long, hot summer we wrote letters as often as we could afford postage. During intercession, the dormitory closed and I rented a room in the tower of the Victorian house across the street. It was a happy experience. My landlady was a dear elderly woman, seventy years old, I'm sure, and had an attic full of *Godey's Ladies Book* magazines, which I read.

And then it was fall. I was back at Read Hall with a new roommate, Ruthy Lehman, and new friends new friends in the dormitory. There were thirty-two of us. Our housemother, Elizabeth Reeder, a graduate student, was pretty, bright, sweet, and absolutely no match for her mischief-making houseful.

We broke rules, climbed up fire escapes, crept around outside the house to look in the dining room window and watch her and her boyfriend—studying very properly. He was a science student, Charles Schwartz, who became a distinguished naturalist and wildlife artist.

She obtained a doctorate and joined him in his work. They married and lived happily ever after. She certainly deserved it after her stint as our housemother.

This was the period when I had four jobs—the typing job, a tutoring job, the NYA job, and work in the kitchen at Read. The first morning there I learned I could not lift a tray with a dozen cups of cocoa so I gave up my prestigious job of waiting tables and was demoted to dishwasher. There were no dishwashing machines.

Dishwashing qualified me for only one meal a day but my partner, Diana, and I worked out a system. Our job before dinner was to prepare salads and as long as we were making forty-eight salads—the number of our regular diners—we felt we could make fifty or fifty-two.

Depending on how the salad course appealed to us, we prepared extras and, climbing the rolling ladder, stowed them away on the top shelf until Lizzie and Miner, our black cook and handyman, went home. The extra salads became our breakfast and lunch.

Then there was the NYA job. I was assigned to work at the alumni office for the staff of three secretaries there. I still recall the disgusted tone of head secretary, Nell, as she greeted me with, "Oh another one. Well, what can you do?"

"I can type," I said.

"Oh you can?" She sounded skeptical. "Well, sit out here and address these envelopes."

A half-hour later, I took the tall stack of addressed envelopes to her and said, "What shall I do now?"

"My God," she said. "We finally got one who really can work."

One of my fondest college memories is of working with Nell, Thelma, Opal, and our boss, Robert E. Lee "Bob" Hill. They showed their appreciation in so many kind ways. On one occasion I had the flu and spent a week in the hospital. When I went back to work and said weakly that I wanted to make up the hours I'd missed, they laughingly told me to "go back to bed, we've already turned in your hours for the month."

I worked forty hours a month for a salary of $10.45. I would take the check to the student loan office, endorse it, apply $10 to my student loan and keep the forty-five cents. A *Vogue* magazine cost thirty-five cents and with the remaining dime I could buy three Mr. Goodbar candy bars. I always meant to save and savor them but usually the magazine and candy bars were finished the first night.

It was well that I was self-supporting. My parents could afford very little help. My mother sent me a total of $10 my entire senior year but not all at one time. I still have some of her letters beginning, "Enclosed is 50 cents. I wish I could send more."

Getting a student loan made education possible but it wasn't easy. Each semester was preceded by a stern talk from Dean McKee beginning, "We may not be able to help you this time." I would agonize until I received the word. The second time it happened, I was so obviously relieved that the loan manager reached over and patted my hand.

"Don't you worry," she said. "We'll always approve you."

The loan manager was Christine Hauschild, an angel. Years later a roadside park was named for her. We would stop and eat our lunch on the way to football games and I would say a quiet prayer of thanks for this lovely lady.

It is no wonder that socialist and communist sentiments abounded on campuses in that era. One of my papers for journalism class was written in praise of Russia, which had, I'd read, a policy of providing education for students with both need and merit. I looked around at the prosperous students, so often pretty, brainless girls interested only in parties and frivolity, and it just didn't seem fair.

Another J-school paper which has survived the yellowing of time was titled "The Newspaper and The Chain Letter." Chain letters were the get-rich-quick scheme of the day.

"Just send a dime to the name at the top, add your name at the bottom," the letter would instruct. "In time, prosperity will come to you.''

The fallacy was in mankind's inherent greed. While some innocents copied the list of names and added theirs to the bottom, other, less-principled ones put their names at the top so the flood of dimes would come sooner. Eventually the fad fell apart.

Meanwhile, back at the dormitory, it was a new life with a large group of new friends. We'd sit around at night in talk sessions (''bull sessions,'' we called them) and speculate on just which girls, not present, were virgins.

I don't know if there's more sex on college campuses now than there was in our day but it certainly must be easier. We were inhibited by lack of place, lack of money, and the fear that hovered over us like a black cloud: What if you got pregnant? What if you had to get married?

During our senior year, one couple did get married, but not from biological necessity. They simply wanted to marry. Both were outstanding students and campus leaders. They were expelled!

Also during my senior year something happened which had a sobering effect and left a lasting mark.

My friend Cas had been living in her own apartment with a stray dog, Rags, but we still saw each other regularly. One day I had word that she was in the hospital. I went to see her and she seemed very sick, but no reason was given.

I few days later I learned what was wrong. Cas, the worldly sophisticate who knew her way around, had peritonitis, the result of a backstreet abortion. There were no wonder drugs in those days. Within a week she was dead.

It was as if a curtain had come down in my life. I began studying harder, writing more, trying somehow to have the career we'd both talked about. I had another writer-friend, Jetta, who was also a poet and a dancer. One noon in the spring of the year, I came into Read Hall and met up with happy hysteria from my friends.

Jetta had won first prize in the Mahan essay contest and I had won second. The honor was great, and so was the $15 prize. A few weeks later, I won the McAnally Medal, also for writing. I still have the medal, but at the time the $15 seemed better.

In May I made a note in my diary: "I am no longer working in the kitchen, having been laid off due to lack of attendance. It's quite a relief, but I'm rather hungry."

I am struck, while reading my senior year diary, by the number of health complaints I noted—periods of dizziness, weakness, and occasional faintings. Now in my seventies, healthy as a horse most of the time, I can't help but contrast my present state of well-being with my early years. It's possible I was merely suffering from malnutrition.

But there was fun and happiness, despite our poverty. In May we held a dance at Read Hall, and my mother came to Columbia for the weekend. My father, luckily, had gotten a government job out of town and our financial situation was a little brighter.

Mother chaperoned at the dance, and Gary and I took her out into the country areas we loved for a picnic the next day. Our romance was flourishing. Perhaps subconsciously I had been shocked by Cas's death and was made more appreciative of the kind of steady, loving presence Gary provided and the solid, conservative values he represented. My arty Bohemian phase was at an end.

From entries in my diary, we must have had more money for little luxuries, for there are notes of going to the Gem Drugstore uptown for a special delicacy—date nut ice cream. Until then, our big splurge had consisted of going to the Crown Drugstore, one of the early supermarket-type of drugstores, where we could sit in a booth, spend ten cents for a giant milkshake and take the entire evening, drinking it through two straws.

Never did I lose track of my main goal, which was the completion of college, and I appreciated the opportunity I'd had, even though I'd had to crawl, claw, and carve my way.

It is probably impossible for young people today to realize how difficult it was for those of us from families of modest means to attend college at all. My opportunity to get a student loan was a rarity; there were no large-scale, federally-guaranteed loan programs as there are today.

When I finished college, I owed the University of Missouri $400, and when I became a wage-earner, I set about repaying it as a solemn obligation before I spent money on myself.

Very few of the girls in my high school graduating class were able to have any type of higher education. A few, like my friend Mary Felicia went to Harris Teacher College, which offered a good general college education, but required that you teach in the St. Louis public schools on graduation.

During the summer between my junior and senior years at Mizzou, Gary and I enjoyed our really big splurge of the year. Together we scraped up $5, enough for a couple to go to a dance at Meadowbrook Country Club, where dances were held on a beautiful outdoor dance floor with a big name band. We went to hear our favorite, Kay Kyser, and the next year, Hal Kemp.

On one of these occasions, I was powdering my nose in the ladies' room when Ruth, one of the prettiest and most popular girls in my high school class, greeted me. What are you doing now, we asked one another. She had gone on to business school and was working in an office. When she heard I was in college, a touch

*My picture in the Mizzou yearbook proves there wasn't much to smile about in 1935.*

of envy crossed her pretty face.

"I'd have given anything to have gone to college," she said, "'but my family couldn't afford it."

The irony of the situation struck me forcibly. My family "couldn't afford it" either, but I had gone and survived. It would be interesting to know how many girls went to college in those depression years. Not very many. When there was a son and a daughter in the family, the son was the one to be educated.

Commencement day came at last in June 1936. Mother came to Columbia for the ceremony and Aunt Hattie, cousins Grace and Florence, and their families came for the day.

We marched in caps and gowns and I was even in

a news photo, due to my proximity to a popular student, Jack Hackethorn. The headline read, "Hackethorn Finally Graduates." So did Start.

Gary's family took us home a few days later. I had met them earlier in spring and loved his father on sight. Gary's mother had died many years before and his stepmother, Elsie, was much younger than his father, blonde, beautifully dressed and a little intimidating. But his half-sister, Betty, then thirteen-years-old, was a charmer. Also blonde, she was not pretty but was a talented singer, dancer, and pianist, with a real gift for comedy. We hit it off immediately.

"I like you much better than any of Gary's other girls," she said.

Back in St. Louis, according to my diary, I "stared at the tall buildings" and wondered "if I'd ever get used to St. Louis again."

It was a shaky feeling, being out in the world. Even with its insecurity, college and Columbia had been a haven. Now it was over. I had joined the organization about which we'd joked in the dormitory:

The Society for Increasing the Unemployed.

# 13

## *I'll Never Go Hungry Again*

THE YUPPIES OF TODAY and their teenage brothers and sisters can't imagine what life was like in 1936. There were some very obvious differences.

There was no television set, no frozen TV dinners, no microwaves, computers, or VCRs. No nylon hose; even pantyhose was far in the future. No drip-dry fabrics, stretch pants, or spray deodorants. No pastel toilet paper, no aluminum wrap. No Hondas, Toyotas, Volkswagens, in fact no cars of any kind around high schools and few were owned by college students. No diet soda or flip-top cans. No pizza in the Midwest. No air travel to Europe and little anywhere else. No mention of outer space except in a comic strip titled, "Buck Rogers in the Twenty-Fifth Century."

But the biggest difference of all between the Pepsi generation and ours was that there was no money. And no jobs.

"You've got to be kidding," a teenager once said to me. "You mean you couldn't get the job you wanted. You can't mean you couldn't get a job at all."

No, you really couldn't get a job at all.

My first try was at Gardner Advertising. Erma Proetz, vice-president and an advertising woman of prominence had been a speaker at our Journalism Week program. She had stressed starting at the bottom and had urged women students (not men) to polish up on their typing and shorthand skills and be willing to take stenographic jobs to start.

My typing skill was already shiny bright and my shorthand was adequate, so when Mrs. Proetz came out to the reception room I announced that I was ready to start at the bottom. She hemmed and hawed a bit and finally suggested I leave my name and address and they would call me if they had an opening.

There were a lot of J-school grads in the St. Louis area and we all made the rounds of the same places. The *St. Louis Post-Dispatch,* the *Globe-Democrat,* the *Star-Times* (St. Louis was down to three newspapers, the *Times* having merged with the *Star).* There were a half-dozen radio stations, several ad agencies and a few other companies known to be headed by MU grads and receptive to new ones. The Missouri Pacific Railroad and Rice-Stix Dry Goods Co. were among them.

At one time I fantasized that the most wonderful job I could get would be one for a railroad. They were steady companies which had been in existence all my life and we couldn't imagine they'd ever be different. I was lucky my dream didn't come true.

Daily I made the rounds, always ending up at the Missouri State Employment Office, where the woman in charge was kind.

Occasionally I would run into Frank Goeman, another MU grad, in front of the DeSoto Hotel. That was where the Advertising Club of St. Louis had an office with a secretary who, on rare occasions, had news of jobs available. We'd compare notes.

One of the successful MU grads, Charlie King of the *Globe,* talked to me, and his wife took me out for a coke one day and introduced me to the personnel manager of the Retail Credit Union where she worked. But that was as far as it went.

Our financial situation at home had changed. My father had quit his job with the fabulous salary of $218 a month after three months. He also had lost his savings at Suffolk Downs Race Track.

My diary reveals a trace of bitterness. "Now some

people might think such an action foolish," I wrote, "but it's perfectly understandable. Why not pamper your whims and if a few people starve because of it, that shouldn't make any difference. They probably shouldn't have been born anyway."

Gary had a job of sorts that summer. His little sister, Betty, and her partner, Louise Becker, took their act—Betty and Lou, the Harmony Two—to a local beer garden on Grand and Shenandoah avenues. The act went over so well that the manager encouraged other acts to perform and Gary promoted a job for himself as master of ceremonies for amateur competitions. We spent every night that summer there.

Betty and Lou would do their song and tap dance routines to such tunes as, "Is It True What They Say About Dixie?" and "I'm Gonna Sit Right Down and Write Myself a Letter."

A tall, deep-voiced girl named Mildred nightly sang her big number, "You Are My Lucky Star" and everyone assured her she sounded just like Eleanor Powell, the movie star who recorded that number.

There was a group of talented young black singers—we called them, simply, "the colored boys"—one of whom sang "Melancholy Baby" with the high, sweet voice of an angel.

Now and then, Gary's friend, Irwin Johnson sang "The Very Thought of You," and once Gary sang, "Snuggled On Your Shoulder," although it was generally agreed after his solo that he should stick to introducing the other acts.

My parents were eking out a precarious existence, betting at a bookie joint, sometimes winning as much as $4 a week.

And Gary and I had our own game of chance. The company which made Lucky Strike cigarettes sponsored a radio program, ''Your Hit Parade,'' which played the week's ten most popular tunes in order of rank. If you guessed the top three in order, you could win a tin of ''flat 50s''—fifty cigarettes. We both smoked. Almost everyone did—another difference in lifestyle.

By being knowledgeable and sending in multiple entries, varying the various top tunes, we managed to win every week and keep ourselves in cigarettes all summer. Picking the tunes was easy for me. I'd followed popular music all my life and my diaries are filled with the words of my favorites. Appropriately, ''Smoke Gets In Your Eyes'' was our favorite song that year.

Gary went back to school that fall, financing himself in part with a job at a restaurant called The Annex, where he worked from five to midnight each day. And one of my many applications bore fruit. I was hired at Stix, Baer and Fuller—not in the advertising department, but as a salesgirl in children's clothing.

This was a masterful piece of miscasting, as I had

no contact with small children and knew nothing about their clothing. Occasionally, some mother sent her child out alone to do his school shopping and it was a real guessing game as we tried on everything in sight until something fit.

The job didn't last long because I wasn't too good at it. But the $2.00 a day (9 A.M.-5 P.M.) helped for awhile.

"So here I am, at 19," I wrote at the conclusion of my 1935-36 diary, "Clarissa Start, B. J., jobless, possessing nothing but hope.

"I do have the love of a fine young man but even he is 125 miles distant. A lot has happened in the last year and I'm glad most of it is over. I suppose, looking back, I'd do everything the same. As a matter of fact, I had no choice in my decisions. It was all fate. Sometimes I think Thomas Hardy was right. I only hope next year brings something better."

That was written in September 1936. My diaries ran from school year to school year.

Again, as in the case of Washington at Valley Forge, it would have been encouraging could I have seen ahead, although it would have required high-powered lenses for long-range viewing. There wasn't much ahead in the near future. After each day of job hunting failure would come the thought:

"What if I never get a job? Is it possible to go through a whole lifetime and never find work?"

In October luck smiled on me. An employment agency asked me to come in. The supervisor asked if I could really type seventy-five words a minute as I said on my job application. I told her I might even type eighty, which I did on a test at the United Drug Co. later that day, making only five errors on a page, four of them in the first line.

At last I had a job, paying $15 a week. It was some distance from home, two streetcars and a bus away, about an hour's time each direction. The hours were eight to five and in those days everyone worked on Saturday, at least half a day. Sometimes we had to work nights, but then we received thirty-five cents extra. You must put these salaries in perspective. A good lunch in the company cafeteria cost only nine cents!

Not everyone looked poor in 1936. Gary's family was, in my eyes, quite prosperous. They lived in a beautiful home near Tower Grove Park. The first time I went there, Betty showed me around from the paneled dining room through the parlor and front hall to the upstairs library, a forerunner of the family room where the family relaxed. Then through the bedrooms past the hall closets which she opened as she casually identified, ''My white suits.'' On the third floor was a playroom with dolls and life-sized stuffed animals, with emphasis on the Republican elephant.

On the surface it was luxurious. What didn't show was that the house was heavily mortgaged, so that

Gary's father could buy rental property which, in turn, he mortgaged to buy more rental property. He was a lawyer in a suite of offices in a big downtown building. His partner, who later became a judge, the partner's wife, also a lawyer, and young lawyers and clerks rounded out the staff. It looked great. There just wasn't much business.

Daddy Dave, as I later called him, was a self-made man who had "read law" in a judge's office in a small town in Illinois, and then worked his way up to become a power in Republican politics, a state legislator, and an assistant circuit attorney. In that fall of 1936 he was working on the campaign of a candidate for secretary of state of Missouri, L. D. Thompson. We went to a big rally where Betty and Lou, the Harmony Two, entertained. The fiery oratory was directed at "that man in the White House." I kept it a secret that I was still a Franklin Roosevelt supporter.

To partisan eyes, the presidential election of 1936 seemed a lively contest. Alf Landon from Kansas was the Republican candidate. And there was a third candidate whom my parents, by then disenchanted with Roosevelt, were considering. Mother had become a fan of a Catholic priest, Father Charles Coughlin, and his candidate, William Lemke, had entered the race.

I thought Father Coughlin was somewhat radical but not all bad. After all, his magazine, *Social Justice,* had purchased a short story I submitted and sent me a check for five dollars, which financed a weekend in Columbia, visiting Gary and all the Read Hall girls still in school.

Mainly I considered myself above politics. I wrote: "The campaign makes one reel. Republicans support Roosevelt and Democrats like Al Smith are supporting Landon. Roosevelt is called a Communist and Landon a Fascist. Norman Thomas and the *Baltimore Sun* say that everyone's crazy. The two forgotten men are the vice presidential candidates, Knox and Garner.

"Billboards scream, 'Know the truth and the truth shall make you free—Roosevelt' while others read, 'Know the Real Truth and vote for Landon.' Someone asks, 'Who in hell can eat sunflowers' [a reference to Landon's state, Kansas] and someone writes seriously explaining that sunflowers are very nutritious. Earl Browder, the real Communist candidate, is suing. Platitudes are spread on with a lavish hand. It all smells. And that's the election of 1936."

My next diary entry begins, "President Roosevelt was elected by the largest vote, the largest popular vote and the largest electoral vote ever given a candidate in this country.

"He received 500 to Landon's 8 electoral votes, Maine and Vermont. All sorts of rumors are flying— that there will be a living annual wage, higher taxes for higher incomes, that the government will take over private utilities. It is the beginning of a new era. At least we are moving into it more peaceably than they are in Europe.''

For Gary's family it was the end of an era. Nice Mr. Thompson was defeated, as were all the local Republicans. Despite Roosevelt's optimistic claims concerning an end to the depression, it was very much with us and the tenants in the Davidson rental property couldn't pay. Everywhere families were doubling up and property stood vacant.

Like dominoes tumbling, one piece of property after another was lost until the Davidsons had only their house. And while Gary's father went to the office every day, their living expenses were being paid by Betty's job as a singer and dancer at The Irish Village, a midtown nightclub where she received $25 a week.

My job had ended after six weeks, just one week after I had made a small downpayment on a $139 muskrat coat, the fur coat I'd yearned for all through college.

My father had a small WPA job which kept us alive. I continued to send out stories, get rejection slips, and to make applications for jobs.

On Thursday, December 3, 1936, I wrote: "In the face of such momentous news as 'Will the King marry Wally?' [King Edward VIII and divorcee Wallis Warfield Simpson], my news is of little importance except to me. But I finally have a job with a firm almost as old and honorable as the British monarchy, the St.

Louis Union Trust Co. on the second floor of the First National Bank.''

I was hired by the treasurer of the firm, a man with the appropriate name of Alexander Hamilton. He looked at me in a fatherly way, said he noticed that I had graduated from college and he hoped I had not been indoctrinated with communism there. I assured him I had not and added that I had taught Sunday School.

On the basis of that moral persuasion I was hired. As he guided me into the securities cage, a wired enclosure in which I was to work, he said "Of course you take shorthand." I gulped and said, "Sort of," which was the truth.

As I had done at United Drug, I worked on a "fanfold machine," a typewriter which made multiple carbons, but unlike United Drug I could not XXX out errors in orders for aspirin and candy. Records at the trust company, where we dealt with bonds and trust accounts, had to be perfect. Each page was numbered and when an error was made, you went to your supervisor to have that number expunged from the records.

Long after I'd left the company, I met up with a co-worker who laughingly told me that when they cleaned out my desk, they found the dozens of papers I'd hidden away when I couldn't face my supervisor with one more canceled number.

"So you've gone to work for Shylock, the enemy,"

my left-leaning friend, Pert wrote from California. I didn't look at it that way. The company was good to me. The office was like a family and just as at my college NYA job, the older women were kind and motherly. There was a flirtatious young clerk who made life interesting and two nice white-collar proper young men clerks who were kind. All this made up for the fact that my boss terrified me. Looking back, I realize he was all of twenty-six or twenty-seven years old and probably insecure himself.

The king chose Wally as we romantics had hoped he would do, and in offices throughout the land, we gathered around radios tearfully as he abdicated his throne for "the woman I love" and slipped into the anonymity of becoming the Duke of Windsor.

My salary was only $70 a month at the trust company but it enabled me to meet the payments on my fur coat, buy a new pair of shoes in the fashion color of the season, "British tan," and buy my mother a Christmas present.

My budget allowed only a dollar for the gift and I spent it carefully. Mother liked cosmetics and most of them were available at the five-and-ten cent store. I purchased ten items and arranged them in a box. Mother loved it.

There was a new game out that year. My diary recorded that we'd gone to a party at Irving Tietze's house and learned to play Monopoly. Also I had bought a copy of "the best book I've ever read." It was *Gone With the Wind*.

Shirley Temple was the movie star of the year but *Gone With the Wind* provided us with the heroine of the era.

We all identified with Scarlett O'Hara who vowed: "As God is my witness—I'll never go hungry again."

# 14

## The Worries of 1937

THERE ARE MANY PERIODS OF MY LIFE I would not want to relive and it would be difficult to list them in order, but I think the year of 1937 would rank among the worst.

In some ways, the spring of 1937 was a breakthrough as I finally was hired for a job for which I had prepared. I left the ranks of stenographers and typists to become an advertising copywriter, my J school dream.

It was not quite the copywriting to which I'd aspired when I wrote high fashion copy for the *Vogue Prix de Paris* contest during my senior year. It was a job with

the Rice-Stix Dry Goods Company, a wholesale firm
on Washington Avenue, garment industry center of
St. Louis. Their highest style garments were their
Eight O'Clock Dressettes, which wholesaled at $8.00
a dozen.

I was hired by Ralph Schmitt, the advertising
manager—one of the J school graduates who had been
kind to me during an interview in the summer of 1936,
but who had had nothing for me then. Now one of
his copywriters was leaving to get married and her job
was available. Was I interested? Oh yesyesyesyesyes.

My predecessor, Isabel Bauer, was marrying Rudy
Gerber, the assistant advertising manager, and she
spent her final week showing me the ropes. There were
catalogs I'd help prepare, ads I'd assemble to be sent
in newspaper mat form to smalltown retailers who
could not afford advertising staffs and used our
prepared ads.

I would be working for six department heads, six
bosses in addition to Mr. Schmitt. I soon learned that
each was ruler in his or her territory, and each was
temperamental.

At the trust company I'd had only Mr. Schroeder
to terrify me. Now I had Mr. Hennigan, Mr. Lubbe,
Mr. Ladney, Mr. Liberman, Mr. McDermott, and
Miss Pabst. I was introduced to each in turn and
learned of the specialties, dresses, lingerie, millinery,
purses, and a newly added line, Paddle and Saddle

sportswear.

My predecessor herself was intimidating. She seemed so self-confident, so positive, so crisp and businesslike. Her fiance, who sat across from me at an adjoining desk, was gentler and reassuring and, as I later learned, had a delightful sense of humor. His annual project consisted of hanging a huge calendar with an outdoor scene illustration. As the year went on, he painstakingly added people and animals, montage fashion, to the basic scene, so perfectly in scale and dimension and color that visitors would stand contemplating the picture for some time before they suddenly blinked and did a doubletake, as they realized an alligator was emerging from the fishing stream and Tarzan was swinging from a tree over a movie starlet.

Along with my array of bosses to sort out, there was the array of co-workers—Henrietta, who was Mr. Schmitt's right hand; Mary and Harriet, who did mail-order layouts; Elizabeth, Vi, Oscar, and others, now blurred in memory.

I worked there for a year, and within a month I was miserably aware that I was woefully inadequate for the job. Layout had never been my forte; art was beyond me. Writing was, I had thought, my talent, but not writing in sales phrases. I would labor over clever copy only to have Mr. Hennigan cross it out and substitute, ''New! Different! Must be seen to be appreciated!'' In my presence, Mr. Liberman lamented that it was ''too bad we can't afford a really good writer.''

Not only did I find selling merchandise difficult but I wasn't too good at selling myself. At age twenty, despite my feeling of sophistication, I impressed my superiors only with youth and lack of confidence. There were things they hadn't taught me in journalism school and when I made mistakes, they were lulus.

There was, for instance, the black moment when Schmitt was out of town and I proudly produced a series of ads for our new acquisition, kiddie clothes, with a tie-in with *Snow White and the Seven Dwarfs,* the big Walt Disney movie of the year.

My ad featured all seven of the dwarfs, heads outlined at the top of the ad. I had the engraving made and proofs on Mr. Schmitt's desk when he returned.

Then all hell broke loose.

Hadn't I realized that while we could use the name, we could not use the pictures of the seven dwarfs or Walt Disney would sue us? Didn't I realize that it had cost to have that outlined engraving produced and now it had to be done over? Why had I assumed I could go ahead on my own ill-advised initiative?

Through such crises, I had one ally, E. Julian Birk, who represented the engraving firm. It was Julian who dried my tears, comforted me, and told my boss that some of the blame was his for encouraging me and he would assume some of the cost. It was Julian who constantly sought to build up my belief in my ability. He was a dear and I never ceased being grateful to him.

As the year went on I became more comfortable, although I was never comfortable with the office politics and backroom gossip, the smiling face with the knife ready for the back.

Moreover, we all had the economic situation to contend with. President Roosevelt's second term was floundering along making little progress with ending the depression and rumors circulated constantly. Thirty percent were going to be "laid off." All of us would be "laid off for a week without pay." Certain departments were scheduled for bloodletting. An efficiency expert had been hired to see who was expendable.

There was the period when the door to the ladies' room was kept open. This, we were told, was to discourage personnel from loitering, sitting, and chatting. When you went to the restroom, you were to do your business and get back to work. This led me to use up some of my employer's time, studiously working on a design for an office chair with a potty seat so we wouldn't have to leave our desks at all for nature's call.

Pressure breeds counterpressure. Throughout my years of employment it was my observation that the kindly boss got more out of his employees than the tyrant. Few people produce one hundred percent of the time, but if an employee likes his boss, he may try to produce one hundred ten percent of the time.

All this I carried to my patient love, Gary, who, weary of my complaints, was less than sympathetic. "I wonder if you'll ever find a job you like," he said.

He was having problems of his own. He had graduated in June and passed the state bar exam although we had an agonizing moment before we realized his name was out of alphabetical order and appeared one space after it should have. There was no work for him in his father's office and so he made the rounds of other offices without result.

How hard it is to recreate in words the economic climate of that day. Gary agonized over not having the right clothes to wear. He applied for one job, wearing summer "ice cream" white pants, and realized he hardly looked the part of a young lawyer. We practiced all kinds of petty economies. The fall of 1937 was when my father and I played "the transfer game."

On the strength of my new job, we had moved to a slightly better apartment on Virginia Avenue. Daily I took the Bellefontaine car which ran in front of the door and went all the way downtown. But one could get a transfer to another line, and my father figured out that by walking up to the intersection of Delor he could take the Delor bus to Grand, the Grand car to Olive and also go downtown—if he had a transfer. So daily, I got on the streetcar, asked for a transfer, hurried to a back window seat and let the transfer flutter through the window so my father could pick it up. Of course it was cheating but then the poor have always rationalized that cheating the rich establishment is all right. Robin Hood did it.

All went well until winter came. I got on the street car one day, hurried to the back seat, and found the window closed. I tugged and tugged and couldn't open it. Suddenly I was aware that the streetcar hadn't started up. The motorman was on his way back. Red with embarrassment, I mumbled something about not really wanting to open the window but he leaned over, opened it a crack and turned his back, as I pushed the transfer through.

I'm sure we were not the only ones to use this clever scheme and perhaps he, too, sympathized with the ''little man.'' It was well-known among the unemployed that there was a counter in the post office where people would leave transfers to be used by those who couldn't afford a fare.

In our student days, we had talked of having a Thanksgiving Day wedding in 1937, but Thanksgiving came and went and we were far from our dream. We did officially announce our engagement during the Christmas-New Year holiday and Gary had my Aunt Lil's diamond reset (at wholesale) through the kindness of a jeweler in his father's office building.

There had been one bright note in my early months at Rice-Stix. In the lull between the fall and winter catalog, which came out in summer, and the spring catalog, not due until late fall, I spent time mulling over writing topics.

There was a rash of news stories about child prodigies at the time, bright, precocious kiddies whose high IQs brought them into the limelight. I cynically reflected on my own early promise and how now, at age twenty, I was nothing. And I wrote a funny story about it which I mailed to the "Everyday Magazine" of the *St. Louis Post-Dispatch* on a Friday in August.

That Sunday, the magazine published a story by "Jake Yoo," a pseudonym for a staffer, joking about the easy life of the city girl compared to the hard life of the girl in the country. It was intended to arouse the passions of city office slaves and it aroused mine. I wrote a sarcastic rejoinder relating the woes of the city girl, from hanging to a strap as she stood on a bus during rush hour to standing behind a slow eater at the lunch counter and rushing back to punch a time clock. Yes, we punched time clocks at Rice-Stix.

My guardian angel was working overtime. Both of my stories arrived at the *Post* on Monday morning. It was late August when newspapers have little to print. The editor, Don Thompson, was on vacation. In his place was his assistant, Damon Kerby.

Damon was helping orient the son of the publisher

(and grandson of the founder), Joseph Pulitzer Jr., known to the staff until middle age as "Young Joe." Kerby put Young Joe to work reading the mail and my efforts, which might have been returned by a more jaded editor, met with appreciation. Not only appreciation, but publication and pay, the generous sum of $15 each.

When the editor returned, he sent for me. I sat, quaking before him. A man of few words, he looked at me. I looked at him. Finally I said, "Thank you," and left. As I was standing at the elevator, he came bustling out and asked, "Did you get your checks?" "Yes sir," I said. End of interview.

Undaunted, I continued to write bright little stories and he continued to send them back. Finally he wrote a brief note suggesting that I desist, as they had a staff.

Many years later I happened across a little list I'd made at this time. It was headed, "Things That Worry Me This Year of 1937." I read it and laughed a little and cried a little.

What was I worried about in 1937? My job, of course, my lack of ability, its lack of security. A needless worry. Eventually I left it for a much better one. My mother's health was another worry. She lived for thirty more years of health and happiness. Other worries were as needless and nebulous. My future? It's still ahead of me. But the list served a purpose. Finding it all those years later put an end to what I

*Our first apartment, in 1938-39, was at 4040 Hydraulic.*

was worrying about that year.

Rebuffed by the *Post-Dispatch,* I went back to writing fiction. Early in 1938 I got out the rough draft of a novelette, rewrote it, and addressed an envelope to the *Chicago Daily News* syndicate whose name appeared at the bottom of serials in the *Globe-Democrat.* My father took it to the post office but brought it home to ask if I wanted to spend as much as sixty cents to mail it.

"What would they pay you if they bought it?" mother asked.

"Oh, maybe as much as $50."

"And we're quibbling over sixty cents," said mother. "Mail it."

A week later I received a letter of acceptance and a check for $80. My luck had turned. The clouds had lifted. As a writer, I can say truthfully, the sun has been shining ever since.

This magnificent bonanza made something else possible. We began planning a wedding in May. The timing was perfect. The Davidsons had lost their house and would be moving to a small apartment. My father wanted to go to Florida. Since neither Gary nor I would have a home, we might as well have one of our own.

*My wedding party, front row from left: Betty Davidson, Mary Felicia Eiermann, the bride and groom, Marcella Frank, and Ruperta Woodcock. Back row: John Irwin Johnson, Hartwell Stahl, and William Brinkman.*

We rented an apartment at 4040 Hydraulic Avenue in South St. Louis. Living room, bedroom and kitchen, $27.50 a month. We furnished with the familiar brown satin studio couch which my parents gave me and with purchases from Lammert's prestigious furniture store. Aunt Olie and Uncle John gave me $25 for a wedding gift and I told them I would buy a desk with it.

Actually we used it as a down payment on the desk ($25), barrel back chair ($35), broadloom carpet ($25),

*Our wedding day—May 14, 1938—was cloudy, sunny, windy, and calm. The weather was a portent of days to come.*

four-poster bed ($8), springs and mattress ($25) and a solid mahogany chest of drawers ($50). The apartment furnished stove and refrigerator. The Davidsons gave us some depression glass dishes which I sold when I became an antique dealer, and Aunt Hattie gave me a bridal shower which provided such practical items as pots, pans, mop, and broom.

Our wedding was far beyond our financial status. White satin and veil, a flower girl, Betty, bridesmaids Pert, Mary Felicia, and Betty's cousin Marcella, best man, John Irwin Johnson, groomsmen, Bill Brinkman and my cousin, Hartwell Stahl.

For $5 I purchased the satin at Rice-Stix and for $4 each, blue chiffon for the attendants who made their own dresses. Two young men had opened a neighborhood flower shop. They provided a big wedding bouquet of white flowers, and Talisman roses for the bridesmaids, corsages for the mothers, boutonnieres for the groomsmen and potted palms for the church. The entire bill was $16. When we paid it, they gave me a philodendron in a fancy pot.

I regret to say the nice young men went out of business very shortly. If I knew where they were, I would repay them by ordering some $48-a-dozen roses today.

May 14 was a mixed day—clouds, sunshine, clouds again, perhaps a portent of the future. We were married in St. Luke's Lutheran Church, photographed by Carna photographers and returned to the apartment for a reception with one bottle of champagne.

Our honeymoon was a drive through the country (now the suburb of Affton), a hamburger at Medart's on Kingshighway, and home to our apartment. We had neglected to buy food for the next day so we dropped in on our maid of honor and her surprised but resourceful mother, who fed us.

My job at Rice-Stix was paying me $17 a week. Gary's job as a credit chaser for the Crowell-Collier Publishing Co. averaged $7 a week. By careful budgeting, we ate on $4 a week, managing to have steak, veal, hamburger, lamb chops, and an occasional vegetarian meal.

Each payday we put money into little envelopes, labeled Food, Gas, Electric, Telephone, Rent. Gas and electric bills were a dollar or two a month, telephone $3. And of course we both made regular payments on our student loans, which we considered debts of honor.

The outlook was not forbidding but it wasn't promising either. Then something wonderful happened.

My serial story, "Glamor Is Just A Word," began appearing in the *Globe-Democrat.* The competition on the *Post-Dispatch* noticed it.

"Isn't this the girl who wrote some stories for us last summer?" Damon Kerby asked Don Thompson. "Maybe she'd be the one to fill in for Dorothy Coleman this summer." Dorothy, a feature writer and columnist, was going to Europe.

The editors still had my parents' apartment address, but there was no phone there. They wired the syndicate for my new address and phone number and then sent me a wire. "COME IN TO DISCUSS POSSIBLE JOB."

It was only temporary, they warned. I hesitated but then they named the salary. Thirty dollars a week!

"I'll take it," I said quickly.

And thus began my "temporary" job with the *Post-Dispatch.* It lasted thirty-four years.

# 15

## Rendezvous With Destiny

"TO SOME GENERATIONS much is given. Of other generations much is asked. This generation of Americans has a rendezvous with destiny."

He was speaking to my generation. One of Franklin Delano Roosevelt's gifted ghost writers—was it Robert Sherwood?—had written the words but it was FDR who brought them to life. How well I remember the vibrant mellifluous tones with which we had become acquainted in the famous "fireside chats." He always addressed us as, "My Friends." The talks were on radio but they radiated a warmth that could have come from a fireside.

People reacted to Roosevelt in several ways. Some revered him as a father figure, a leader on a pedestal, the champion of the "little man," a person who could do no wrong. Others hated and distrusted him and referred to him with scorn as "that man in the White House." And then there were those of us who sensed that he was, indeed, a con man, an opportunist, a consummate politician, but who were so admiring of his technique that we rewarded him as one rewards a super salesman, by signing on the dotted line—even though we didn't quite believe the guarantee.

After all, we had to trust somebody. And what was the alternative? In 1936 the alternative had been Alf Landon, well-meaning but colorless. In 1940 it was Wendell Willkie, another glib salesman, a personable and powerful businessman, certainly a man with charisma. It was my first chance to vote in a presidential election, as I had turned twenty-one in 1938. I gave it much thought.

In the end, I voted for Roosevelt, canceling out the vote of my dyed-in-the-wool Republican husband.

The summer of 1940 was also the year my young husband spent two weeks at Camp Custer, Michigan, as a newly commissioned second lieutenant.

The commission had been at my urging. As early as 1939 I was sure our country would eventually be at war, although there were many high-ranking political figures and pundits who scoffed at this idea. Even Dorothy Thompson, the columnist who was the ideal of those of us in the lower ranks of women writers, laughed at the idea of "Little Adolf" Hitler aspiring to make his Germany a world power.

Dorothy Thompson had an influence on a tiny part of my life as a writer. I was to have a byline on my newspaper work and I immediately suggested my new name, Clarissa Davidson. Too long, said the editors. Besides, I was established as Clarissa Start.

Established? After two published stories a year ago?

"Forget about it," mother said laughingly. "Look at Dorothy Thompson. She's had two or three husbands and she's still Dorothy Thompson."

"Mama, I'm not going to have two or three husbands," I said with the positive assurance of youth.

But Clarissa Start it was and that it has stayed through two married names.

My stories were frivolous froth, icing on the solid stuff. The *Post-Dispatch* in those days had a distinguished reputation—"one of the ten best newspapers in the country," it had been called, and it was a respected bipartisan, if liberal, voice.

One day, a few weeks after I'd joined the staff, a wave of inner-office communication swept through the building. "Bovard's resigned," I was told when I asked the news.

"Who's Bovard?" I replied, revealing that I hadn't learned everything in journalism school. Oliver K. Bovard was the managing editor and a famous and controversial figure. He was in disagreement with the powers of the Pulitzer Publishing Co. over their support of Roosevelt, not because he thought Roosevelt too radical but too conservative—a "mere Kerensky," he said, likening him to the Russian pre-revolutionary figure.

His resignation caused a great stir, so much so that we were all asked to remain after work for a five o'clock meeting, at which we would be told what everyone already knew. I was less than enthusiastic about staying late but it was an order.

To my chagrin, Ben Reese, the city editor, circled the room looking for alien spies and singled out Bill Isam and me.

"Who are you?" he asked sternly. "I edit the 'Weekly Whizzer,' sir," said Bill who was in charge of the newly created page for children.

"I work on the magazine," I identified myself.

"Out," said Mr. Reese with a gesture of the thumb and we left.

Bill and I laughed in later years about being booted from the top secret meeting. The next day as I was going out to lunch, Ben Reese, a big, burly, imposing man came down the sidewalk on Twelfth Street and stopped directly in front of me.

"I want to apologize," he boomed. "Don Thompson tells me you're a new member of the staff. I'm sorry I asked you to leave." At least I knew who the new M.E. was—Ben Reese, a big man in many ways.

In October, Don Thompson stopped by my desk

to tell me that my job would be permanent; Dorothy Coleman was not returning. My salary was to be raised to—oh joy!—$40 a week!

Working for a metropolitan daily was an exciting experience, partly because you knew the headlines before they hit the street. Increasingly the dark clouds of war hung over the horizons of Europe. They darkened my diary, no longer a scrawl in a lined notebook but neatly typed on copy paper on company time.

> Monday, Sept. 25, 1938.—It's beginning to look as if things will start popping in Europe any minute. Britain and France after first deciding to throw Czechoslovakia to the wolves have done an about face and said No more concessions for Hitler without a guarantee of peace. Personally I think they should beat Hitler to a pulp and destroy Germany while they can. Roosevelt has written a note, asking that the nations not abandon plans for peace, as he said, outside countries as well as those involved will feel the results of the catastrophe that might follow. Everyone agrees that war would be the most horrible thing ever witnessed on earth but peace at any price will only avert it for a little while. I know I'll hide my darling in the closet before I'll let him go to war.

My sentiments were naive but typical of the am-
bivalence of the times. Most of my generation were
strongly pacifistic by childhood indoctrination. Movies
showed the horrors of war more than the glory. Erich
Maria Remarque's *All Quite On the Western Front*
represented the German view of the futility of combat. The French-English-American side on film gave
a lot of attention to the ''hinky-dinky-parlay-voo''
romances of the Charmaines and the U.S. doughboys,
but they too were somewhat realistic.

A serial story in the *Ladies Home Journal* had a great
effect on my thinking. ''I Saw Them Die'' was written by a woman who had been a nurse in World War
I and her graphic reminiscence of such scenes as the
bombing of a hospital and parts of bodies hanging on
trees ''like gruesome Christmas ornaments'' impressed
me deeply. Not for us, we vowed.

Were we influenced by our university professors?
I'm sure they tried. I recall a history professor who
seemed pro-German and a philosophy professor who
would urge us to march in May Day parades as
students did at eastern universities. But for the most
part we laughed it off. Who wanted to form a protest
parade on a May day when you could go on a beer
bust on Hinkson Creek?

The closest I came to parlor-pink sentiment was to
attend a rally for a socialist candidate. We all thought
socialists were fine and Norman Thomas, their peren-

*Gary and his father, Edward G. Davidson.*

nial candidate, a nice man.

And so the stories of Hitler's audacity alarmed us, but not to the extent of wanting to change the status quo. Not my newly married status quo.

We were happy in our little apartment on our limited budget and now and then we even gave a party. One was a costume party and because Gary had a new tiny mustache which gave him a slight resemblance to Hitler, he wore his khaki uniform, combed his hair across his forehead and assumed an Achtung! Heil! stance. We all thought it was very funny.

We also had an educational project going that fall, as Gary organized a class in criminal law, attended by friends. That was a subject for jokes, too. "This week we're into murder and next week we get to

*My mother posed for Gary's camera in August 1949.*

rape,'' I reported to co-workers.

My parents were still a source of concern. They had gone to Florida right after our marriage, tried to establish themselves on the farmland in which they'd invested during the boom. When money ran out, they hitchhiked back to St. Louis. My mother's penciled account of their step-by-step walk still gives me chills.

I met them at the bus station as they were able to ride the few miles across the river. I was shocked at mother's burned skin, rough hands, and shabby clothes. We found them a cheap furnished room.

Our small incomes were stretched to help not only

*Our first house, on Murdoch Avenue in Shrewsbury.*

my parents but Gary's family, too. They presented a more respectable appearance, but had to borrow from us from time to time.

Gary had left his magazine credit job and connected with a law firm, Gleick and Strauss, in a downtown office. Like his father, he had a respectable front but little income. His salary was $50 a month but that was better than that of the young man who shared his office and received only desk space and no money. He later left and became a highly successful TV news director.

Betty was singing with a band, Buddy Kay, at the Casa Loma ballroom in South St. Louis and we basked in her fame as she received ovations for her "A-Tisket A-Tasket" (just like Ella Fitzgerald) and her "Old Man Mose" (just like Betty Hutton).

I continued to write newspaper serials, 25,000 words for $80, but eventually reasoned that I was doing much better writing about 3,000 words for the *Post-Dispatch* for $80 in two weeks. I gave up my fiction career.

My specialty in those days was humor, the light little bits of satire which Thompson called "think stories," along with interviews with jazz figures—Benny Goodman, Glenn Miller, and others.

Gary continued to look for better jobs and war kept threatening.

*My first dog, Suellen.*

August 31, 1939—The tension has been building in Europe over Hitler's demands for Danzig and the Polish Corridor. News broadcasts interrupt all the programs and the situation looks bad. I was positive that Chamberlain would slice up Poland and hand it to Hitler as he did Sudetenland. Gary was equally sure Hitler would be sufficiently bluffed and back down, for, as Dorothy Thompson said in a broadcast, "He's sitting in on the biggest poker game in history and he's holding a pair of deuces."

One big card is the fact that he's signed a nonaggression pact with Russia, as yet unratified thus making the democracies worry. An eventual war seemed inevitable, everyone voicing the opinion that we should stay out of it.

> Meanwhile Gary is taking a course to make him
> a second lieutenant in the reserve corps . . . they
> have a legal department. . . .

That was all the news except that we had a canary.

My entry of Sept. 4, 1939, related that a state of war existed between Germany and France and England, that we listened to Chamberlain and King George and that when the band played "God Save the King," Skipper, the canary had swelled his yellow feathers and sung along with them.

We bought our first new car in the fall of 1939. Until then we had owned two, a disintegrating Model T we'd called Naughty Marietta and an aging Model A Ford. As repair bills mounted we opted to take the plunge and spend $675, the price of a beautiful maroon-colored Studebaker Champion.

As another sign of our affluence, we went to Florida in January 1940 with my parents and Aunt Olie and Uncle John. We found Miami prices staggering but after dickering, managed to rent an apartment for the six of us for $35 a week. It was near a good restaurant where fifty cents covered a dinner consisting of shrimp cocktail, steak, baked potato, vegetable, salad, dessert and coffee, and if you arrived before 6 P.M. a free Manhattan cocktail. One night Gary and I splurged on a seventy-five cent dinner at a top seafood restaurant.

I wrote stories with the help of hotel press agents—one on an Egyptian prince, another on an English bartender who was a nephew of Winston Churchill. Thus we had a chance to view high life at the headliner spots and one night we even saw Walter Winchell, the legendary gossip columnist. We went to a jai alai game, played miniature golf (the new craze), had fun.

We had been married two years when I got the nesting urge, not for a family—that was not yet financially possible—but for a home.

Amazingly we had saved enough for a down payment on an acre of ground in Sunset Hills, priced at $1,000. I knew exactly the kind of house I wanted, a Cape Cod with dormer windows. We had an architect draw up plans and estimate costs. His figure was discouraging—$7,000—but we dreamed.

Not long ago a friend said to me, "Some dreams are not meant to be realized." I never did get the Cape Cod house.

I was probably influenced by the Cape Cod where Gary's cousin and her husband lived. Jo and Vernon Reger were older than we and often had us over for an evening of talk and lemon pie.

Jo's right name was "Dimple" and a more inappropriate name could not have been found for her. A nurse, she wore pants long before anyone but Marlene Dietrich wore them. She was witty, profane, and we adored her and her quieter husband, Vernon.

It was Jo and Vern who came up with an alternative. Friends of theirs were moving from a rented house on Murdoch Avenue in Shrewsbury, a nice little suburb. The rent was just $30 a month, only a little more for a whole house than our apartment rent.

We moved in June. Gary went to Camp Custer and I was terrified to stay alone, but our nice neighbors, Andy and Beulah, who lived next door, looked after me. We heard our first country music, "You Are My Sunshine" played on Andy's guitar.

Daily we drove downtown, over the Murdock cutoff. That winter, a new house was taking shape and when the For Sale sign was put up, we stopped just to look.

It was not quite a Cape Cod, but it was cute, with a bay window at the end of the big living room. It had the fresh new smell of a new house. And it was only $6,150.

Within two months we had sold our acre of ground, making a $200 profit and qualified for an FHA loan. We courageously took on payments of $52 a month and on March 1, 1941, we moved into our home.

How I loved that house. Coming home at night we could see the branches of the big oak tree silhouetted in moonlight against the new bricks and, as Gary put the key in the lock, I would reach out and pat the walls. Our very own house.

That spring we planted a Paul's Scarlet climbing

rose against the garage wall and two lilac bushes—
seventy-five cents each. I grew marigolds and zinnias
from seed and my father planted tomatoes on the lot
next to us.

We soon knew all the neighbors—Bill and Peg, the
couple next door, who had built the house; Olive and
Clyde; Bill and Verna; Lucille and George; and Paul
and Helen.

There were five mothers who lived with the young
couples, and two teenagers—Billy, Bill and Peg's
nephew; and Helen and Paul's son, "young Paul."

Out of all the nights and days of that year, a few
flash up in memory. Like the fall night when we were
sitting on the front steps, holding hands and Billy and
Young Paul walked by.

"Look at the love birds," they teased. We laughed
and waved.

Billy and Paul both attended Webster High School.
Both wanted to be airplane pilots. Paul kept badger-
ing his mother to let him join the RAF.

"Look, mom, I only need the signature of one
parent . . . ."

"No, no, no! If and when we get involved but not
before. . . ."

Young men were being drafted into service for training. There was a song, "Goodbye, Dear, I'll Be Back
In A Year."

We looked at the two handsome boys crossing the

street to Paul's house. Mercifully we could not look ahead to the pictures we would clip from the papers a few years from then:

"Local Boy Awarded DFC" . . . "Plane Shot Down Over Frankfurt" . . . "Shrewsbury Man Missing."

The weather was still balmy. It was just starting to get cool. We stood up to go inside.

"It's almost cold," Gary remarked.

"Yes, but I don't mind. I can hardly wait for our first Christmas in our own home."

It was just two months away. December 1941.

# 16
## Army Wife

A FEW YEARS AGO at a meeting of the Webster Groves Historical Society, my husband, Ray, and I were talking with a young newspaperman who told us he was working on a historical novel.

"Really?" said Ray, who is something of a history buff. "What period are you writing about?"

"The 1930s," the young man said.

We looked at each other, trying to keep straight faces.

"It's a time we remember rather well," Ray said. "If you have any questions. . . ."

"Just remember there was no television then," I said.

"Oh, I know that." The young man reacted rather quickly.

On the way home, Ray and I got to talking about the things a young novelist might not know about the 1930s—not big things like the absence of television, but little things.

"I hope he doesn't have his heroine bake chocolate chip cookies," I said. "There weren't any chocolate chip cookies then."

I did a lot of cookie baking in 1940-41 because we had a farmer who delivered fresh eggs, twenty-five cents a dozen and fresh butter, twenty cents a pound. There were two new recipes publicized that winter and I liked them so well they've been a part of my cookie baking ever since. One was for Russian tea cookies. The other was for Toll House cookies, or chocolate chip cookies.

I was baking chocolate chip cookies on a Sunday afternoon, December 7, 1941, when the phone rang.

"Can you get it, honey? I'm baking."

Gary came back to the kitchen, a strained look on his face.

"Aunt Lu says to turn on the radio. The Japs have bombed Pearl Harbor." In answer to my question: "It's in Hawaii."

> December 8. It seems like something from Or-
> son Welles. Even this morning seemed unreal,

sunny and windy, so bright and clear that it seemed later in the day as we drove the new express highway into town. Most of the local staff had come to work at 5 A.M. and the first extra edition was already out. Everything was building up to the president's speech at 11:30 A.M.

A little after 11:30, I went down to the washroom, hoping I could hear something from the KSD office. The door was open and I could hear the president's voice so I stood in the doorway. Maggie and Fay and Lucianna from the society department were there and they motioned me to come in and sit down. We sat without a word. The speech was interspersed with cheers and applause. We all sensed what he would say as he neared the last paragraph which began, "I am asking the Congress of the United States . . . ."

The copy boys looked at each other and grinned. Mrs. Ruhl started to cry. Lucianna, whose husband is in the Navy somewhere in the Pacific, leaned forward, her face paper white. . . . The speech ended "a state of war has existed between the United States and the Japanese Empire." There was applause and "The Star Spangled Banner" and at the first note, we all got up and walked out very fast without saying a word.

On Tuesday morning, December 9, Gary received a telegram termed an ''Alert,'' advising officers to wind up their business affairs and be in readiness for a call. Gary priced uniforms at Boyd's—$150. Four days later, he received a letter edged in red, marked Very Important, from the War Department. He was ordered to Fort Francis E. Warren, Cheyenne, Wyoming. We groaned.

That night it snowed. The next morning, Gary went to Jefferson Barracks for his physical and I sat home, looking at the snow and playing the Bing Crosby record of the ''Star Spangled Banner.'' I felt like crying, but I said to myself, ''Save your tears. You may need them later.''

No one talked any more about, ''Goodbye, Dear, I'll Be Back In A Year,'' but no one anticipated a war of the length we were to experience. Gary left on January 7, 1942 and returned in February, 1946.

I do not believe there is one of those four years I would want to relive.

For many people of our generation, World War II was the highlight of their lives. Men who would have led humdrum lives as clerks in dull jobs suddenly were potential heroes, embued with the glamour of a uniform and a dangerous mission, even though they might end up as a clerk in a dull war office job.

Every romance suddenly became high drama. Weddings were hurry-up affairs because ''he has his orders.'' For some young brides, the honeymoon was all they had. Others are now going to senior citizens meetings with the boy who wore a pair of silver wings or praised the Lord and passed the ammunition.

An English woman once told me a bit wistfully that the period when the bombs rained on Britain and they thought every day might be their last, stood out in her memory as the happiest period of her life. The Yanks were there and as the saying went, ''It isn't that foreign girls have anything the hometown girls don't have; it's just that they have it here.''

''It was marvelous,'' my English friend recalled, misty-eyed. ''We weren't supposed to go to dances on American bases so they'd sneak us in. We'd climb into the lorries all dressed up in our best frocks and hide under the tarpaulin, and they'd drive us right past the sentries.''

The stratagem probably fooled no one but added spice to the adventure. Wartime makes its own rules and for many, the love affairs, both sanctioned and extracurricular, were more exciting than anything that could happen in peacetime. Everyone was an actor in the drama. And in truth, we did not know whether or not we would survive, those who went away and those who stayed at home.

Each January 7th, I go through my own commemoration of that awful day, usually untrimming the Christmas tree, and thinking to myself that whatever the day brings, it can't leave me feeling as low as I did that day.

Gary left at 6 A.M. in our little red Studebaker and I went to work on the bus. My assignment took me to the City Hospital that afternoon for what I thought would be a routine one-hour interview on the shortage of nurses. But the supervisor assigned to me enthusiastically took me on a tour of the hospital, including a look down into the operating theater for a sight of real blood. Feeling a bit queasy after that, I was taken on an exhaustive tour of nurses' quarters. I made comments properly, long after I'd run out of questions to ask. At quarter to five, the supervisor took me back to her office and said brightly, "Now, we can have a nice long chat."

By the time I reached the transfer point for the puddle jumper county bus, always erratic in its schedule, there were long lines of people. I finally reached my stop, hiked over the hill, got home and found the furnace had gone off. We had a new addition, called a "stoker," which required daily removal of the "doughnut," a clinker formed by the stoker's action, and I had neglected to remove it. Also, our new puppy, Suellen (named for the character in *Gone with the Wind*), had been penned in over-long and had had an accident.

Well, I told myself, I'd have some hot soup and regroup. We were out of soup. Well, just toast and

*Gary and I at Fort Warren,
Wyoming, in 1942.*

milk. The milk was still on the back stoop, frozen and pushing out of the top of the bottle. (No cardboard or plastic containers then, novelist.)

I reached the door just as my mother came up the drive from her little house a few blocks away. She thought I might need cheering. "Mama," I cried, and burst into tears as she hugged me.

The pop tune of that spring was, "Miss You, Since You Went Away, Dear." I wore out our record. I also used up all my vacation time with a trip to Fort Warren in February and a second trip in March, when Gary was transferred to San Francisco and we assumed he was on his way to beleaguered Bataan or Corregidor. We drove through Utah and Nevada and spent my birthday at a lodge on Lake Tahoe amidst heavy snow drifts.

It is hard to convey the feeling of wartime in early 1942. There were air-raid warnings and blackouts and people honestly expected to be bombed. There were reports that Japs had been sighted off the coast and enemy agents captured. Those hindsight moralists who feel Japanese Americans should not have been interned do not understand that it was hard to tell the good guys from the bad guys, the gardeners from the

*A few weeks after the end of the war, when Gary was stationed on the West Coast, I flew to San Francisco to be with him. I had just landed after an all-night flight when this photo was taken.*

saboteurs, and everyone hated and loathed the Japanese aggressors and torturers of our captured men. We could not have looked ahead to the day of the Toyota and Ikebana flower arrangements.

While the German holocaust is relived on television annually, and we annually apologize for Hiroshima, little is ever said of the Bataan death march. But the early war in the Pacific was very real and to those of us who had friends killed there, it was very horrible.

The feature stories we wrote at this time were less frothy and more war-oriented. St. Louis had its own war hero in those early days, Lt. Cmdr. Edward "Butch" O'Hare, who shot down six of eight Japanese bombers surrounding him in a combat mission in the Pacific. He received the Medal of Honor and returned home to St. Louis for a celebration and parade in his honor. I rode in the parade and received my first front page byline on my story, a big thrill. O'Hare was later killed in action. The Chicago airport is named for him.

Gary and I assumed each farewell was our last, but instead of being sent to the Pacific, he was sent to Pasadena, in charge of what everyone called in those days "a colored car company."

The forty young black men under his command were mostly from farms in the south and only a few had ever driven a car. Gary gave each one a quick rundown in how to start, steer, and stop the trucks and command cars and they started down the scenic coastal highway from the Presidio.

In Pasadena they were assigned to the Southern California Sector, headquartered at the Huntington Hotel. They were called the Huntington Commandos by less fortunate officers passing through. The car company was mostly a chauffeuring service.

It made no difference that the young men who couldn't drive also knew nothing about car maintenance, or that Gary's only experience with cars had been to say, "Fill it up." (There were no self-service pumps then, young novelist.)

If unqualified for his job, he was a kind, understanding leader and his men who were transferred away wrote him letters imploring him to get them back. "You are my dear and only commanding officer," wrote a young man named Hosea.

"How do you handle them?" Gary was asked by people in the service and in the community, who had, frankly, anticipated riots and disturbances from black troops, incredible as that seems now.

"I treat them like human beings," was Gary's dry retort.

Pasadena had integrated schools even then, and there was less racist feeling there than in many places, but the military offered little opportunity to blacks.

After six months of separation, we decided I would take a leave of absence and go to California. We rented an apartment, I became an army wife and soon found out it was not for me.

In my few years as feature writer I'd grown accustomed to deferential treatment and it was hard to realize that, as the wife of a second lieutenant, I was supposed to stand back as my superiors went through a door or got on an elevator.

In addition to this, I quickly came to grief for doing what my husband was doing, treating blacks as human beings.

At Thanksgiving it was customary for an officer's wife to have dinner with her husband's company. I considered myself lucky. Gary told me they had a good cook and moreover, they served butter, then not

*My most glamorous portrait.*

available on the market. When I remarked at a meeting of officers' wives that I was looking forward to dinner with the men, the Southern-born wife of the general took me aside.

"My dear, I don't believe you should go," she said. "But, I've already accepted," I protested. "The other wives are having dinner with enlisted men."

"But these are Nigrahs," she said. "I don't believe you should."

Naturally, I went and did so again at Christmas. This time I was even more brazen. There was a morning program and then a lull of several hours until late afternoon dinner. By now, Gary had an assistant, a black lieutenant with a pretty wife. They were an attractive, educated couple—a black man had to be pretty special to get through OCS then—and we found them more congenial than many other co-workers. They lived at some distance across town and she had no place to wait except the garage, so I did the obvious thing and took her home with me.

It all seems slightly ridiculous now but at the time I looked on it as a victory of principle. I have a letter from my mother, warmly commending me, and for many years I exchanged Christmas cards with the lieutenant's wife.

Meanwhile, I tried to reinstate myself in the good graces of the general's lady. When she announced a fund-raising project involving sewing and asked for volunteers, I raised my hand.

"Not you, dear, you're only a lieutenant's wife," she said, smiling. "May I have a captain's or major's wife, please?"

A captain's wife reluctantly volunteered and the general's wife said to me, "You may be her assistant."

Our project was doll-making, soldier and WAC dolls. The general had an aide whose wife had been a fashion designer. She made a pattern and we cut out heads and bodies, sewed them together, embroidered faces and then stuffed the dolls. We made each one a sharply tailored uniform complete with button-down collar and shoulder epaulets.

Doll clothes are always harder to make than people clothes but doll tailoring of this scope was absolutely insane.

About ten of us met daily in our simulated factory and the sewing machines whirred noisily and we labored mightily. From time to time, the general's lady made an inspection tour.

"I don't like this one," she said one day. "He doesn't have a neck. Take the head off and give him more neck."

After she had left, one of the braver wives stood up, waved an arm imperiously and said, "Off with his head!"

I do not recall how many dolls we made or what we charged for them. I do remember that the profit we showed for our good cause—Army Emergency Relief—was so small that we estimated we could each have donated $10 and done better.

I was so thoroughly sick of them that I didn't buy a doll and have always regretted this. I wonder if any are still in existence, selling at exorbitant prices at antique shows.

This was only one of my efforts at volunteerism. I also worked a few days each week at the telephone in the office which found housing for servicemen's wives and helped with problems, a kind of social service job. And in February I was the volunteer public relations director for the Red Cross, culminating my efforts by writing a full page feature story for the local newspaper.

"Very nice," said the volunteer director. "Now if only you could just get one like that in the paper every day. . . ."

Looking back I realize now that my year in California was wasted. I could have taken a job in the Lockheed defense plant or at a movie studio and enlarged my income and experience. Instead I looked forward to bingo night at the officers' club, shopping trips with other army wives or an occasional show or movie. We saw the topical hit, *This is the Army,* and when the film *Casablanca* came to Pasadena, I went to eight straight matinees.

Now and then we went to the Palladium Ball Room, where the big bands—the Dorseys, Glenn Miller, Benny Goodman and others played. Gary was an early jazz enthusiast and finally persuaded me that Lunceford was better than Lombardo, Basie better than Busse. Now and then we'd go to The Hangover on Vine Street to hear Bob Zurke play "Honky Tonk Blues" or to an obscure club off Cahuenga Boulevard where the King Cole Trio played. It was led by Nat "King" Cole.

Back home my friends were all having babies. I was happy for them but miserable for myself.

Like the duration of the war, my childless years were unpredictable. I couldn't see into the future and the birth of my son in 1951. The future seemed to hold little for me. One day I opened the mail and found a letter from my editor, Don Thompson. He was shorthanded, he wrote, and besides that, no one could take my place. Would I consider coming back?

Quicker than you could say El Capitan, I was on that Santa Fe economy class train, heading home. I looked on it as no mere coincidence that Gary was promoted right after I left.

# 17

## And Finally Peace

W ERE OUR EMOTIONS somehow numbed during those days of World War II? If not, how could we stand to read the daily newspapers? I have heard of others of our generation speculate that if the events of that conflict had been brought into our homes via television nightly, as were Korea and Vietnam later, there would have been less universal support for our leaders.

But support them we did, with a feeling that, "Of course we're going to win." Only occasionally did we sense the terror of, "But what if we don't?"

The casualties were usually reported on page three

of our daily. Years later, I would sometimes ask for the bound files (now on microfilm) and turn the pages of 1944 and 1945 with wonder and disbelief at the scope and number of the dead, wounded and missing. There were days when page three looked like a high school or college yearbook, with row upon row of postage stamp size pictures of fine young men.

You scanned them until you found a familiar name and face and then shuddered or sighed or cried. Now in my sunset years, I read the obituaries. When you have lived most of your life in a large community, gone to school there, and been active in business and church and social life, there's almost always someone. And in those days of late 1944, there was almost always someone.

In the fall of that year, I had lunch with Donnie Steward, a friend from the trust company. She was married now and worried about her husband, Clay, age thirty-eight. He'd been drafted and sent to infantry training camp in Texas. He was hardly infantry material and I soothed her fears.

"It will be months before he's ready to go overseas," I told her, "and the war will be over by then." It was a phrase we used often in the early optimism of that winter.

Five weeks later I took a second look at one of the postage stamp pictures. Donnie's husband had been wounded in action at a place we were just starting to

hear about—Bastogne. The Battle of the Bulge. Luckily, he returned.

Shortly thereafter we had news of our doctor whom
we adored. As he wrote in a letter to me, "a pudgy,
paunchy practitioner" was hardly the one you would
picture as parachuting behind the lines but there he
was. He was captured at Bastogne and, because he
was Jewish, we worried doubly. Later he was to tell
us that he had been treated well by his captors and
when he escaped on a prisoners' march to
Czechoslovakia, he found hospitality from German
farmers along the way.

We were especially prayerful over the two neighbor
boys, Billy and young Paul. We saw Billy's picture—it
was larger than the small casualty ones. He was in
the South Pacific and had been awarded a Distinguished Flying Cross.

Young Paul's mother, Helen, and I had become
close friends. It had started at the first neighborhood
party to introduce us.

"I read the most marvelously funny story on dieting
in yesterday's *Post*," Helen said in her enthusiastic
bubbly way.

"Thank you, I wrote it," I replied.

Paul senior, as we called her husband, was a traveling salesman for Wonder Bread and Cake. "The
twinkie salesman," we called him. He was gone a lot,
so Helen, and I and her pretty daughter-in-law,

Jeanette, married to young Paul just before he went overseas, went to dinner and shows and bowled and drank to console each other.

Gary's little sister by this time was a professional band vocalist, Betty Day, traveling the Midwest. From time to time I'd spend a weekend with her. One was in Kansas City.

"I'd better tell you," mother began when I came home. "Yesterday there were cars parked all along the street. . . ."

"Young Paul," I said, and mother nodded. He'd been shot down over Frankfurt and was missing in action. They hoped he'd been taken prisoner.

Many years later when Helen entered a nursing home, I managed a sale of her household possessions and bought for myself three small sauce dishes, green bordered with pink rose centers. They were all that remained of the set that Paul senior had smashed against the kitchen wall in his fury.

But this story, too, ended happily. Radio hams throughout the country were picking up messages from German prisoner of war camps and relaying them to anxious families. From the Stalag Luft where he was held, a man in Ohio picked up young Paul's name and called to tell his wife he was still alive, before the government knew of it.

I stopped off in Ohio to interview the radio ham on my way to Camp Lee, Virginia that summer. Gary was finally headed overseas. It was typical of the military that he traveled to the East coast so he could travel back to the West coast to go by ship via Australia and on to India and then Iran.

He now knew a little about operating a fleet of cars so it was no surprise that he was put in charge of a railroad, in the town of Dizful, distinguished, he wrote, by the fact that it had recorded the hottest temperature in the world. Periodically he tried to transfer to the Judge Advocate Division to be a lawyer and in the closing months of the war he succeeded.

We wrote letters almost daily but it was hard to bridge the two worlds, that of the military and the civilian. Ours was a world of petty annoyances, rationing of meat and sugar and gasoline and shoes. Overseas, in his case at least, was a life with the necessities, but one haunted by loneliness and boredom. Many men in positions such as his were not in much danger but many would have preferred action to inaction.

At home we coped with rationing in various ways. Dickson Terry, one of the writers in our office had six children and shoes were a constant need. My parents and I didn't need many pairs of shoes but mother couldn't live without coffee and my father loved sugar, so we traded shoe coupons to Dick for coffee and sugar. Mother and I joined the lines early on Saturday morning at the meat market and learned to cook liver, kidney, and hearts.

I smoked in those days and while cigarettes weren't rationed, they were in short supply. On lunch hours, we'd line up at the end of a queue extending from Katz Drug Store on Seventh and Olive to the corner of Eighth and Olive. In an hour, you would move patiently down the street, into the store and around the four sides, eventually reaching the cash register where you exchanged your quarter for a package of whatever they were selling that day.

My brands were Camels or Chesterfields but some days I'd receive the mentholated Kools or off brands such as Twenty Grands or Rameses. There had been a brand of condoms with a Rameses label and there was much speculation about the relationship of the two products.

Few people complained about rationing because it was for "our brave boys overseas." Sometimes our concern was ludicrous.

Once I saved up six precious packs of Camels to mail to Gary. He was on the move and months later the cigarettes came back, stale and unsmokable. Later I found he'd had plenty of cigarettes. It took a while to adjust attitudes when the war was over. "Canned peaches," I'd exult as we went shopping only to have him groan, "Oh no, I never want to see any more canned peaches."

We drank a lot of rum in those days. "Rum and

Coca Cola,'' like the title of the Andrews Sisters juke box best selling record, and also rum and pineapple juice and other combinations that reminded us of college days.

Sweet muscatel wine was also available, and no doubt many Americans acquired their taste for wine in those days.

I learned to drink beer, which I had never liked, even in my childhood when every family made *heimgemacht* in the big stoneware crocks we sell as antiques today.

My beer taste began one night when I was coming home by bus, and a plump little man across the aisle leaned over and said, ''Don't you work at the *Post-Dispatch?* I'm Black on the copy desk.''

Blacky parked his car at the end of the line and offered to take me home so I wouldn't have to walk the last mile. There was a catch to it; he always stopped at Ralph's Tavern midway.

''What do you drink?'' he asked the first night.

''Scotch and water.''

''I'll be damned if I'm buying you a 40 cent Scotch and water. No, you can't buy your own. You'll drink beer like I do.''

So I drank beer, at first a sip or two, later a bottle or two. It's an acquired taste and I acquired it. It's a rare occasion now when I drink Scotch and water.

Blacky was to become a wonderful friend, counselor,

shoulder to lean on and cry on during despondent moments. It was good to have a man to talk to, and Blacky was always good for funny gossip. Like the story about a mutual acquaintance who took a girl to a hotel room only to learn she insisted on sex to the tune of "The Jersey Bounce." It was a pop tune but he couldn't find it being played on the radio that night. Frantically he twirled the dials until he finally made connections—with the song and the girl.

Another top tune was "They're Either Too Young Or Too Old." I thought of this one day when an elderly (like sixty-year-old) co-worker invited me to dinner (his wife was out of town) a few hours after I'd turned down a copy boy who wanted to take me to a movie.

They were mostly too young when I visited Betty and the band, but we had marvelous times. One New Year's Eve I took the train to Memphis where she was performing at the Claridge Hotel. We entered the lobby and a sea of young servicemen, mostly Army Air Corps, shouted "Betty-Betty-Betty!" It was like something out of a Betty Grable movie, a hilarious weekend of rum and Coca Cola and an atmosphere of live-it-up, tomorrow-we-die, as some of them did.

I spent much time with a friend, Elizabeth Brinkman, whose husband, Bill, a high school friend of Gary's, was overseas. Elizabeth, a librarian became acquainted with a regular reader, Charles Kober. He

*My sister-in-law, singer Betty Day (Davidson), was a hit with the GIs in 1943.*

invited her home to meet his wife and she invited them both over to meet me. Soon we had a group going, augmented by friends and neighbors. Charles wrote a silly poem, which began, "The day before the day before it's Christmas 1944." For the next twenty years we dated the beginning of our Saturday Night Crowd by those lines.

Partying kept those of us on the sidelines from dwelling on our frustrations. Like many a man, I wanted to join what seemed like the big adventure of our generation. Virginia Irwin, from our magazine staff, had joined the Red Cross and later was accredited as a correspondent overseas.

I had the job of rewriting some of her stories and it increased my dissatisfaction with staying at home. But the local Red Cross rejected me—physically unfit because of a thyroid deficiency—a trifling thing but a blow. I knew how men felt about rejection. Our new friend, Charles, had been drafted and then released because, as a lawyer used to many years of sedentary work, he couldn't take the pace of infantry marching in Texas.

"They wanted to Section Eight me," he said, referring to the term for discharging the emotionally unfit. "I didn't want to be released and they figured anyone who wanted to stay in was crazy."

Our next door neighbor, Bill Sargent had a similar experience. Years of easy living and work in his finance company had not fitted him for rugged military life and he, too, was sent home, with a pension to salve his bruised ego. It all seemed an awful waste. Bill volunteered as our neighborhood air raid warden and enjoyed himself going around from house to house ordering us to "douse those lights."

In the spring of 1945 we were told we were winning but it was hard to believe. The war had gone on so long we felt it was with us forever. Then one night in April, my phone rang.

"Get down to the office to help get out the special edition," Al Offer, one of our magazine editors, told me. "President Roosevelt has died and our worst fears are realized. Harry Truman is president."

This was not an isolated reaction to Truman's ability. How he enjoyed proving his disclaimers wrong.

We were recovering from the shock when a greater one came, also with suddenness. The Germans had surrendered. The war in Europe was over.

Gary had his orders to return to California and we assumed he would go to the Pacific. But in late summer the bomb was dropped on Hiroshima. Some people, like my second husband, Ray, who had worked on the Manhattan Project, or A-bomb development, knew the war was over but for most of us, the impact was not as obvious.

A group of us had made a date to go to dinner one August evening, at a nearby restaurant, The Tulip Box, where you could get that rare treat, a real steak. I was on the local bus when the announcement came over the driver's radio that there would be important news in a short time.

The first to arrive at The Tulip Box, I was sitting at the bar, sipping a frozen daiquiri when the stunning announcement was made. The war was over. The bartender fixed himself a drink and we clinked glasses in silence, and smiled.

Soon the restaurant was bedlam as people crowded in to celebrate. In our group was the Kobers' long-time friend, Ed Adams, a Scotsman who took much kidding on his thrift. He was serving on the gas rationing board and as the waiter took our orders, he gave him an advance tip, some of his own much coveted gas coupons. The delighted waiter gave us superb service and big thick steaks.

We all swore that Eddie knew gas rationing would end the next day.

# 18

## Parenthood and Politics

CONTRARY TO THE OLD SAYING, absence does not necessarily make the heart grow fonder, and prolonged absences are hard on a marriage. It's a wonder more relationships didn't come apart during World War II. I'm sure many couples looked at each other, as Gary and I did, when reunited, warily, as if studying a stranger.

Even our letters had degenerated from their early expressions of devotion. I would write of a household decision and he'd criticize it from his thousands of miles away. I'd defend myself and my annoyed letter would cross with a loving one from him. Long distance communication was difficult.

Among things we argued about was where we were going to live at the end of the war. He favored California, which I had heartily disliked, and I was considering Chicago, which he thought was out of the question.

My dalliance with Chicago was fleeting. I'd had happy visits there with friends, Al and Franny Weisman, and one day Al, an advertising executive, wrote me an excited letter outlining a job possibility.

An editor friend of Al's was looking for a writer to take over an advice column, which would be syndicated. Al thought my chances were good. I had filled in, during vacation time on the Martha Carr column for the *Post*. Martha was the newspaper's invented name and had been written by a long series of women and a few men. My letters were different from the standard serious advice of most newspaper columns, lighter in tone, sometimes flip and this, it seemed, was what Al's editor friend had in mind.

After considering all the angles, I declined. Eventually the editor found an inexperienced but bright woman named Eppie Lederer and she did very well— and still does—writing the column bylined Ann Landers.

In the summer of 1945 Gary was sent back from Iran and stopped over in St. Louis on his way to San Francisco. We were sure he was going to the Pacific. But the sudden end of the war kept him in San Francisco and at long last, he was assigned to legal duties.

I flew out in December. I have a picture of myself at the airport, in black suit and velvet turban, arriving at 5 A.M. after an all-night flight. I'd taken my first plane trip on an assignment the year before and loved flying. No more trains for me.

"I don't know where we'll stay," Gary apologized. "The town is filled up. I'm on the waiting list at the St. Francis but they weren't too encouraging. We may have to try a private home."

We went to the St. Francis first. The desk clerk took one look at the uniformed man and his weary wife and assigned a room. Moreover, they sent a bowl of fruit and a gardenia corsage to me.

We had a wonderful reunion. The tune of the time went "Kiss me once and kiss me twice and kiss me once again—it's been a long, long time." Happily we relived our 1942 visit to San Francisco. In February, he came home to St. Louis and we renewed our life with no talk of California, Chicago, or other controversial subjects.

This is not to say all our problems were over. I'd acquired a different lifestyle with the habit of staying downtown for a few drinks with my boss and co-workers after hours. Virginia Irwin had returned from war correspondence and with newcomers to the staff, Jean Lightfoot, Dick Terry, Peter Wyden, and others, we gathered at Myrtle Schertz's restaurant next door for shoptalk and beer.

The nightly joke was that I, the little housewife from the suburbs, had to catch the 4:25 bus and go home. Often I missed it. Gary would drive home from his office in Clayton, the growing area his father recommended, and was understandably annoyed when I wasn't there.

Our social life also was peopled with strangers augmented, to be sure, by old friends, but the parties were noisier and livelier. In many ways, life then was a repeat of the roaring twenties after World War I. Our group was strong on costume parties, everything from "come as a character from Li'l Abner" (the popular comic strip) to the circus party where I persuaded my reserved husband that we should dress as monkeys and hang from a tree as guests came up the driveway. Actually, Gary wasn't always dignified; he could clown with the best of them when he relaxed among people he knew.

Eventually the parties and the new friends strengthened our marriage as shared fun does. Then two more things happened to keep us from being subjects in a magazine feature of the time, "Can This Marriage Be Saved?" These two saving events were parenthood and politics.

We'd wanted a child for a long time and were almost resigned to adoption. The agency to which we applied put us through a discouraging series of interviews which seemed designed to prove we were too intelligent and too successful to be acceptable parents.

Two friends, Katie Dye and Marian Willier, were going through the same agonies. Mutual misery brought Katie and Russell, Bob and Marian, and Gary and me together in friendship. In the fall of 1950, Katie told us, almost with apology that she was pregnant. That winter while my parents were in Florida and we were relaxing alone, we went to visit Katie's baby girl with news of our own. I was in the early stages of morning sickness and couldn't have been happier.

Bob and Marian did make the grade as adoptive parents and their two little boys, Katie's daughter, and our son proved what the adoptive agencies had told us all along—we were terribly nervous parents.

But if anyone were to ask me my greatest achievement in life it would be that human being who, with his family, has brought me more joy than anything else in life.

The happiness started even before birth. Pregnancy was a lark. After the first queasy weeks, during which time I was teaching a writing class for the University of Missouri extension department, racing to the ladies room during break time and wondering just how late into the evening "morning" sickness could last, I never felt better.

I prepared eagerly for natural childbirth, the big thing then, and our great doctor and good friend, Saul

Dworkin, went along with my whims. Later on, he told me he'd known all along that heavy anesthesia would be necessary. I didn't remember a thing from 8 P.M. October 4 to 5 A.M. October 5. But the Lamaze exercises have helped me to relax for sleep ever since.

As a little boy, Bruce would beg me to tell the story "about how for the longest time they didn't bring me." And I would go through the narrative of waking up to realize I'd had my baby and hoping it was a boy and ringing for the nurse and then waiting and waiting while heels clicked down the hall, turning off at other rooms (it was 5 A.M. feeding time) until finally a tiny, stooped nurse arrived with my bundle and I said the words Bruce always laughed to hear: "I never thought I'd have such a beautiful baby!"

He was also a noisy and colicky baby and there were times when I felt the adoption agency had been right and I was too old and edgy, but we all survived and by spring I was back at the office. Mother took care of Bruce by day and I joined her at night.

Surely no baby ever had two more devoted slaves. We shared his bath time, played with him, took turns holding him as he went to sleep listening to recorded music, of "The Teddy Bear Picnic" and "Bobby Shaftoe's Gone to Sea." Sheer bliss for all of us.

One evening Gary came home from the office to tell me of a coffee-time conversation he'd had with some other lawyers.

"There's a newly created State Senate seat," he said. "One of the representatives has filed for it but some of us think a lawyer should be in the race and we all agreed to hold back for whichever one of us decides to run."

"That's fine just so it isn't you," I said. He had run for magistrate in the election just past in a field of nine candidates in which he'd finished fourth. I'd found it very boring.

"Well, uh—as a matter of fact. . . ."

"Oh no," I said. But then I rallied. "Okay, if you want to run, I'll give you one night a week of my time to go to meetings and campaign for you. But that's it."

By the next summer I was giving seven nights a week, plus Saturdays and Sundays, attending meetings in five townships, listening to the same candidates make the same speech, being charming to wives of committee members, showing Bruce's baby picture, cooing over other people's baby pictures, making phone calls, writing letters, and ringing doorbells. My competitive spirit had been aroused and we were out to win.

There were times when I went beyond the call of duty. Like the Sunday when we were just finishing noonday dinner and the phone rang. An eager partisan urged that we attend a church dinner in Mehlville. We raced to reach it, found ourselves led

*Bruce and Gary.*

to the fried chicken line and when we reached the serving table, I heard my husband say graciously, "I'll just have cake and coffee but my wife loves fried chicken." I gave him a meaningful look and sat down to my second big Sunday dinner.

He was the underdog in the campaign and his opponent was well-known and well-liked. But we worked hard all that blistering hot summer at the old-fashioned business of getting out the vote.

Computers probably have revolutionized the process of record keeping, but in our day there were printed lists of registered voters in each precinct of each township. His race covered five. We checked the lists for familiar names, wrote or called, and asked our friends to call their friends. Then I typed letter after letter to all those strange names on the list.

Voter lists were interesting from another standpoint. It was fascinating to note how many of my co-workers, all loudly praising or criticizing and often condemning all politicians, had never bothered to register to vote.

In the final weeks of the primary campaign, we went door to door. We canvassed the stately homes in University City, a long walk apart, climbed to third-floor apartments, went around the suburbs and then to the sparsely populated rural area.

Many of our friends did the same thing. Our neighbor, Helen; our doctor's wife, Lee; the Saturday Night Crowd; and Bob and Marian.

"I tell everyone I was in the army with Gary," Bob would laugh. "I don't tell them I was in the Pentagon while he was in Iran."

On the last hot night before the primary, Helen and I and Dorothy Moore, a writer friend who was in the midst of buying a newspaper in St. Clair, Missouri, finished walking the last precinct as darkness descended.

"If Gary Davidson doesn't win after we've given our all, there's no justice," Dorothy said.

I later figured out that I had personally rung doorbells at 400 homes. I also worked outside the polls handing out literature and I am still very polite to all those workers who do.

Then came the colorful experience no one has today. Today's voting machines give quick returns and winners are predicted ten minutes after the polls close.

In those days, precinct workers laboriously counted paper ballots, bagged them up and took them to the county courthouse where the results were tallied and certified.

Gary's office was across the street from the court-house. There was no air-conditioning and the windows were open, so I could hear the loudspeaker booming out the returns as they came in. I divided my time between lying on the sofa, running to the window for the periodic reports, and sometimes dropping to my knees to pray.

The vote seesawed back and forth—400 for his op-ponent, 410 for him, then 625 for his opponent and 600 for him. Soon it was 2,780 for him and 2,760 for his opponent. A cliff-hanger all through the night. But by dawn he was in the lead and holding. I washed my face, went down to the office at eight and just before noon took his call with the final unofficial results. He had received 10,400 votes to his opponent's 10,000. The 400 votes may not have been the individuals I'd contacted but, I always felt they were the margin of victory.

The general election was anticlimax to the primary. The district was only slightly Republican but the top name on the ballot was that of Dwight D. Eisenhower and we were confident it would be a Republican year. It was, and we celebrated by going to Florida with Jan and Charles and home by way of New Orleans.

The trip back had one incident of historical significance in the changing world.

We were near Memphis on the last night of our trip. It was a dark and rainy night and we recalled from a previous trip that there were few places to stay near Memphis.

In the 1950s that phenomenon known as the motel was just coming into being, filling the need between the hotels, too expensive for those on modest budgets, and the roadside tourist cabins which had taken the place of the tourist homes of the 1920s.

We stopped at one shabby motel, decided it wouldn't do and then stopped at a filling station to ask for help.

"There's a new place just opening up on the next highway," we were told. "They say it's pretty nice."

Skeptical but willing to try, we drove to the new motel. We couldn't believe our eyes when we walked into the lobby with carpeted halls, were shown to a beautifully furnished room, and were even given a jug of ice, an unheard of luxury at that time.

"What a great place," we agreed. "Wouldn't it be wonderful if there were something like this in every town."

Eventually there was. I later interviewed the young man who had saved money from a movie popcorn stand to open his first motel. It did so well, Kemmons Wilson started a chain naming them all after the place where we'd stayed—Holiday Inn.

# 19

## This Old House

SINGER ROSEMARY CLOONEY, recorded a tune in the 1950s and, while she never knew it, it had a great impact on our lives. The song was "This Old House."

We had been the first in our group to buy a house, the ranch style in Shrewsbury, but soon all our friends were buying homes. Charles and Jan waited the longest and they were the most particular. We began teasing them that they would never reach their goal of saving enough to buy for cash as prices kept soaring just beyond their reach.

The $7,000-$8,000 range we'd considered too high in 1940 was only half of what houses were selling for in 1950. At our 1950-51 New Year's Eve party, I wrote a ten-year prediction of ridiculous speculation including house prices of $50,000!

Eventually Jan and Charles built a house, an elegant one for about half that figure.

We were invited to a party there one May evening in 1954. But en route we made a detour. We were thinking of buying another house. My parents were still with us, living in two rooms in the dormer wing upstairs. We had a bedroom and a room for Bruce on the first floor, but now we found we were going to have another baby.

If the baby were a girl, we'd need more room. Besides, I'd done everything I could think of in the decorating line, changing carpeting, color schemes and slipcovers. We had even acquired our first antique, a corner cupboard which dominated our dining room.

One of Gary's fellow lawyers preached the wisdom of acquiring antiques and that started us to thinking of older houses. Maybe a three- or four-bedroom, two-story in Webster Groves, which borders Shrewsbury and has good schools. We'd like a little more ground, too, perhaps an acre with trees.

Bill Brinkman, who worked in the real estate department of a bank, called with a suggestion. Probably not what we wanted, he added hastily. It might be too big—five bedrooms—and maybe too much ground—two acres. And possibly too old—it had been built in 1867. But the price was reasonable. Would we look?

So, on a May evening with Bill and Elizabeth and Ed and Ginny, we stopped by the house on North Gore. It didn't make a tremendous first impression, just a big brick house on a hill. It was far from the street and seemed to me to be awfully close to houses on the street to the rear—nine of them with back fences forming the border (although the trees obscured them).

We entered the house into a hall with front stairway. The owners took us into the living room to the left, a big room, thirteen by thirty-six with two fireplaces. I was unimpressed.

"Where's the two acres?" I asked.

"Here," said Carolyn Ward, leading me to a window. I looked out the window and gulped. There was a slope of lawn down to the street with two huge evergreens and a hedge along the walk. Elizabeth looked over my shoulder.

"It looks like a park," she said.

"Yes," I breathed, as I stood there, absolutely enchanted.

We followed the owners, Tom and Carolyn Ward, through the rest of the house but very little registered. I remembered a front and back stairs, a kind of little hidden room in back, four marble fireplaces and massive antique furniture.

On the dining room table were galley proofs of a

*"Mrs. Queen Clarissa lives there" a neighbor's grandson once said, pointing to 300 N. Gore in Webster Groves. It was a lovely house, made for gracious living and parties. It was also fun for the boy who grew up there.*

book. Carolyn had written a novel, *Mistress of Thornhedge,* and it was being published. That impressed me.

We thanked the Wards and left, uncommitted. When we reached Charles and Jan's, the others regaled them with descriptions of this unbelievable house. Who in the world would want a place like that?

Ed, an engineer, had a number of comments on the probable state of the plumbing and electricity. Gary and I sat side by side on the sofa, saying nothing. Finally, I leaned over and whispered, "What did you think of it?"

"I kind of liked it," he whispered back.

"I did, too."

We looked at each other and grinned like conspirators. The next day we talked about what it would be like to live in a really historic home surrounded by a park. We called and told the Wards we'd like to come back and see it by day.

A few weeks later, a major happening put all thoughts of moving out of our minds. I woke up in the middle of the night with strange sensations. A few days later, my doctor stood at my bedside, tears in his eyes, telling me there was no way to save the baby. She was born two weeks later and lived only momentarily.

The whole summer was miserable. Not only was I brokenhearted, but I had gained weight I could not lose. Then I acquired a miserable case of poison ivy. I felt that all the calamities of Job had befallen me.

That summer of 1954 probably tops the list of periods I would not want to live over. I buried myself in work and the do-gooder volunteer enterprises I'd become involved in.

As a stroke of irony, I received an award from the

*I received the "Woman of the Year" award from the St. Louis Women's Chamber of Commerce in 1955. From left are Frank Eschen of KSD and KSD-TV; Joseph F. Holland; Mrs. Oswald Zesch; and me.*

Women's Chamber of Commerce as Woman of the Year for 1954.

"What a year," I snorted. "Nothing but failure."

It had been unsuccessful for the Wards, too. No one wanted that old house. Every now and then I'd drive up Gore, turn on the sidestreet, and go slowly by, looking up at the solid brick walls. They seemed comforting and homey. And the grounds were beautiful in all seasons.

In the spring of 1955, we listed our house with a

big real estate company, at a big inflated price for the time, $17,000. It seemed ridiculous but everyone was asking high prices. Not long ago, this dear little house sold for $85,000—and fast.

When our contract expired with no results, Tom Ward's brother Bill, interested in selling the house on Gore, offered to sell ours. Within two weeks, we had an interested couple with parents who liked the in-law quarters and also the yard. Unlike one prospect who had said, "The first thing I'd do would be to cut down that big oak tree," they liked the tree, and I liked them. The deal was made for both houses and we planned our move.

We celebrated mother's seventieth birthday in March, a month which marked a different milestone for me. I turned in a tentative set of columns titled, "The Little Woman," Gary's teasing name for me. They were about house and home and the funny sayings of a certain three-year-old and my observations on being a woman.

No one thought a reporter could sustain a personal column for long. Several had tried and failed. Mine lasted for the next seventeen years.

And one of the best sources of material was "This Old House," a home which proved to be an absolute joy.

Gary researched it at the title company and found we were part of a long list of owners and occupants.

It was built by John and Mary Fulton. He was a lawyer like Gary and much later, I found another odd coincidence; like me, he was born on March 28.

The house had known good times and bad. A florist had planted quantities of shrubbery. Someone else had rented it to multiple families as a rooming house. One owner had been a patron of the arts and housed Municipal Opera singers there in the summer. One of them, an Italian tenor, had undertaken to build a circular driveway in front. Only after it was encased in concrete walls did they discover it was too narrow for cars. We had assumed it was built for carriages. By the time we bought the house the drive was unsightly broken concrete with weeds. Eventually we had it filled up and grassed over.

We started out small, very small, as our funds were minimal. Gary and Uncle John painted the living room. We bought the cheapest wallpaper available for the front hall, but its roses and leaves looked just right for fifteen years. Bruce, not quite five, helped me soak and scrape old wallpaper from the bedroom walls. When smoke seeped through the parlor wall one night, we decided to line two of the fireplaces.

Little by little, we added to our sparse furnishings from antique shops and house sales. There were some big additions, a pair of mirrors from an old house in the Lafayette Park area, a pair of crystal chandeliers made to order. But this was done much later. In the beginning we lived in sparsely furnished rooms with draperies made by my loving hands.

The house gained a sort of immortality by being included in a book on old St. Louis homes by Elinor Coyle. *The Golden Age* featured it and other homes built in the Victorian era.

If ever there was a golden age to my life, it was that period from 1955 to 1960. Gary was reelected to the Senate in 1956 and, as a lawyer, loved the work of making laws. He was gone from Monday through Thursday each week but we managed to crowd family fun and social life into weekends.

On Thursday nights he and I would visit until a late hour, recapping all that had happened that week. Often we were interrupted by calls from constituents with causes to champion, problems to discuss.

Although I worked at the newspaper daily and often had dinners or speeches to make in mid-week, I still managed time with Bruce. As he grew older, we no longer had the bath, bedtime story, and music routine, but after dinner, we'd go to his room to play games and read. He was an enthusiastic reader and a newfound friend, Virginia Rosenmeyer, a librarian, would bring him books she thought he'd like. *Beady Bear, Curious George, Winnie the Pooh,* and *Wind in the Willows* were favorites.

Ours was a neighborhood of young children. The Chaffees, an army family who lived down the street, had four: Dorothy, Jan, Billy, and Johnny. There was Charlie McNamara and Doug Cairns and then the newlyweds next door, George and Dee Helfrich, had two little boys, Mike and Mark. On the next street were Jeff Smith, Scott Hunter and his little brother, Bruce, called Little Hunter to distinguish him from our Bruce. The parklike side yard gave up its perfect lawn to become a baseball diamond.

But there was still a garden for me; on spring mornings I'd be working in it as early as 5:30.

After struggling to landscape it on my own, I called in an expert, Harriet Rodes Bakewell, who worked wonders, designing a formal rose garden around the brick patio which Gary and I had laid laboriously, several rows of brick each year. Our irregular-shaped yard had baffled me but she pulled it together with a crescent-shaped perennial border. The wooded area bordering our nine neighbors had wildflowers in spring, fragrant mock orange bushes and giant catalpa trees like huge bouquets. Along the front walk were several varities of tulips and peonies planted long ago by a former owner.

It was a great house and garden and we showed it off on seven house tours in the fifteen years we lived there. Each one was a frantic experience of in-depth cleaning and after the first three, Gary said firmly, "No more." We had just remodeled the kitchen and I protested that I'd like to show off our work.

"All right," he said, "if some group wants to tour just the kitchen, you can let them." It was a short time later that my neighbor, Inez Comfort, called and said, "Our Kappa alumnae chapter is having a kitchen tour and we were wondering. . . ." Of course we did it.

It was a marvelous house for big gatherings. At Christmastime we went all out with garlands of greenery on the stairs, holly wreaths at the front door, and a big lighted star which Gary constructed for the second floor between window and roof.

We had started having open house on a small scale in our first apartment and home and it grew until we had 100 to 200 on the Sunday between Christmas and New Year's. We served eggnog and cookies, cheese balls, shrimp, turkey, and mother's rolls. At Halloween it was a "spook house" as we led the little trick or treaters through dark halls with dangling paper skeletons.

We hosted garden club meetings and church groups and the neighborhood improvement association and political coffees—activities proliferated in our busy lives.

When first we toured the house, the Wards' son-in-law had assured us we would enjoy "gracious living" there, and "gracious living" became our family joke. Sometimes the hectic pace and slapdash housekeeping resulted in less than gracious living. But then we acquired household help, first a weekly "ironing lady,'' then a German-born Gisela, a dynamo at housecleaning, and after she retired to her own home, black Mary came five days a week.

''Now this is gracious living,'' said Gary when we came home to a clean and tidy house at the end of the first week.

Mary was replaced by Mattie Wardell, a jewel of efficiency. Our relationship did not get off to an auspicious start. We hired her through an ad and had not met until the end of the first day when I came home to find her seated in the kitchen.

''Hello, you must be Mattie,'' I said brightly. ''How are you?''

''Tired,'' she said, pronouncing it ''Tard.'' A cigarette dangled from her lips and her look seemed to me hard and unfriendly.

We were at odds the first few months because she was often late. The late arrivals annoyed me so much that one day I waited until ten and when she arrived, I exploded.

''I'm not going to fire you now because it's just before Christmas,'' I said, ''but if you don't straighten up, I'm going to fire you right after Christmas.''

All the way to work I felt miserable. What a terrible thing to say. How would I have reacted on the on the receiving end? When I got home that evening, I sat down with Mattie.

''Look,'' I said, ''I'm sorry. I didn't mean it. I'm not going to fire you, but I would appreciate it if you could get here earlier.''

Mattie turned out to be punctual, reliable, and loyal. She not only worked hard but she took responsibility. I'd come home to find she'd washed curtains or polished silver without being told.

"Not that they needed it," she'd say with irony, "but I knew you were fixing to have a party this Saturday so I thought you'd want things to look special."

Her phone messages were accurate and beautifully written, spelling and punctuation flawless. It prompted Gary to have me inquire about her education. Only fourth grade, she said, "but I read a lot." "Borrow any of our books you want," I said.

Sad to relate, during one of our vacation absences, my father had a quarrel with her, fired her, and she refused to come back even when I pleaded.

But occasionally she would come to help with an open house, laughing and kidding with our friends she'd come to know. This lasted until I moved to the country which she designated as being "Plumb Nelly—plumb out of town and nelly out of this world."

We still keep in touch. I took the grandsons to visit her on one of their trips here. Occasionally we have a long telephone conversation, commiserating with the signs of growing old together.

And I often reflect that Mattie was one of the happiest associations to come out of that old house.

# 20

## I Led Three Lives

I HAD BEEN BAKING COOKIES when I heard of Pearl Harbor and I was baking cookies on a December night in 1955 when a phone call again changed my life.

It was the German consul calling from Kansas City to ask if I would be interested in joining a group of "distinguished church and welfare leaders" on a tour of West Germany in February. We would be the guests of the *Bundesregieren,* the West German government. All expenses would be paid.

After some debate and discussion, it was cleared with my editors. The family decided Bruce's routine of nursery school and home could go on without me. Friends and family would augment my parents who were always there even when Gary was away.

I was not too enthusiastic about visiting Germany. All my post-World War I education and indoctrination along with our World War II experiences had colored my views. But after all, it was a trip to Europe. Maybe I could stop over in England.

The invitation had been maneuvered by my friend, Marlene Maertens, German-born refugee and 100 percent American citizen whose life story I'd related in a series on displaced persons. She and another friend, the Rev. Dr. O. Walter Wagner, director of the Metropolitan Church Federation of St. Louis, were in Germany preparing for participation in the Kirchentag, an international church festival, and would be there to greet me.

A press release named the sixteen in our group, five men, eleven women. With amusement, Gary said it looked like a dull trip. With delight I wrote on our arrival to let him know we'd been subdivided into three groups and mine consisted of myself and three of the men.

Moreover, the three men were charmers as the clergy in top positions often are. The Rev. Dr. Earl Adams headed the National Council of Churches. The Rev. Dr. Robert Van Deusen was head of the National Lutheran Council. The Rev. Roy Smith was a Methodist minister who had been a World War II chaplain.

*The church-welfare tour of West Germany in 1956. From left, the Reverend Dr. Earl Adams, the Reverend Dr. Robert Van Deusen, and the Reverend Roy Smith.*

Our group represented the Protestant Church and welfare. Another group of three was Catholic Church and welfare. The third group consisted of nine women in public life, presidents of the League of Women Voters, Catholic and Jewish women's organizations, and political and farm leaders.

We toured independently, joining up from time to time, and when I returned home to the speechmaking circuit I told my favorite story.

Conscious of the high rank of my colleagues, I tried to stay in the background. As we met with each German group, we would identify ourselves, the men speaking at length on their work and the religious movements in America. I usually spoke briefly identifying myself as journalist, welfare volunteer, housewife, "und mutter." At one stop, I added lightly that, "You might say I lead three lives." Earl Adams added that I was much too modest, that I had been designated a "woman of the year."

The next morning at breakfast, we opened the newspaper. "Ich Lebe Drei Leben," read a top headline. "I lead three lives," said Woman of the Year Frau Clarissa Start Davidson of St. Louis, Missouri, USA. The story told of my activities as a journalist, welfare volunteer, housewife "und Mutter" and concluded with a brief paragraph, "Accompanying Mrs. Davidson are. . . ."

The men teased me unmercifully for the rest of the trip.

"Come on, Drei Leben, you have three lives to give," they'd call out as we climbed towers, trekked through three-foot snowdrifts at a servicemen's retreat at Berchtesgaden, and toured camps of the mounting number of East Zone refugees.

It was not only educational, as I had hoped, but we learned of the German miracle of economic recovery and the genuine gratitude for the help of our country. It was also fun, as we discovered *Fasching,* the German Mardi Gras carnival, and the joys of *konditoeri*—whipped cream pastries—and the friendship that can be formed with people of another language.

Along the way, I fell in love—with Germany. It was an uneasy feeling at first, a feeling of disloyalty. Did it mean we were condoning or excusing Hitler, ignoring the Holocaust? By no means, nor were the German people. But there had been a resistance movement and many of our church leader hosts had been a part of it.

The trip made a tremendous change in my life. I had always dreamed of going to Europe "some day." Probably I would have gone on one of those conventional guided tours, the seven countries in ten days, "if it's Tuesday this must be Belgium" kind. Instead, we were immersed in the life of another country, traveling and communicating on our own. The language barrier was less than it was in London— where we did stop on our way home. From the first night when I walked the streets of Bonn—with the eerie feeling I'd been there before—to the last sight of the grandeur of the Alps surrounding Garmisch, I felt at home. I made peace with the German part

*The trip to Germany led to a book on Martin Niemoeller, here with Marlene Maertens and me in 1959.*

of my ancestry hitherto ignored, as I watched German women running, rarely walking, and thought, "Why that's just like Mama, just like Aunt Olie."

This first trip led to a second and a third. One of the German resistance leaders we met was Pastor Martin Niemoeller, famous even in our country as the outspoken critic of Jewish persecution, the man Hitler called his "personal prisoner" in Dachau concentration camp.

My friend, Marlene Maertens, had known him in Germany and arranged for our meeting in Frankfurt on our last day of the tour, a day when I broadcast to our home station, KSD.

The next year, Martin Niemoeller and his wife, Else, visited St. Louis and we enjoyed a less formal visit.

"I feel as if I've made a new friend," she said on parting, "and it isn't often at my time of life that one makes new friends.''

I saw them off at the airport and on my way home began thinking how someone should write a book about the Niemoeller story. The next day Marlene called me from Philadelphia.

''Just before Martin left, we began talking of how someone should write his story,'' she said, ''and we think you're the person.''

Marlene made all the arrangements, finding a publisher in New York, arranging for financing for the trip, providing me with background information. I learned something of the age-old question, ''What is truth?'' on that project. A book at the public library called *I Was In Hell With Niemoeller* purported to tell of his experiences in the concentration camp. After I had copied most of it, laboriously on the typewriter in those pre-copier days, I learned, from Niemoeller himself, that the book was a hoax. He had never met the man who wrote the book and fabricated it all.

I spent a month in Wiesbaden, Niemoeller's home then, learning the true story. It was a combination of business and fun, too, for Gary and Bruce, then not quite seven, went along, and we enjoyed the scenery, the *konditorei* and the warm, buoyant Niemoeller family life together.

A German journalist was preparing a book on Niemoeller at the same time; we met at luncheon one day. I was quite nervous because obviously his

*Trips to Europe were a great joy to all of us.*

qualifications for such a book were superior.

*God's Man,* the story of Pastor Niemoeller, was published in the fall of 1959 within a few weeks of the German book. For the only time in my life, my byline was Clarissa Start Davidson. Both were reviewed in the prestigious *Saturday Review;* the reviewer compared one anecdote which differenced slightly in a time reference.

"These books are only five minutes apart," he concluded, "but it seems to us the Davidson book gets there first with the most."

The book was a critical success but my only financial gain was the trip to Europe. That was enough. It gave us courage to try a trip in 1963, Europe by

*Bruce and cow on Rigi Kulm, Switzerland.*

Eurail we called it, our own seven-countries-in-three-weeks plan. We saved hotel costs by traveling at night sleeping on the train. Rome to Zurich, Zurich to Innsbruck, leaning out of train windows to buy food from vendors or enjoy an accordion serenade on a summer night in one station. We made friends with other families who had read *Europe on Five Dollars a Day* and were proving that traveling on the native economy could offer more than the grand tour on the fancy hotel circuit.

It was on our return home that Gary lectured me on economics. At that time, his legislative income of $1,500 a year scarcely paid his office expenses and on weekends he tried to augment it. My salary, almost ten times his, kept us on a pleasant though carefully budgeted streamlined lifestyle, and provided such luxuries as travel. It was a tribute to our love and maturity—his especially—that we never thought "your" or "mine" but "ours."

"If you can save $1,000 to go to Europe," he said to me after we had spent that amount on our Eurail jaunt, "you can start saving for your old age. From

*Helen Beck, left, is shown with my good friend and household manager, Mattie Wardell, in 1968.*

now on, I want you to give me $25 a week of your salary to invest."

I was forty-six years old then and old age seemed a long way off, but I agreed.

We bought a few shares of utility stock with my first week's offering. It wasn't always easy to come up with $25, especially when a specialty shop sale would have shoes at $5 a pair or a cashmere sweater marked down from $25 to $15. Or when friend Helen and I would lunch in splendor at the Mayfair ($1.50 for a prosperity sandwich!) and take a cab back to work.

"The Untouchables," a gangster TV series, was popular then and occasionally Gary would borrow the jargon of the underworld.

"The boys are getting restless . . . you haven't paid off lately. . . ." I would grumble or make excuses but I would come up with $25.

As I live now, still not extravagantly but less stringently budgeted on a dozen kinds of small monthly checks, including a nice one from the utility which split to 250 shares, I thank my sensible first husband. I only wish I'd learned much earlier in life that it can be as much fun to save as it is to spend money.

"Meanwhile back at the ranch" was another catch phrase of the day, and meanwhile back at the brick home, life was busy. I literally did "lead three lives."

Travel led to talks before groups and so did the book. The first talk I gave on *God's Man* was to the Friends of the Columbia, Illinois, Library, across the river from St. Louis. The chairman was a bubbly energetic woman named Julie Lengfelder and we discovered over luncheon that we shared a March 28 birthday, that we had children the same age, and our husbands both liked to play baseball. We soon became close friends.

"Do you ever listen to your windshield wiper?" was one of Julie's flights of fancy. "Swish-swish, swish-swish . . . and think that it's like the ticking of a clock, seconds of your life ticking away?" I did indeed and it often seemed I couldn't run fast enough.

Someone must have asked me to list my activities during that time period for I came across the list recently and was staggered at the page-long, single-spaced listing.

If I joined anything I became president: The Women's Advertising Club, Theta Sigma Phi journalism alumnae, Missouri Press Women. I was chair-

*Gridiron co-authors Bea Adams and Clarissa.*

man of the St. Louis County Child Welfare Advisory Committee and several other groups, honorary member and advisor for Beta Sigma Phi international sorority for working women, chairman of the Nellie Salmon Day Care Center, established by a legacy from a black schoolteacher in Webster Groves through the DAR.

Extracurricular activities weren't all solemn meetings. Once a year I became a chorus girl in the Ad Club's Gridiron show, a popular event attended by 1,000 women in evening dress. Eventually I also became co-author of the show with Bea Adams, its creator, and we had marvelous times writing its satire and skits.

For an anniversary show, some of us veterans resumed our chorus girl roles in a Western saloon setting. Bea and I still quote our favorite kernel of corn from that show: ''I miss the old spittoon.'' ''You always did.''

The leggy picture of me in the news account prompted a friend, Mildred Michie, to have the St. Louis baking industry name me Miss Cheesecake of that year. During the close of one legislative session, tradi-

*This can-can girl had a lot of fun during the 1959 Gridiron show.*

tionally attended by wives, I was seated in the dignified decorous state capitol senate chamber when a page approached and handed me a message.

"Greeting to the Cheesecake Maid," it read. I looked up to see the lieutenant governor, Ed Long, who was presiding over the senate, shaking with laughter.

The Democratic Party dominated Missouri politics in those days, but even in his minority position, Gary had won respect and made friends. There is less partisanship inside politics than outside. My own newspaper rarely had a kind word for Republicans, which led Gary, commenting on the disparity of our incomes, to remark, ''The *Post-Dispatch* supports me whether it agrees with me or not.''

I went along to meetings of our Jefferson Township Republican Club and even wrote a fund-raising musical show on one occasion. We were active in our North Webster Improvement Association, went to meetings of the Boy Scouts and DeMolay. When Bruce entered first grade at Bristol School, Julie Yarbrough persuaded me to be the classroom mother.

In our early married days, we had a truce on religion. I was a Lutheran, Gary a Methodist and neither of us wanted to change. When Bruce was born we decided to compromise and visited churches to make a mutual choice. The Sunday we attended the First Congregational Church, the Rev. Dr. Ervine Inglis spoke on the church's early opposition to slavery and how they'd been called ''black abolitionists.'' As we walked down the steps, Gary turned to me and said:

''Well, you black abolitionist, I guess this is it.''

After a merger of Congregationalists and the Evangelical and Reformed denomination, our church became the First United Church of Christ. It was a powerful part of our lives. I taught first and second grade classes, we both served on boards and later tried the challenge of teaching a high school class. Gary did

*Despite my hectic lifestyle, I managed to have lots of fun with Bruce.*

*My mother, Ada Start, enjoyed her grandson as much as he enjoyed her.*

not talk much religion but he lived it.

Last year on his birthday, I phoned my son to ask if he and his wife were "going out on the town to celebrate."

"Actually," he said, "Gail's going to choir practice and I'm going to a Scout meeting.

I smiled to myself, thinking that somewhere along the line we did something right.

Then there was my third life, as writer, which made everything else possible. It was an ideal job for my whirlwind lifestyle. While an occasional new editor would try to pin me down to a regimented schedule, I usually could come and go as I pleased. A school program, teacher's conference or Scout Mothers' tea could be squeezed in by saying to our understanding secretary, Mae Tavenner, "I'm on assignment—gone for the day."

During the war years I traveled often to other cities to interview theater headliners coming to St. Louis —Tallulah Bankhead, Lunt and Fontanne, Bea Lillie. There was less travel now but I interviewed celebrities when they came through town—Zsa Zsa Gabor, Joan Crawford, and with trepidation, Katherine Hepburn who was not temperamental as pictured, but gracious and charming.

In political years there were wives of gubernatorial or presidential candidates; once I tried to keep up with Martha Taft as she campaigned for her husband, Senator Robert Taft. When Vice-President Alben Barkley became engaged to Jane Hadley of St. Louis, I went to his Kentucky home to interview him. He was a charmer.

"Now I don't want my picture taken," he said, "but if you must, take it from this side. It's my good side."

"The Little Woman" column was increasingly important for its rapport with other women trying to "lead three lives," at job, at home and in volunteer work. We all tried to be superwomen in those days. Often we suffered from what Anne Lindbergh described as *zerissenheit,* German for torn-to-pieceshood.

*One of the great joys of my life was in sharing the platform with Eleanor Roosevelt during the fiftieth anniversary festivities at Mizzou's School of Journalism.*

In speeches I quoted a poem titled "When I Have Time," which lamented the lack of time for important relationships. I was talking to myself but other women listened and agreed.

A big event of this period was the University of

Missouri School of Journalism's fiftieth anniversary in Columbia, Missouri.

I was honored to be a speaker at the week-long event, in a group headed by Eleanor Roosevelt. I'd long been an admirer of hers and I enjoy recalling one small incident which might have given the former First Lady a moment of embarrassment.

It was the first luncheon in the week and she approached me at the head table with a question:

"Is one of the women in charge of this event named Jane?"

"No," I said. "The chairman is Peggy Phillips."

"Oh dear . . . I have a note left at my hotel which reads, 'Mother and I are looking forward to seeing you.' It's simply signed Jane and I can't think who it might be."

I promised to cogitate and all during lunch, I delved into my subconscious. Suddenly a trivia fragment surfaced. A Columbia, Missouri, nationally famous singer had been paralyzed in a plane crash, courageously fought her way back to active life and had been a guest at the White House.

I tiptoed quietly to the other end of the head table.

"Mrs. Roosevelt," I whispered. "Isn't Jane Froman a friend of yours?"

Her face lighted up with recognition and relief.

"Of course, of course. She lives here . . . why didn't I remember? Thank you so much."

What a great lady she was, with so much of the human touch, even to the forgetfulness we all experience.

My long-time friend, Marian Willier, was my roommate for a week. We both were impressed on arrival by a red carpet at our door, a message of greeting from our student escorts and a big bowl of fruit.

"Ah, fame," I said, biting into an apple. "I suppose you'd trade it all to be a student again?

Marian, zipping up a designer dress, gave me an eloquent look. "Are you kidding?"

I agreed. I remembered how, as a student, I would have traded youth for that apple. Even then I was glad I wasn't young any more.

# 21

## Winners and Losers

MY BELOVED FATHER-IN-LAW, Edward G. Davidson, died in 1947, but his spirit was with us all those political years and often we'd quote some of his wisdom, including one of his favorite sayings:

"They told you this job wasn't permanent when you took it, didn't they?"

Every candidate seeking political office knows the job isn't permanent, but every successful candidate hopes to stay in office long enough to achieve a goal, seek an appropriate time of retirement, and leave with dignity and praise. A few lucky ones have that happy experience but many end their careers in defeat and disillusionment.

Gary's two terms in the state senate had been most satisfying for him. Spurred on by my interest in child welfare and mental health and by all those do-gooder committees on which I'd served, he worked for improvements in those fields. He and two other St. Louis County Republicans, Senators Hartwell Crain and Charles Witte, sponsored and passed a bill for special education of handicapped children.

Later I was to comment bitterly: "And a grateful electorate responded by defeating all three of them in the next election."

It was not a case of the citizens voting them out or voting anyone else in to replace them, however. It was 1960 and the victory belonged to the man who headed the ticket, John Fitzgerald Kennedy. Everyone else rode in on his coattails.

Senator's Crain's wife, Minnie, died that summer. We had become good friends and Gary and I went to the funeral parlor to pay our respects. The Democratic convention was in progress and before leaving home we learned that Lyndon Johnson was to be chosen the vice-presidential nominee.

When we arrived at the funeral parlor, a priest was leading prayers. I started to kneel with the others but Gary stopped to talk to Crain so I stayed by his side.

"Did you hear about the convention," Gary muttered. "They've chosen a vice-president."

"No. Who'd they pick?"

"Lyndon Johnson," Gary said with a grin, for this political maneuver was viewed as a cynical compromise.

"Well, I'll be damned," said Crain, shaking his head.

When we left to go home, I voiced my criticism.

"I hope when I'm lying in my coffin and they're praying over me that you aren't off in a corner talking politics."

Gary only laughed. "If you die while there's a convention in progress, you can be sure I will," he said.

The next day we rode to the cemetery in a limousine with other state senators, all Democrats. One, an elder statesman, was a Catholic. Gary asked how they liked the ticket and to a man, including Senator Kinney, the Catholic, they were gloomy. They didn't think Kennedy had a chance and they looked on the addition of Johnson as an insult to voter intelligence.

"He's a playboy," Kinney said of Kennedy. "A lightweight. Catholics will never vote for him just because he's Catholic."

How wrong he was.

We didn't take Gary's opposition very seriously in 1960. His biggest struggle to date had been the primary in 1952 when he, as an underdog, had defeated a man of experience and good standing in the party. The district was primarily Republican so the November election had been less of a contest.

*Gary found a constant and loyal supporter in former St. Louis Mayor Aloys P. Kaufmann.*

In 1956 there was no primary opposition, the reward for having established ourselves as good party members. The big race had been for committee posts in our township and we had worked hard for a pair of able newcomers who had won.

The Democratic opponent that year had been Ed Wright, the mayor of another community. He was a lawyer, able, and respected. Gary had actually felt sorry about defeating him.

Now in 1960, again there was no primary opposition and the Democratic opponent was a young man without experience or any special qualifications. It should have been a shoo-in.

We did not expect religion to be an issue. Protestants everywhere were affirming the fact that they would not vote against Kennedy because of his religion. At the Metropolitan Church Federation, the clergy urged us to avoid discrimination.

So it was with amusement rather than concern that Gary quoted his opponent as saying, ''You know my name is John and I don't have a middle initial, but I'm thinking of adding a 'J'. I think it'll make me sound more Catholic'' Actually he was a Mason and a member of the same religious denomination as ours.

He didn't need this little stratagem as it turned out. Everything was straight-ticket voting that year. We had our first inkling of it when I set about to canvass a key precinct, mostly made up of St. Timothy parish.

I was a bit uneasy to find that this normally Republican district gave every evidence of going Democratic.

'We normally vote Republican,'' said voter after voter, 'but we have to get Kennedy in this time. No, we don't want to risk losing our vote by splitting our ticket. Sorry.'' I understood the political yearnings of Catholics. After all, I still remembered my grandmother during the Al Smith campaign. Our managing editor, a Catholic, took his religion seriously. When I was named to the board of Planned Parenthood, he called me to his office and told me to resign. When I resisted, he said I could stay on but was never to mention the name of that organization in column or story. I served one term and then declined to be renominated.

The *Post-Dispatch,* which at that time had the reputation of being an "independent" newspaper, usually supported the Democratic candidate for president. I took a lot of kidding from co-workers who told me I

## ELECT

### E. GARY
# DAVIDSON

REPUBLICAN
## STATE SENATOR
**7TH DISTRICT, ST. LOUIS COUNTY**

**SENIORITY COUNTS . . . . . .**
...Davidson is the only Republican candidate who would outrank all other St. Louis County state senators of either party.

*The photo above was used on the back panel of this campaign folder for the 1960 election.*

was the token Republican on the staff.

"We make her wear her Ike button on her girdle," my co-worker Mary Kimbrough said during the Eisenhower campaign.

I had made the transition from my liberal leanings in the Roosevelt era to being what I considered an "independent." But when one is in political office, it is mandatory to support the whole ticket, rascals and all.

I worked very hard at being fair and impartial in my professional life. Sometimes I succeeded too well.

*This* Post-Dispatch *photo certainly doesn't do Pat Nixon justice. She was a very gracious subject for my interview.*

I wrote a story on Mrs. Ernest "Buffy" Ives, sister of Adlai Stevenson, during one campaign. Some time later she was a guest of honor at our Ad Club Gridiron dinner. At the reception she approached me and said with consternation, "Your mayor's wife tells me you're a Republican. I can't believe it."

My assignment in 1960 was to interview Mrs. Richard Nixon when she visited here. I was most impressed by her charm, her graciousness, and most of all, her discipline. A reception for garden club members was held at the National Garden Club headquarters at Shaw's Garden in St. Louis, and Mrs. Nixon greeted hundreds of women. I stood in the background watching as she spoke to each one personally, looking only at that woman and never letting her eyes wander off in the distance as those in that position so often do. My political button that year read "Pat Nixon for First Lady." She was a true lady.

Kennedy charmed much of the press and they were kind to him. Those reporters assigned to the campaign came back, laughing over stories of his philanderings, the kind of stories that ruined subsequent candidates. His never appeared in the press.

We sensed it would be a close election nationally,

*Gary's aunt, Lulu B. Wilson, joined us at a political reception for Vice-President Richard M. Nixon, then running for the presidency against John F. Kennedy.*

but hoped our district would follow its usual Republican pattern.

On election night we normally gathered at the committeeman's house to listen to returns coming in by phone from precinct workers throughout the township. It was a gloomy night, as the results came in, close but not the margin needed.

"That precinct, too?" the committeeman would say in disbelief. "But we always carry it. Where's that polling place? Oh—Immacolata."

We carried our home precinct with effort. Almost every voter came out that year. The last one was carried in on a wheelchair.

I rarely relished the day after election. If I were on the winning side I was all alone in our office. Being a loser was worse.

Bruce was a fifth grader and his class was having a Share-a-pet day. Mothers were invited to come and bring the family pet, a rash project now that I look back on it. We had a kitten, Mrs. Black by name.

I didn't want to face anyone, but finally I put on my raincoat and went out into the gray drizzly atmosphere. Clutching Mrs. Black to my bosom, I walked into the classroom, late.

"I just thought. . . ." I began. And then the circle of sad, sympathetic faces was too much. I started to cry.

The whole winter was a low. My parents had gone to Florida, following a family fracas. Gary's Aunt Lulu, of whom I'd never been too fond, had come to live with us. It was my idea. She had cancer and the people with whom she had lived and served as housekeeper for many years did not want her. She had no place to go until a nursing home had a spot for her.

"Are you sure?" Gary asked dubiously. I was sure.

It worked out beautifully. She was a great help and we became close friends. I admired her courage, her refusal to give in. Unfortunately, her spunky nature collided with my father.

Their quarrel was over the election but it was actually a conflict of personalities. My father left, taking my befuddled little mother to Miami, where she terrified him by slipping away in the middle of the night to be found by the police.

It was not the last time. My parents came back in spring and one night about 1 A.M. the phone rang.

"She is? Well, bring her here," I heard Gary say.

"It's Granny," he explained to me. "The police have her. . . ."

"Granny? Why she's in her bed. . . ."

"No, she isn't."

In a state of shock I went down to the back door in time to see the police car roll up and my mother in nightgown, one shoe, and one slipper, run nimbly up the steps.

"Good night, Mrs. Start," said the driver.

"Good night," she replied cheerfully.

To this day I have no idea how they knew who she was. A neighbor worked at the police station nights and perhaps he recognized her. Or perhaps she was able to tell them.

She was like quicksilver in her movements. We took precautions with a system of locks to her room. My father slept with a string tied from his wrist to hers. It was a worry.

But the election defeat overshadowed all other problems.

There was still hope because a new senatorial district was created for 1962 and it seemed logical that the one man with experience would be chosen by the party. However, the committeeman of another township in the district, had ambitions.

A handsome, charming young man, he persuaded one committee woman to change her vote. This created a two-two tie in the five townships leaving only his. It wasn't quite ethical but he voted for himself, and was elected in the contest with the Democratic nominee.

However, that was committee machinations. In

1964 the committeeman (now state senator) filed for reelection. So did Gary. And so did a third candidate, a state representative who aspired to move up to the senate, and who had money, prestige and newspaper support.

It was a vigorous three-man race but hardly an even match.

When we learned our own committee people for whom we had worked so hard had defected, it was the end.

We knew it was simply the way politics works. You win some and lose some. With all its flaws, it is not a bad process, democracy at work with all its human failings and pressures and greed.

With the backing of his new state senator, our committeeman became a judge.

I took the defeat much harder than Gary did.

A friend, Marian Hausman, newspaper publisher and fellow writer, commiserated with me. Her father had been a state senator and a political power for many years. She told me how her mother had reacted when he, too, was betrayed by his supporters.

"Father got over it, but Mother never forgave," said Marian. "Years later after many of the opponents were dead, she would pass a cemetery and say, 'There he lies, the old so-and-so.' "

I remarked to friends of one of the committeewomen, "Someday we'll be in an old folks home and she's going to wonder why I pushed her wheelchair over the cliff.''

Gary was more philosophical. ''Vengeance is mine, saith the Lord,'' he was fond of quoting. ''It's just politics. You can't blame them for doing what's for their own benefit.''

At the time I identified more with the motto attributed to Bobby Kennedy: ''Don't get mad. Get even.''

But gradually Gary's rational attitude prevailed and my resentment simmered down.

I never had the opportunity to push the committeewoman's wheelchair over the cliff. She died at a young age.

Some of the others involved in our defeat later suffered sorrows so devastating that I was glad I hadn't wished them ill.

Time heals all wounds or, as the flip side goes, time wounds all heels. Some of the brightest rising stars are like shooting stars, fizzling out of sight.

Watching a nationally televised convention many years later, I saw a stooped, gray-haired man announcing our state delegation's vote. Idly I wondered who he might be. When the name flashed under his picture, I whooped and called to my husband, Ray, to see how the once-dashing, handsome committeeman had changed.

The Biblical psalmist wrote, ''I have been young

and now am old, yet have I not seen the righteous for-saken.'' It sometimes seems that the unprincipled flourish like the green bay tree, but what goes around comes around. One of the blessings of old age is be-ing able to look back and see that the devastating ex-periences were not that important in the big picture.

I'm still an avid follower of the political scene, a true ''independent'' now, a Reagan-Bush supporter, who votes for Dick Gephardt and enjoys the mellow writings of former Democrat Senator Tom Eagleton. I sorrow for the losers though I may not have voted for them, admire the dedication of the fine people in politics. And I'm terribly glad I don't have to relive that part of my life.

# 22

## *Days of Wine and Roses*

"THEY ARE NOT LONG, the days of wine and roses."

The line comes from the same poem as, "I have been faithful to you, Cynara." *Cynara* was the title of a movie in my youth. *The Days of Wine and Roses* was a film of the 1960s.

The musicians we were listening to on a June night in 1965 did not play the romantic theme. "Wipe Out" was one of the songs they played. "The Age of Aquarius" was another. Our son was host to his junior high school friends and, as a real prestige feature, I had agreed to hire the live combo in which he played guitar. Listening to them in my own home was better than listening, as I usually did, parked in front of a

*"This old house" was the scene of a warm dinner party in observance of the golden wedding anniversary for my parents.*

house at their practice sessions or driving them to some remote suburb to play at someone else's party.

You had to sit at some distance, no matter where you were because the decibel level was too loud for middle-aged eardrums. Gary and I had chosen to sit on the patio in the rose garden. Occasionally I would notice lights flickering on and off in one of the bedrooms and I would go on patrol.

"How are you doing, grandma and grandpa?" I would call as I went up the stairs.

I wasn't concerned about grandma and grandpa but I was concerned about one couple who seemed to be disappearing into dark corners of the house.

We weren't rigid disciplinarians, but we had some idea of how much freedom children should have. Luckily, drugs were not a big problem in those days.

We had heard of a neighborhood party which had ended in an alcoholic brawl and Gary had sternly cautioned Bruce on how to behave under such circumstances.

"Take your date and leave," he advised. "If she won't go, leave and call her parents. I'm talking to you, not just as your father but as your lawyer."

We really had no cause for concern for Bruce or his friends, who were mostly well-behaved top students. In his early days he'd had a tendency to select, or be selected by, the bad boy of the class. Once around fourth grade age, I came home to find a little boy exiting hastily with a bottle of beer left as evidence. Quite disturbed, I called his mother and was aghast to be told, "Oh yes, he frequently comes home and tells us he had a beer at your house. He says you and Mr. Davidson give it to him."

"Why we wouldn't . . . why I never. . . ." I sputtered, finally ending with, "I don't believe he'd better come here while we're not home."

Amusingly, at a neighborhood party soon after that, I had a long talk with a charming woman.

"Do you know who that was?" Gary asked me later. It was our beer drinker's mother. "His father's a nice guy, too," Gary said.

Parents often say fatuously a child never gave them a minute's worry. With Bruce it was true. If anything, I thought he spent too much time studying. One sunny Saturday, he and his friend, Doug, spent the whole day at schoolwork indoors while Doug's mother and

I talked on the phone wishing the boys would go out and play. Quite a switch. Both boys are lawyers now.

Perhaps Bruce was challenged by a student adviser in junior high. The adviser told another boy he could make good grades easily. Then, turning to Bruce, he said, ''You'll have to be satisfied with B's.'' Bruce never made less than an A from that time on.

His special ability was in mathematics, a real touch of irony to me. While my father was an engineer, I rarely balanced my checkbook; Bruce must be a throwback, we decided. When he went from junior high to Webster High School, he was selected for an advanced math class with an outstanding teacher, George Brucker, who had received a national award for teaching.

Bruce and his grandfather were not only alike in ability, but they were friends, too. I had to admit that while my father hadn't been the best of fathers, he was a good grandfather. Regularly he brought home a fresh supply of baseball cards, just then beginning to be collected. He and Bruce talked sports, listened to radio and TV together. Mother was becoming increasingly senile, but she was always sweet and gentle and fun.

''Granny does the twist much better than you do,'' Bruce told me one day as he and my mother danced to a Chubby Checkers record.

Politics was out of our lives now and after some

discussion, Gary decided to take a job offered him as director of a newly established Legal Aid Bureau. For the first time in our married life, he had a substantial salary. It was not a carefree job. He had a dozen bosses, the members of the board—all lawyers with differing points of view, and usually he returned home exhausted after their monthly meetings. But he was doing the kind of work he enjoyed—helping people— and it made an easier transition from his other public service.

He still made regular trips to Jefferson City, as editor of *Legislative Digest,* published by the Missouri Council of Churches with commentary on legislation which had church and state reference.

Our numerous activities resulted in numerous friendships and acquaintanceships, but our close ties were still to the Saturday Night Crowd, the seven couples whose social life dated back to "the day before the day before it's Christmas 1944."

There had been changes in our group. Lou and Louise changed to Hal and Louise. Lou had been killed in a car accident early in 1963 and widowed Louise had married widower Hal Qualls in 1964. Our Shrewsbury neighbor, Paul Claus, had died after a long illness, and in 1966 his widow, Helen, married John Beck, the widower whose son and daughter-in-law were Helen's next door neighbors.

John had nine children and not all of them approved

*Helen and John Beck's wedding reception in June 1966 at 300 N. Gore.*

the remarriage. There was enough dissension that Helen talked of calling it off. As her confidante, I gave her a stern lecture:

"John loves you and you love John," I told her. "You go ahead with your plans. Many years from now when you die, his children and grandchildren will grieve at your funeral because you'll have won them all over and they'll love you, too."

I didn't think of this until more than twenty years later. John had died by then, and Helen had cared for him lovingly through a long illness. After five years

*The Saturday Night Crowd. We loved parties, especially costume parties.*

in a nursing home, she died, and it was at her funeral that I remembered my words, because there were John's children and grandchildren grieving; she had won them over and they had grown to like her.

I was fifteen years younger than Helen but called myself "the mother of the bride," for we had the wedding reception on our lawn, a happy and festive occasion.

Then another loss came to the Saturday Night Crowd. Charles, our clown prince, the life of our parties, was stricken with Hodgkin's disease. While we realized the gravity of the situation, it was still hard to believe that he was dying when we were called to the hospital one rainy Sunday afternoon in September 1966.

The others from the crowd came and went. I stayed on until almost darkness, taking comfort from the fact that Charles had squeezed my hand when I urged him to take medicine from his nurse.

That evening we watched a movie on TV, *The Bridge On The River Kwai*. I tried to absorb myself in the plot but found myself praying for Charles, the helpless, hopeless prayers you offer beseeching the Almighty to spare this fine person for just a few more years, asking the inevitable, "Why, Lord?"

The movie was over at ten. I prepared for bed, thinking, "Now I can pray without interruption." But as I lay down, a strange thing happened. I was overcome with a sense of joy and happiness, a feeling that everything was all right.

"You don't have to pray anymore," I could almost hear a voice telling me.

My prayers had been answered; he was going to get well. That was my interpretation. But in the morning came the call. Charles had died the night before. The time? I asked. It was 10:20, his brother-in-law told me, almost exactly the time when my heart had been filled with joy and happiness and the feeling that my friend was indeed, released from his suffering.

It was still a sad time for us. It rained a lot that fall and the car radio played "Lara's Theme" from *Dr.*

*Zhivago* a lot. Charles and Jan had seen the movie and talked of it and it all seemed to tie together in an overwhelming feeling of sorrow.

Added to this loss was a sense of our own mortality and the knowledge that we were all aging and ailing.

Gary had a heart condition. A conference with our long-time doctor friend that fall gave it a label—''angina''— but much later I found the bottle of tiny pills had a prescription date several years earlier, so he had known about it longer than I.

''Smoke less and drink more,'' Dr. Dworkin ordered.

We began having an old-fashioned cocktail before dinner, a pleasant prescription. But Gary found it difficult to stop smoking. I'd started smoking at age fifteen and continued through college because everyone smoked. The year I turned thirty, I had an annoying series of sore throats and laryngitis, and decided to give up cigarettes ''for a while.'' That was December 1947 and I never smoked again. It was so easy for me that I was a bit impatient with what I viewed as Gary's lack of will power. But then, I reasoned, he had so few faults he was entitled to one indulgence.

I made an effort to have a less hectic home environment. We went to fewer duty banquets, spent more evenings by the fire with our Siamese cat, Zsa Zsa, and when I could persuade Gary, our outdoor dog, Spot.

At ten each night we watched the news on television. We knew the anchor men and the woman weather forecaster, so it was like ending the day with friends. Gary would start to bed and I would linger behind and stand in front of the big oval mirror over the parlor fireplace. It reflected across the hall and living room into the big mirror over the fireplace there. And reflected back was my face in the oval mirror and so on, into infinity, it seemed.

I tried to take pleasure in the beauty of our home and the serenity of our lives, but in the middle of the night I would wake up with the gloomy thought, "We are one day closer to death."

Strange. Now, many years later, I never have that thought.

We went to a Legal Aid conference in Scottsdale, Arizona, that fall. A much older woman lawyer chided us for not going to a nightclub featuring "go-go" dancers, but Gary didn't feel up to it.

Go-go dancing was the in thing then. Jane Langenbach and I enrolled in a YWCA class for exercise and go-go dancing. As usual I was trying to lose weight. My goal—my fiftieth birthday in March.

Saturday, March 4 was one of those typically frantic days in our household. Mother needed medicine from the doctor. Bruce had to go to a talent show with his combo. I was working on a speech to give out of town and another at home. Gary was preparing for a meeting in Kansas City and Bruce for a band concert in Cape Girardeau. We were rushing off in all directions.

How trivial it all seemed when I thought of it later.

We went out to dinner, a civil service banquet with friends John I. and Charlotte Johnson, but came home early. We had to teach Sunday School the next morning.

But the next morning I was awakened by a noise and found my husband in convulsive movements and then suddenly still. He was dead on arrival at the hospital.

In the months that followed, I found out what many another widow has learned—that I was not the central figure of the universe, the person around whom the home centered.

He was.

The funeral and the days following were a jumbled blur. It was comforting that those TV anchor people and the mayor and judges and senators and community leaders were among the 750 who signed the funeral parlor book. Betty Hearnes, the governor's wife phoned. Friends from near and far gathered around my son and me with love.

"He went out like a star," my sister-in-law Betty said softly of her brother.

And I was left in the dark.

## 23

## *The Single Scene*

"IF THEY ASKED ME, I could write a book," sang one of the characters in *Pal Joey,* a musical of my show reviewing days.

I wrote two books about my experiences as a widow. *When You're A Widow,* later published in paperback under the title, *On Becoming A Widow* was a serious and spiritual book. More than twenty years later, it has been reprinted and is still selling. The sad fact is that there are new widows with the same old problems.

My second book, *Second Song,* was a lighter treatment of the singles scene written some years later. It "told it like it was." The first, written six months after Gary's death, was filled with tremulous hope and the conviction that the worst was over.

As widows go, I was a lucky one. Many widows have financial problems; mine were minimal. Many widows have lifestyle adjustments; my life was little different except for the aching hour of 5 P.M. when I would find myself standing by the window waiting for the second car to pull into the driveway.

Many women have trouble with children; my son, 15, became suddenly mature and responsible. He was a blessing, never a problem.

Many widows complain of a gap in social relationships. A life built around a husband's career leaves a widow bereft of both husbands and friends. I had many friends from many circles and especially our close supportive Saturday Night Crowd.

I was the fourth widow. Two of the others had remarried. Jan, the most recent, was finding Charles irreplaceable and those of us who had loved his bright personality could see why. She became my special confidante. We would get on the phone each night at five, cocktail in hand and assure each other we weren't drinking alone, a no-no for widows.

Jan was the one who urged me to write a book for widows because, as she said, "no one understands like another widow."

A writer writes of necessity, of an inborn compulsion, and in times of stress, writing is great therapy. I found myself jotting down notes in moments of despair. In six months time I had a file of these notes simply labeled "Widow."

Faced with a week's vacation time and nothing to

do, I performed a crash job of putting my notes into book form. When I read what I had written, I was appalled. This was intensely personal, not what I had started out to do at all.

At the time I was writing a column for the magazine, *This Day,* put out by Concordia Publishing House in St. Louis. I called my editor and asked if they might be interested in looking at my manuscript. Within three weeks it was scheduled for publication. A new day had begun for me. I could say in truth, ''The Lord never closes a door without opening another.''

There had been another change in my life, too.

''If I died, you'd marry again in six months,'' Gary used to tease me when I talked of how awful it would be to be a widow.

I didn't marry, but in six months I had met someone. It was a romantic meeting at the Strassenfest celebration in Columbia, Ill., where my friends, Bill and Julie lived. Within a few hours of meeting Charlie, an air force retiree who collected antiques, liked to garden, had the same religion, politics, and—amazing coincidence—was born on Gary's birthday, I was enchanted.

''Enchanted'' is probably a good word for it. For the next five years I experienced a no-win situation with a person who was outwardly charming, but given to moods of black depression and strange irrational behavior.

"He drinks too much," I thought at first, for he certainly did. "If he'd just go on the wagon."

Late in our relationship he gave up alcohol, but he was still a troubled soul, impossible to understand. One day, as I was whimpering to myself, "What am I doing wrong? What can I do to make things right?" a great light dawned.

"You dumbbell," I addressed myself. "You're not doing anything wrong. He's doing everything wrong. What are you, some sort of masochist that you're letting yourself in for this?"

A psychoanalyst perhaps could have explained it, proving that I'd had a poor relationship with my father and wanted to continue a pattern of rejection. Or perhaps I had guilt feelings over my husband's death and didn't feel I deserved a second chance.

I didn't seek analysis but I prayed a lot, mostly in the vein of, "Please Lord, do what's best for him and best for me." My prayer was answered though it took me a long time to realize it.

It wasn't all bad, that period from 1967 to 1972. My life changed in many ways. In the fall of 1967 my mother broke her hip and died within ten weeks. She died as she had lived, quietly and without trouble to anyone.

I was sure my father would never recover from the loss and at first he was difficult to live with, making scenes whenever I went out, communicating his disapproval to Bruce who took to asking, "Why do you have to date? Why do you want a boyfriend?"

Some widows give in to tyrannical parents—or tyrannical children—and stop trying to make a new life for themselves. I explained to Bruce, gently but firmly, that while I loved him dearly, I had no intention of making him my whole life and that some day he would thank me for it.

More than ever I was grateful for a job and outside interests. I had been appointed to the Missouri Governor's Commission on the Status of Women and in that capacity was invited to the White House for a tea, a coffee, and a luncheon. Bruce went along on one occasion and literally rubbed elbows with the president, when he and Lyndon Johnson collided as they raced to be first at the table where chocolate chip cookies were being served.

A fellow member of the commission, Sue Shear, took her daughter on this trip. As a working Democrat, she secured special treatment for us at the office of Sen. Stuart Symington, who arranged for a tour of the Capitol sights for our children.

Bruce had a teacher at junior high who idolized the Republican leader, Sen. Everett Dirksen. When Senator Symington asked Bruce, "And what would you like to see?" Bruce promptly responded, "I'd like to see Senator Dirksen's office. He's my hero." Symington smiled—a little weakly.

I covered many of the events related to the growing "woman's movement." Like many of my generation, I sometimes found it hard to understand what
all the fuss was about. Those of us from the depression generation had always worked and found that if
you took advantage of opportunities, you could have
success on an equal footing with men—if you wanted
it.

I didn't want it. I liked my woman's role, the one
which included being housewife "und mutter" with
the freedom to go to school plays and luncheons and
to leave the office early when I was having guests for
dinner. When a chance came to sit in as editor on
several occasions, I found I didn't like being an executive. It was a headache and also a bore.

I liked assignments like the one for Julie Nixon's
wedding to David Eisenhower, even though it was
more work than fun. I managed to maneuver admis-
sion to Dr. Norman Vincent Peale's church on Sunday morning, where I sat in the balcony looking down
on the heads of the Nixon family. But the press was
barred from the ceremony that afternoon and the
reception later. My only brush with the famous was
in holding Barbara Walters' ladder as she reported
our outside view of the church for network television.

The next year I was invited to a luncheon for press
women at the White House where the Nixons greeted

us personally.

It was the "Little Woman" column which was the most rewarding. My fans were responsive, sometimes overwhelmingly so, as when I received 1,200 letters after my husband's death. My average was 400 a month exceeded only by that of our top TV personality, Charlotte Peters.

"If a man from Mars landed and asked me to take him to my leader, I'd take him straight to you," wrote one partisan fan.

On the other hand, a column in which I lamented my inability to tell a flower from a weed brought a letter with a picture of Ann Landers labeled "flower" and one of me labeled "weed."

Oh, well, you can't win 'em all.

When my Newspaper Guild benefits included five weeks vacation, I began traveling more with my librarian friend, Virginia. We toured Germany where I made a new friend, Anni Oberwallner, through my widow book and Anni introduced us to Munich and the Oktoberfest. One year we drove down the beautiful coast of Yugoslavia. Charlie joined us for his fiftieth birthday in Dubrovnik but left us abruptly.

Friends suggested tactfully that I try to find someone else. That's not easy to do for a middle-aged widow. And for all his faults, Charlie was charming, and often delightfully entertaining. We went to auctions and his phrase, "We buy junk, we sell antiques," later became

*My new friend, Anni Oberwallner, introduced me to Munich.*

the title of a book I wrote.

Meanwhile my father had come out of his grief and met someone, too. At the Cardinal baseball senior citizens day, he became acquainted with a lively widow, Harry Jane Gruenert. Within a short time she had my unchurched father joining her Lutheran church, listening to religious radio broadcasts, and tithing his Social Security. I was amazed, amused, and admiring.

Bruce, too, had someone. The summer after high school graduation, he went on a YMCA trip to Bogota, Colombia. In the group was Gail Stephens of our neighboring suburb, Kirkwood. Now when you have an only son you can't help but worry about what your daughter-in-law will be like. Will you like her? Will she like you?

I couldn't have invented a more ideal mate for Bruce than Gail. An added attraction was her nice family: her father, Bob an engineer with McDonnell-Douglas; mother, Barbara a talented artist (who had done a painting of our century house with her art class); and her brother, John; and sister, Julie. For four years Gail's mom and I cheered the romance on, trying not to be too obvious.

Another piece of luck was the navy ROTC scholarship Bruce received which paid his tuition to Cornell University in Ithaca, N.Y. He left for college that fall of 1969 and with my father away much of the time with his lady love, I was really alone.

It was that year that I decided to move from the house I'd planned never to leave. The change was a big one. A one-story house surrounded by ten acres of woodland. Charlie and I were in one of our friendly periods and I took him on a drive-by.

"Buy it, it's right for you," he said at first glance.

Without his approval I might not have bought it. But it was right, not for us, but for me for the next seventeen years.

My house movings always seem fraught with complications and this one was a real three-ring circus. Selling the Webster house was an on-again-off-again affair, but eventually another widow antique dealer, twenty years my senior, bought it.

On New Year's Eve, 1970, Charlie was hospitalized with a heart attack and while I made daily visits to Scott Air Force Base hospital, cold weather set in and the pipes in my new house froze, necessitating daily visits there, too.

These problems melted away and the Women's Ad Club honored me as their Woman of the Year, with

*The "Woman of the Year" kept one eye on Mayor Alphonso Cervantes, the other on the forty-five pink geraniums.*

a banquet and forty-five pink geranium centerpieces (eventually planted at the new house).

In March 1970 I moved, with more than a little help from my friends. At the Webster end they packed books, bric-a-brac, and picnic lunches, and made it all a moveable party. At the High Ridge end, there were friends, too—Joe and Pat Whealen, longterm political acquaintances who were my new neighbors. I turned to them with numerous cries of "Help!"

And Charlie and his red truck were a great help, too. On sunny summer days he cleaned the pool, cut the grass, and spaded the garden.

That fall the romance soured again. It was at this time that an old acquaintance called. Stella Chaney Brown wanted me to speak to her Parents Without Partners chapter. Why not? Maybe I'd meet someone.

I'd been named Ecumenical Woman of the Year by the church federation and it seemed appropriate that my first PWP romance was Jewish. He was handsome, fun, a Pearl Harbor veteran, a nice solid citizen

*Stella Chaney Brown built my interest in astrology.*

with a dear teenage son. It lasted about a year. There were several others of shorter duration. No one special.

If I had it all to do over again, what would I change? Not Charlie. For all his faults, he was unforgettable. Not PWP or any of my other experiences. What I might change would be my own attitude, which actually is the thing you can change most readily in any situation. I wish I had relaxed and let things take their course rather than trying to bend them to my own desires.

In a way the five years of widowhood were similar to my years as an army wife I should have enjoyed the good times.

I've spoken to many singles groups, read many advice books. A recurring theme is that you must learn to live with yourself before you can make a life with someone else. There are worse things than remaining single. But you never could have convinced me of that at the time.

Through Stella I reactivated an interest in astrology. We took a course from Faye Kershaw, an astrologer I'd met whose advice to me invariably turned out to be right. Faye is long gone but I still seek an actual update from an astrologist, Lee Amato. We both decided the Reagans were astrology followers long before the news stories appeared.

I don't try to make converts on the subject but I encouraged anyone with a mild interest in the subject to read Grant Lewi's book, *Heaven Knows What,* an interesting analysis of personalities by sun-moon sign combinations.

Some are amazingly accurate, if not especially flattering. Of my own combination (Sun, Aries, Moon, Gemini), he says bluntly, "This is the talkiest sign of the Zodiac." Too true.

Many who espouse astrology believe in reincarnation. My ego tends to reject the idea that there's ever been another me. On the other hand, research by Edgar Cayce is intriguing to read.

"Do you know there's a theory that people are reincarnated in groups?" I told the Saturday Night Crowd. "We probably enjoyed Bacchanalean revels back in ancient times together."

There's also the provocative belief that if you do not work out your problems with someone in this life, you will be presented with the same person and problem in the next. The chilling thought of spending another lifetime with some of my problem people prompted me to try to start getting along with them in this life.

*The Jour de Fête at Ste. Geneviève in August 1967 found these good friends in celebration. From left, George and Jane Langenbach, Julie Lengfelder, Charles Stemmler, and me. Bill Lengfelder is standing.*

Birthday coincidences have always interested me. Gary and Charlie had the same birthday and some similarities. My second husband's mother and mine were both born March 30, as was my grandson Scotty. My son's father-in-law and my second husband share May 20, as did Gary's sister. Family birthdays often cluster together in the same month.

Luella Sayman, grande dame of St. Louis business and society, annually gave a party for her Aries friends on her April 5 birthday. We were a lively group, all with Aries qualities of leadership. I sense a kinship with other Aries. I always admired the showmanship of brewery magnate "Gussie" Busch (like me born on March 28), not to mention my fondness for his product Michelob.

But it was my birthday twin Julie Lengfelder who was especially close. During my widow period, she often came to the country to spend Friday nights with me. I remember one occasion when I was startled to see her wearing what I thought were my new pink bedroom slippers.

But no, when I went back to my bedroom, there were my slippers. She'd bought an identical pair by coincidence. We were to discover we bought matching lamps, matching sweaters, and, more important that we often reached the same conclusions. We shared many enthusiasms from Beefeater gin to the TV series "Upstairs Downstairs."

On my wall hangs a framed verse Julie gave me. It reads:

> What made us friends in the long ago
> When first we met? Well, I think I know
> The best in me and the best in you
> Hailed each other because they knew
> That always and always since time began
> Our being friends was part of God's plan.

It was Julie who listened to my sad stories of my on-again-off-again romance. Now and then I'd turn to Faye Kershaw, too.

"What do the stars say? Am I never going to meet anyone?"

She assured me I would, when the signs were right—"by the middle of next year," she encouraged me during a black moment in 1971.

It was in May 1972 that several people sent me an auction bill for a sale to be held in Lonedell, Mo. I was thinking of turning my accumulation stored in my barn into an antique shop. The auction was tempting but I had a tentative date with one of my PWP fun friends to clean my swimming pool. Then he called and canceled.

I showed up at the Belew family auction as did one of their cousins, Ray Lippert. He hadn't intended going either because he thought it would sadden him to see the dismantling of the farm where he and his family had spent many happy summers.

But a few hours before the auction, a California cousin called to say he'd be in town and they arranged to meet in Lonedell. Somehow—by coincidence or divine plan—Ray and I found ourselves side by side.

By the end of the day we knew each other's life stories. He was a widower with a grown son and daughter. He'd been happily married and what a change that was from the bitter divorced men I'd known.

He'd grown up in South St. Louis; like Gary, he'd graduated from Roosevelt High and from Missouri U. He and his roommate, Sherwood ''Skeets'' Beesley, had ''majored in poker,'' he laughed. He'd graduated from Journalism School but war work had taken him to the DuPont Company's participation in the atomic bomb development, and after the war he'd worked for the Monsanto Co. Now he was enjoying retirement, Florida in the winter, fishing in the summer.

Interestingly, I had just about come to terms with my life. In the solitude of my country home, I'd begun thinking, "Hey, this being single isn't all that bad."

Yet the day after meeting Ray I found myself saying to Bill and Julie, who'd come over for dinner:

"I've just met someone I think I'm going to marry."

"Really?" said Bill with amusement. "Does he know it?"

He didn't. But in a short time he had the same idea.

## 24

## *The Second Time Around*

W E'VE BEEN MARRIED almost eighteen years and each anniversary I make the same silly joke:

"And to think they said it wouldn't last. They said a playboy like Ray could never settle down to a homebody like me."

So I'm not home very much.

Ray couldn't say he wasn't forewarned. The man who had retired to spend his days fishing in the summer and sunning in the winter soon found himself transporting antiques to shows and bailing me out of crises in my three-ring circus lifestyle.

Ever the aggressive type, I hadn't waited for him to take the initiative but had invited him to the opening of my Blue Barn antique shop in June. He was out of town but sent a gracious note suggesting a date in July. I replied with an invitation to a July 4 party at my house and, when he accepted, I invited the other guests.

My advice to widows: widowers of mature years are

*It was a lovely wedding; my friend, Helen Biedenstein helped cut the cake and ease the nervousness.*

shy and out of practice. Don't be afraid to pursue them; they'll never know it.

By September love was in bloom. At that time I left

on a trip to Europe with Julie Lengfelder, Virginia Rosenmeyer, and Stella Chaney Brown—four women in one Volkswagen—touring six countries in three weeks. I left Ray with a few "honey-do" tasks. Harry Jane had an earache ("Pick up prescription at drug store"). Bruce's German shepherd, Moose, had an ear infection ("Drops twice a day"). And Webster Groves was threatening to sue me if I didn't have the thorny hedge trimmed along the acre I still owned in my old hometown. Because Webster had a ban on burning, Ray had to transport the clippings to the country in his fancy Chrysler Imperial.

Neither the car nor he would ever be the same again.

Like the prince slaying the dragons, he passed all the tests and even found time to write long, loving letters to me. When four of them were awaiting me in Florence, Italy, Virginia said, "You'd better cancel all your plans, fly home, and marry him."

But I continued to provide an obstacle course. After I returned to the United States he and I drove to New Orleans to pick up the VW I'd bought in Europe. On the way home, he followed in his car, but somehow I lost him. He'd had a flat tire and arrived at my house only an hour or two late, but I agonized so much over the incident that I decided perhaps marriage was a good idea.

Early in December he faced the last dragon. I'd

*As if the joys of an Acapulco honeymoon weren't enough, we also learned from the newspapers that everybody else was freezing.*

decided in my innocence of country living to hold a pre-Christmas sale at my antique shop. The day before the date a horrendous ice storm moved in. Customers came to the sale, but Ray ended up driving timid women in their cars to the top of the icy hill, then hiking downhill to get the next one.

The ice persisted. Later in the week he called to see how I was doing, I said, "Not so good. I'm out of people food, I'm almost out of dog food. The dogs and I are eyeing each other hungrily. Worst of all, I'm out of beer." He came to the rescue, only to slide into a ditch. On the day we got our marriage license, we crawled uphill.

The wedding was on December 21, the longest night of the year, as friends teasingly reminded us. It was held before a packed house in my High Ridge church. I wore a blue velvet dress I'd made and was "given away" again by my father. My friend Helen Wilhelm planned the reception. Attendants were Ray's daughter, Harriet, son, Ted, and wife, Margy, my son, Bruce, and his fiancee, Gail. It was officially fiancee, for Bruce told me just before my wedding that

*Bruce and Gail had a wonderful wedding also, after which the mothers proved they could cut up with the kids.*

his was set for May—a perfect happy touch.

We had two honeymoons. We took Bruce and Gail with us to Acapulco over New Year's; Harry Jane and my father to Florida a month later. On both trips, freak snowstorms marooned us for a day or two, the first in Waco, Texas, the second in Unadilla, Georgia.

Perhaps this was an inkling of things to come. Over

the next few years we were marooned by snow and ice storms in the country, sometimes as long as three weeks. But it was still a beautiful place to live. In winter, life centered around the fireplace with my Siamese cat Zsa Zsa and five dogs.

How did we acquire five dogs? It just happened. Bruce brought his part-German shepherd, Moose, home for college for a summer vacation and she became a dropout. Butch, a beagle from the house on the next hilltop, moved in. We kept two of their pups, Smarty and Missy. And then Blacky, a stray, wandered up one day and decided he liked bacon for breakfast, too.

The scenes I remember most happily are those of autumn when the trees were brilliantly burnished and we'd walk down into the woods, the dogs happily yelping and thrashing through gullies of dead leaves, Moose retrieving sticks and trying to run uphill, carrying branches as long as she was.

In summer, life revolved around the swimming pool. We had breakfast there, used it as our cooling system in midday, and often watched a full moon reflected in the water at night. It was the setting for parties for Ray's church choir and our annual "singles party" for friends from my PWP days.

Somehow we never quite achieved the tranquil existence we'd envisioned as retirement. Then, as now, the pace became as hectic as when I led three lives in suburbia, with the juggling of writing, antiquing, garden clubbing, flower show judging, house sales, and speech making. Ray describes our morning scramble as "getting my little girl off to kindergarten," as he fixes my lunch and hands me my mittens.

"Find a place you want to be 'from,' " he said when we were house hunting, "because you're *from* High Ridge most of the time."

He's more the homebody, doing the cooking, shopping, laundry. He had performed these chores as a widower and I explain to envious women that I didn't want him to lose his skills. It's a liberated marriage of two people secure enough not to stick to stereotypes. Also he's a better cook than I am.

Second marriage isn't successful for everyone. There are certain hazards. Unlike first marriage in which young couples establish a pattern together, second timers have years of habits. To merge patterns and families isn't always easy.

Obviously common interests and backgrounds make for success. Like Arline and Hiram Riek who met at a Masonic lodge function and merged their lives and interests. Yet Helen and Bill Biedenstein who met when she was a middle-aged Protestant widow and he a young teacher in a Catholic school have overcome great differences gracefully and lastingly. In contrast, some of the most likely to succeed second-time-arounders are now divorced.

Often marriages, first or second, fall apart over one of the two big issues, sex and money. Not being

*Life at High Ridge involved lots of time in the pool, and lots of dinner parties, too.*

Masters and Johnson, we don't advise on sex but we have lots of advice on how to handle money in a second marriage.

The plan we established was to have a joint household account to which we contribute equal sums of money and from which we pay food, utility bills, insurance, and home repairs.

Our dwelling places have belonged to me, first the house in the country and now our flat in town, but Ray contributes by sharing bills, even to costly home renovations, as well as contributing his own sweat equity as any homeowner would do.

The most important thing, we felt, was to keep our individual savings intact for our children. Our wills stipulate that we leave nothing to each other but loving regard and that our estates go to our children and grandchildren.

We also have separate checking accounts for personal expenditures so that it's no concern of his if I splurge for an ultrasuede suit or an orchid plant and what he does at his Friday night poker game is strictly his business. Gifts to our children, including cash, are also private and separate.

Now had I married a childless millionaire, I might have felt differently about it, but under our circumstances, it wouldn't seem right laying claim to Ray's savings nor he to mine. Actually we're very flexible and do not split things to a gnat's eyebrow. We realize much of our plan is built on trust. But if you don't trust a person, you shouldn't marry that person.

We've been especially lucky to have understanding children. We'd both lived alone for five years and our children had sorrowed over our loneliness. Now they were happy for our happiness. Harriet continued to live in Ray's family home with her ninety-two-year-old grandmother, and we soon became close. Our sons moved away but we traveled regularly to visit them.

Ted and Margy lived in the Upper Peninsula of Michigan, then California and Wisconsin before returning to St. Louis. Bruce and Gail were moved by the navy from San Diego to Newport to Charleston, S.C., to Memphis to Virginia Beach. Bruce's four-year commitment to the navy stretched into his present countdown to twenty-year retirement. Along the way, the navy enabled him to get a law degree. Gail is one of those wives who deserves a medal for creating a home in each new post.

Her parents moved, meanwhile, to Houston where her father was a part of the NASA space program.

We visited there and took another trip along the California coastline to see Ray's Lippert cousins in that area. Our many friends who now live in Florida provided welcome snowbird stops in winter time.

And then we traveled to Europe, as does many a person enjoying those twenty-four karat golden years. Many retirees have discovered as we did that you don't have to be rich to travel. Our foreign journeys are strictly "on the cheap." No grand hotel guided tours or advance reservations. We drive back roads, stay at gasthauses, pensions, small hotels. There's one in the Loire Valley with service and cuisines equal to the best in Paris.

To those of us who recall staring in wonder at a fragile biplane in the sky, being jetted to foreign countries is magical.

"I can't believe it," said Louise as we sat on a balcony overlooking the Moselle River. "Is this really little Louise Brinkman from Accomac Street in South St. Louis?"

We were touring Germany and Australia with Louise and Hal. Every morning we packed lunch with surplus from bounteous breakfasts and picnicked at noon at a scenic spot, as Ray, the self appointed wine steward, uncorked a bottle of the local specialty.

We chose not to drive in England in 1984 and instead took a conducted tour with friends Doris and Jules Orabka. After circling England, Ireland,

Scotland, and Wales, we spent a week in London, visiting my friend, Phyllis "Pip" McHallam, exploring parks, gardens, Harrod's department store, and having tea at the Ritz.

On another conducted tour, we enjoyed Denmark, Norway, Sweden, and Finland. An air traffic controllers' strike gave us concern as to whether we'd be able to get home on schedule.

"Let's not go home at all," Ray suggested. "Let's charter this bus and go to Germany. Our friend Anni will show us around Bavaria and then we'll head down to Italy. There's a nice hotel in Genoa. . . ."

We'd spent a week in Genoa in 1977 when one of Bruce's navy deployments took him there. Near the railway station is a hotel with a tower and we settled down like natives. Daily Ray would visit the same shop for a loaf of bread, cheese, and wine. We'd lunch in our tower room, then walk the cobblestone alleys to the parks. One day we saw a funicular trolley winding up a hill, took it and found a beautiful scenic view far from the sights in tourist guide books.

I'd taken one cruise in my widow days and felt out of place among the honeymooners and golden wedding celebrants. But Ray and I have had two wonderful Caribbean cruises and one around Hawaii. Nothing like the "Love Boat," friends warned us. All old folks. But Ray came back with a surprise for me—a color slide taken on my camera on a day when I was

*Travel is one of the big benefits of the golden years. Some people benefitted more than others, as this slide from Ray's camera revealed.*

otherwise occupied. It was a picture of him with a cute bikini-clad fellow passenger sitting on his lap!

The book I wrote on second marriage was titled *Second Song* but for all its fun, even a happy second marriage is not all harmony. Any marriage has problems and in a second marriage there are sometimes double the problems.

In many ways an expanded family is a joy. I'd always wanted a daughter and Ray's daughter, Harriet, has been one of my blessings. Harriet is a school librarian and we share an interest in books, gardening and antiquing. We telephone daily and it's great to have someone ask, "And what did you do today?" Harriet even took in Bruce and Gail's dog, Windy,

*One of the joys of country living was being able to romp with Moose and the other dogs. My granddog Windy is at right.*

when they could no longer keep her. Like the mother in my favorite comic strip, ''Cathy,'' I'm grandmother to a dog.

I had no nieces or nephews, so embraced Ray's niece Babs, her husband, Lee, their children and now grandchildren. Ray in turn began attending the annual Davidson family reunions up in Carrollton, Ill. He proudly tells of my son's accomplishments and together we share the fun of each other's grandchildren.

But expanded families mean expanded problems. Today's aging generation often finds itself responsible for those still older. Even younger family members can become ill. We went through a heartbreaking period while Gary's younger sister, Betty, was dying of cancer. I was the one who took her for her many chemotherapy sessions, but Ray cooked for her and

*Ray and his daughter Harriet—now my daughter, too.*

her mother and comforted me over the agonizing ordeal.

In turn, I've tried to be supportive in his crises.

"I sometimes feel as if I'm living in the midst of *As The World Turns*," he sighed when his son and daughter-in-law separated and then divorced. His son married again, a lovely young woman, Pam, with children, John and Jennifer, and our family expanded a little more.

Divorce can be as hard on parents as it is on the participants. It is one of the subjects seniors discuss when they get together, for many families experience it. We tried hard not to take sides, not to make judgments and to accept change. But we continued to see our former daughter-in-law and her family, whom we'd learned to love.

One worry above all haunts the remarried widow and widower. What if I'm left alone again?

Our scare came in 1979 which Ray dubbed "the year of the knife." It was while we were traveling with Hal and Louise in Germany that Ray realized something was wrong. In January he consulted our doctor. The diagnosis: cancer of the stomach.

Ray survived the operation, thanks to the skills of doctors, the prayers of friends and family, and his own sunny spirit and the incentive to live to go fishing with his grandsons. But his 215 pounds went down to 145 and weakened muscles led to a ruptured spinal disc, neurosurgery, and then a double hernia. During another hospital stay, a doctor (not his own) glanced at his thin and wasted right leg and made the callous comment, ''That'll never come back.''

''That's what you think,'' was Ray's angry unspoken reaction. As soon as possible, he began walking, carrying firewood uphill, and exercising his weakened leg until today it is almost the size of the other. He does push-ups, climbs steps, dances.

But there's always something. In a Christmas letter one year I wrote, ''We look on it as a good year when the eye doctor says, 'Your cataracts are no worse,' and the dentist says, 'I think I can save this one.' ''

A threat of glaucoma necessitated laser surgery for Ray. The prescribed eyedrops may have been responsible for heart attack symptoms later that year, doctors said. Again he came through.

The same age as Ronald Reagan, Ray had a skin cancer operation the same day as the then-president, and two other similar medical procedures the same days as Reagan underwent them.

On the day I picked up Harriet's dog, Windy, at the vet's hospital and we heard on that evening's news that the Reagans had brought their dog home from

*In 1974 Bruce was a boot ensign. Today that hat holds a lot of scrambled eggs.*

the hospital, we decided the coincidence had gone about as far as it could go.

We continue to celebrate survival. On January 29, 1989, we had a party to celebrate the ten-year mark of Ray's recovery. Our guests were High Ridge neighbors Joe and Pat who had weathered their own health problems, Nancy, whose husband had died of cancer, and Betty and John, who haven't let John's loss of a leg slow them up on building their own house. We popped the champagne corks and drank a toast.

But we felt a little like the college basketball coach who retired amid much television coverage. ''If you

had your life to live over again, what would you do?''
the interviewer asked.

"I wouldn't do it," he shouted. "I just plain
wouldn't do it at all."

Parts of it I wouldn't either.

# 25

## *Don't Throw Anything Away*

" "TWO WEEKS AGO ago I retired," former President Ronald Reagan began his first press conference after leaving office. Quickly he added, "Boy, am I glad that's over!"

Ronald Reagan has been an example for many in our age group, but never more so than in his desire to keep on being active and useful after retirement.

I could hardly wait to retire, planned for it for the last seventeen of my thirty-four years at the *Post-Dispatch*. But I kept emphasizing that I wasn't retiring to do nothing. I was retiring to do something different.

I tacked up a sign, "Today is the first day of the rest of my life." It reminded me that the future still lay ahead.

Often I meet people who say, ''But what do you and Ray do all day long? How do you fill the time?''

I'm genuinely sorry for people who are bored in retirement. There is so much to do that we never get caught up. A Beetle Bailey cartoon attached by magnet to our refrigerator sums it up:

''How can a guy with nothing to do get so far behind?''

People deal with retirement in varying ways. Our friend Roy Brandenberger in California became a consultant for the big firm he'd served as executive. Doing part-time what you once did full-time is an easy way to make the transition.

When George Langenbach sold his car agency, his wife, Jane, got tired of having him underfoot. ''Go down in the basement and invent something,'' she told him. Soon his house stabilizer became the Perma-Jack Co., requiring them to fly around the country setting up franchises. They became so busy, she eventually made him retire again.

The ''thousand points of light''—the volunteer activities praised by President Bush—provide new jobs for many. Our friends, Melba and Art Loewnau, have regular days at the hospital, wheeling patients to therapy, delivering mail, performing many helpful chores.

Another friend, Dolly Sutton, began making phone calls for Meals on Wheels and ended up as a full-scale coordinator of that most worthwhile project.

The senior citizen organizations themselves keep many a member busy. Florence Muelken assured her husband, Ollie, she'd quit after two terms as AARP president but let herself be drafted for a third term. Lea Allen is as busy on the residents' board of Friendship Village as she was in advertising.

And then there are those of us who turned a hobby into a business. My own switchover was fortuitously timed. The collecting of antiques was once the exclusive interest of a few. Now the buying of one person's trash and selling it to another as treasure has become a booming business nationwide and many elders are profitably engaged in it.

My antique business began in a small way in the barn on my country property. It was an awkward white building which I painted blue, providing my business with a name, The Blue Barn.

I'd collected antiques for my century home, had attended antique shows, visited shops, and read books. I knew absolutely nothing about making out sales tax returns, keeping an inventory, buying, selling, pricing. Years after I had an established business, I read a book on how to start one and was amazed to learn I should have had $10,000 and a course in cost accounting. Mercifully I didn't know this at the time.

I called the county courthouse, asked how to start a business, and was told ''You write the state revenue office for a tax number. You collect sales tax and pay it.''

That's all I knew. Everything else was on-the-job training.

I cut the ribbon at the Blue Barn entrance in June 1972. By fall I was participating in my first antique show. My stock was pitifully meager, but my fellow dealers were marvelously kind. Betty Towne of the Pink Plantation in Foristell and Macky Boedeger of the Pine Door in Alton still laugh at my naivete.

"Do you have any tickets?" Betty asked me.

I thought she meant tickets to the show. No, she meant sales tickets. I didn't have, so she gave me a book of hers. We still do shows, one of them side by side, the Pink Plantation and the Blue Barn. And now I have so much stock I never get it all unpacked.

The Barn itself was never a winning proposition because of the remoteness of our area. I abandoned regular hours and was open only on special occasions. Once a year I would invite regular customers for a Saturday-Sunday sale. Then, because we'd made so many dealer friends, I began having Friday night previous parties for dealers only. To my surprise, they bought more than the customers.

Now and then someone asked me to sell a houseful of things. My Aunt Hattie died and cousins Grace and Florence asked me to clear out her house. My hairdresser, Max, moved to a nursing home and I helped him. Then I held a sale for my daughter-in-law's grandmother. And so on.

One day a total stranger called and asked if I did sales. Of course, I replied, with my customary confidence.

I learned a great deal from this, my first real house sale. One thing I learned was never to underestimate a sweet and presumably helpless little old lady.

"How much should I get for this dining room set?" she asked.

"Oh, maybe as much as $1,000," I said, guessing high.

"Ha, I already sold it to the new owners for $1,600." Then, with a sharp glance, "Are you sure you've done sales before?"

That set the tone. Mrs. P. was in charge. Throughout the sale I could hear her voice, loud and clear:

"I don't know why she put $35 on that. You can have it for $20."

She kept quoting "Mydaughter," as in, "Mydaughter said if you don't get $10 for that I ought to keep it."

At the end of the sale I met the infallible Mydaughter.

"Your mother is charming," I said weakly.

"My mother is nuts," she snorted. "But thanks for helping her."

*Joan Komlos setting up a house sale.*

Success breeds success. One sale led to another. There was The Pink Lady who had painted everything in her house pink. There was the modest bungalow in a modest part of town where we sold marble statues and fine art glass. I asked dealer friends to help me appraise. Jane Langenbach began helping me for fun and laughs. "Only chance I get to see you," she'd say.

But the estate and house sale business really took off after Joan Komlos came into my life.

My neighbor Pat once said Joan was sent by the Lord and Ray supports that theory.

"He looked down and said, 'That girl needs help,'" said Ray. "He saw I couldn't be of help to you any longer."

Joan owned the beauty shop I visited after Max retired. Her interest in antiques stemmed from her Aunt Sadie who had filled a house with a collection of everything.

When Aunt Sadie and Uncle Louie moved to a nursing home, Joan asked my help in pricing the contents of their home. It was unbelievable. On one basement shelf were thirty butter molds, on another two dozen lamps. Dishes, dolls, Aunt Sadie had 'em all.

Family made their choices and a five-day auction took care of the rest. It served to whet Joan's interest in antiques.

"I'd like to help you with your sales," she said one day. "I'm selling the shop and I'd like something to do."

"Oh, I don't do enough of them," I said. "They're so much work."

"If I helped you, you could do more," Joan said.

Soon we were doing one a month. We've cut down a lot now, as they are work, but we've had some hilarious experiences. Hairy ones, too. But most of the outcomes have been happy with satisfied customers who recommend us to others.

A few have been pains in the neck. One man took to popping in on us suspiciously at all hours and, at the last minute, removed choice items we had advertised. It was at this sale that Joan began calling us Partners in Crime. We shortened it to P.I.C.

Some people have delusions of grandeur about the worth of grandma's possessions. We explain gently that we cannot sell at Neiman-Marcus prices as we do not deliver, gift wrap, or offer payment by Master Card.

Some really throw us a curve by selling to friends, relatives, or prospects viewing the house before our customers arrive. This violates our rule: NOTHING IS TO LEAVE THE PREMISES AFTER WE'VE STARTED PRICING. Another rule is even more important: DON'T THROW ANYTHING AWAY. It makes an antiquer turn pale to find a wicker plant stand or blue graniteware in the dumpster.

We understand the confusion, indecision, and guilt feelings that go with dismantling the home of an elderly relative. We assure people that we will save family pictures, important papers, and turn over money or good jewelry, if found. It's amazing how much money we do find, sometimes a stray five or ten in a birthday card, sometimes hundreds of dollars in a hat box.

On other occasions, our finds are discreetly ignored. Who would have guessed that that proper little old lady had all those pornographic books or once posed for a life class? Some discoveries are touching. Beautiful nightgowns still in the tissue-filled boxes, although the owner was wearing patched flannel pajamas.

The house-and-estate sale is a national pastime. In the east they call them "tag sales." The high cost of new merchandise, especially new furniture, has increased their popularity in recent years. Many young

*The regulars are in line at 5 A.M. for a 7 A.M. sale.*

couples furnish their homes from them.

But an equal number of customers are professionals, regulars who attend all of our house sales and a large number of the others advertised.

Who are they? Well, there's one couple in their seventies who drive a Lincoln and are always first in line. They act as "pickers" for dealers but periodically have sales of their own. Some are owners of shops. Some are private collectors and, of course, eventually every collector becomes a dealer, interested in upgrading his collection.

We know who is interested in tools and who will come to a sale with vintage clothing. Or Christmas ornaments or quilts or costume jewelry or jazz records.

Our sales begin at seven in the morning and often the regulars are in line by five A.M. Some of our competitors who conduct sales spread them out for four or five days, but we employ a one day blitzkreig method. Our sales are over by two P.M.

"What do you do with what's left?" we're often asked.

There usually is nothing left. If there is, a buy-out person buys it as a lot and disposes of it at an auction.

Some of our regulars follow flea markets or shows.

Many senior citizens combine winter resort travel with business. We ourselves do antique shows and Ray has often likened us to the "carnies" or carnival operators who come into town, set up a show, and then take it all down and go.

We have narrowed our show participation down and conduct most of our antique business at the co-op, the Ice House in Eureka, where thirteen dealers share space in a 100-year-old building which once was an ice-making plant. Here we take turns minding the store, each working nine days a month, selling for one another in an amazingly smooth operation. Joan and I each have our own rooms now—the Blue Barn and Aunt Sadie's.

Most of us have patient husbands who help our cottage industry.

"I'm a nickle-an-hour workman," Ray sighs as he helps polish silver or refinish furniture.

There are times when I wonder how I ended up doing this.

"I always thought when I retired I'd do something noble like join the Peace Corps or do church work," I told Joan one day. "How did I end up cleaning junk out of basements?"

"You are doing something noble," Joan assured me. "You help people who need help and we do it honestly and efficiently."

There is a fascination to the "junque" business,

something of the treasure hunt and the never-ending process of learning.

My role model in retirement, along with Ronald Reagan, is Red Skelton, who, at seventy-five years of age, still performs, writes, paints, and does all this on an average of three and one-half hours of sleep a night.

Someone asked him why he works so hard at his age.

"I have a government to support," he said. "Actually I've never worked a day in my life. This has all been fun for me, and if I stop having fun I'll quit."

A good thought for every retiree who didn't really retire.

## 26

### Keep the Moving Parts Moving

THE YEAR I REACHED SIXTY-FIVE, I fell apart physically. It started with a bad cold just after New Year's, went on to a digestive complaint—was it diverticulosis or diverticulitis? My doctor said reassuringly, "Everyone over sixty-five gets it."

Then my back went out. One of those cute lists was making the rounds. Headed "You Know You're Old When . . ." it included the clue, "When your back goes out more than you do." Mine did.

My back had long been a problem. During the 1960s when ballerina skirts were fashionable, I stepped gracefully back from a restaurant table, caught my heel in the hem and toppled.

Years later, working on the swimming pool filter, I stepped nimbly back and fell off the retaining wall.

This time, an X-ray technician summed it up: "No sign of trauma. General deterioration due to age."

"My aching back" was a snappy rejoinder at one time. With me, it was an accurate description. Once I consulted a fancy specialist. His cheery conclusion: "You're just wearing out in spots."

In 1980, the year after Ray's neurosurgery, we went on a cruise and he loved to describe how we walked the deck of the rolling ship, locking arms, he on the left, I on the right, with our bad legs on the inside and our good legs on the outside— "looking like a couple of peg-legged sailors," he put it.

Then came 1982, the year I reached sixty-five, and I really did a klutzy thing. A *Post-Dispatch* retiree, a dear little lady of ninety, was moving from her home to a retirement center and asked my help in selling her household goods.

Ray had something worse than a backache at the time; he had shingles, more painful than cancer or neurosurgery, he said. So when I bought some of Mary's things, I handled the moving of them myself, including carrying two sewing machine bases from the second floor of her house down to my car. Ouch!

For weeks the only way I could get out of bed was to roll over onto the floor in a crouching position and then slowly, painfully, walk my hands up my calves, knees, thighs until I was upright. I climbed stairs, hand-over-hand on the rail, pulling myself up. I took

*My aerobics class at Chris Wille's Dancercize really "Kept the moving parts moving." My classmates ganged up on me to surprise me with a birthday cake.*

eight aspirin a day, cried myself to sleep, and, never a heroine in pain, decided, "If I'm going to feel like this the rest of my life, I'd rather be dead."

Then a friend suggested a chiropractor. Dr. Kelley took X-rays and said briskly, "The good news is you have no trace of arthritis," something which surprised me because I had a squeaky knee which I'd referred to for years as "my arthritic knee."

The bad news was that I'd dislocated my hip. I was not "wearing out in spots" as the eminent specialist had suggested. I had a tricky socket and Dr. Kelley thought he could straighten it out in time.

At first it was twice a week, then once a week, then twice a month. I still go once a month, not to Dr. Kelley, for he and his wife retired and built a home in Maui, which we've visited. Dr. Reva Minor, the beautiful young woman who bought his practice, takes care of me once a month. I think of it as "getting my wheels realigned."

The marvelous part was that after a few weeks I was no longer going hand-over-hand up the ramp from Dr. Kelley's office, but skipping uphill and walking without pain.

The next winter we went on a cruise, one of the joys of the twenty-four-carat years. I love everything about cruises, the food, the scenery, the food, the entertainment, the food, the shops, the food. Well, actually the big problem is that every cruise ends with my weighing six to ten pounds more.

On this one, a Holland-American cruise, morning exercise classes were part of the program, so I signed up to counteract the inevitable fattening up.

"We'll do aerobic exercises at the end," said our pretty young teacher, "but if any of you find it's too much you can drop out."

I had no problem with anything including some jumping jack and striding steps. In fact I felt great.

"When do we do the aerobic part?" I asked.

"We just did," she said.

That was all there was to it? Then why did some of those young people look so winded? I began feeling good about myself.

Back home at the neighborhood supermarket, a poster caught my eye. DANCERCIZE . . . aerobic dancing exercise classes, with Chris Wille. Fenton Methodist Church. Eight weeks for $28.

Hmm, why not? I made a call, mailed a check, reported on a Monday morning wearing some ancient black tights and leotards and found myself in a church gym with forty to fifty young women, mostly aged twenty-five to thirty-five. Many had toddlers in nursery class there.

Chris, a human dynamo with charm, explained we'd do fifteen minutes of warm-up stretching, thirty minutes of dancing and fifteen minutes of cool-down exercises, which were very important.

At the first session we were to take our pulse. I'd learned this little maneuver in Red Cross classes in World War II, but was never too good at it.

"All done? Now multiply by two," Christ said. "What did you get? Over 100? You might consider some changes in your life style—not smoking, maybe? Change in diet? Around eighty? You're in the normal range, sixty to eighty, not to worry."

I was sure I'd made a mistake. Mine was forty-eight.

"You're supposed to double it," a classmate said.

I *had* doubled it; it was twenty-four at the half-minute.

Much later I learned that Chris's resting pulse rate was also in the forties, as is that of many trained athletes. It means you're in condition. Hey, how's that for a little old lady in Reeboks, who was ready to turn herself in a year ago?

Chris's class isn't for sissies. The dance routines are vigorous, fast-paced, done to Michael Jackson and all those other shriekingly loud songs that my husband dismisses as "that yanh yanh yanh music." But some of the steps were the simple old shuffle-off-to-Buffalo, grapevine, and fan kicks we'd learned back at Community Center dancing school in the twenties.

The cool-down floor exercises were harder, but after a while I found myself doing the bicycle, sit-up, push-up things better than I'd done at Miss Gunther's gym class in high school. Toward the end as I was tiring I'd pretend I was in the Russian ballet and would be sent to Siberia if I failed. It was also encouraging to note that some of the young girls dropped out. Of course, some of them were pregnant.

My biggest problem is identifying the music. I go back to the days when lyrics were important. "Why is he singing, 'I'm back, I'm back?' " I'd ask. "No, no, it's 'I'm bad, I'm bad.' "

Rarely do I think of the age differences, except now and then. Like the day one student said to another, "You graduated from Lindbergh High? So did I. What year? 1972?"

"I'm in class with a girl who graduated from high school the year I retired," I told my husband.

When icy weather made driving difficult out our way, we had to walk half a mile uphill for the mail. Usually I made several stops to catch my breath. The winter after I started Dancercize I walked to the top of the hill without stopping. What a feeling of exhilaration! I wasn't getting older; I was getting better.

Dancing isn't for everyone, although we have lots of company at the couples dances we attend once a month at the Turner Hall in Columbia, Ill. The bands play the golden oldies and we waltz and jitterbug just like World War II. The encouraging thing is how good so many of our generation are in an era when few young people seem to know how to dance.

Other friends our age have become vigorous walkers, as have the young. My son jogged his way through the New York Marathon.

It's a health conscious age, far different from our youth when the indolent cigarette-smoking youth sneered at any exercise except elbow bending at the bar, and the worst thing you could call a girl student was a "Phys. Ed. type."

But whether you go out for the Senior Olympics, as our friend, John I. Johnson does, or just join the marathon through the mall, the important thing is to follow my husband's dictum:

"Keep the moving parts moving."

# 27

## Nursing Homes

"**Y**OU LOOK FORWARD to getting older?" a friend said, "to ending your days in one of those awful nursing homes, strapped to a chair, wearing diapers like a baby?"

Of course not. Few people want to live in nursing homes, not even the people who have to be there.

Fortunately, old age doesn't necessarily mean being institutionalized. According to Hugh Downs's commonsense book, *Thirty Dirty Lies About Old,* fewer than one in five older persons lives in an institution. Eighty percent live in their own homes or with relatives.

My traveling friend Virginia dreaded the thought

of going to a nursing home, giving up her apartment and the garden she tended so lovingly. She had her wish. A happy celebration of her eightieth birthday, a sudden stroke days later and within a month she was gone, as she would have wished it.

My close friend and neighbor Helen outlived two husbands and continued to get along in her own home until the day she broke her hip and lay on the floor, unable to crawl to the telephone. Fortunately her stepson, who lived next door, noticed her morning paper still on the porch at noon and went over to investigate. After hospitalization, Helen quietly made the decision to enter a nursing home.

She lived there five years and those of us who loved her found it heartbreaking to see her deteriorate after a series of strokes robbed her of the ability to communicate.

Time after time, I ended my visits to her, sitting in my car, hitting my fists in my lap and raging, 'Why Lord, why can't you take her. This isn't living.''

But dying is a part of living, just as the drying of leaves on a tree is a part of nature's cycle, a less lovely phase than the leafing out in spring and the canopy of summer. The old person in diapers, dependent on others, needs love and laughter as much as the baby in the same situation.

The saving grace, the thing that kept me going back to see Helen in her helplessness was the sense that she

*When Ray reached middle-age his goal was to live long enough to take his grandsons fishing. He has made it—and then some.*

was aware. Once, as I got up to go, I leaned over and kissed her and said, "God bless you, Helen." With tremendous effort, she stammered out the words, "God bless you, too." It was the first thing she'd said in months. I laughed and cried all the way to the car.

A lapse of memory or loss of speech doesn't mean a total absence of mind. My husband tells a beautiful story of his mother who, in her growing senility, would ask the same question as he picked up his father and her each evening to take them to dinner at his house. As they passed a certain church landmark, she would ask, "Will Harold and Em be there tonight?"

His brother Harold and wife Em were vacationing in Florida and nightly he would explain this patiently and she would say, "Oh yes, that's right." They returned just before the Christmas holidays. Plans for the family party were under way, and suddenly, Harold died in his sleep.

The family decided that mother would not be told; it would confuse her and be painful to have to repeat and repeat the sad news. But the first evening, on their way home, Ray suddenly realized he was driving the same familiar route, past the church.

Almost frantic, he wondered what he would say, how he would answer when the familiar question was asked. But as he made the boulevard stop at the church corner, to his amazement, his mother turned to him and asked, "Will Em be there tonight?"

"And from that moment on, she never mentioned my brother's name," he relates. "It was as if she knew without being told."

He, too, went through a sad period of visits to his mother when she would speak to him and his father without recognizing them. And yet on his last visit to her, she smiled at him and said, "My beloved son"— like a benediction.

Our family dealings with nursing homes began with my Aunt Olie. Childless, Aunt Olie and Uncle John lived in their upstairs flat into their eighties, tending their garden and keeping their house immaculate. They were an extended part of our immediate family, always present on holidays and special occasions.

Uncle John loved good food and wine. Entertaining them was my way of repaying them for caring for me when I was a child, coming up with my college tuition that first year, taking us into their home when we had no place to go.

Uncle John failed suddenly, a spell with his heart and a few days later, a quiet slipping away. Aunt Olie

adjusted to living alone. I came by several times a week
to take her shopping or do her banking. I tried to get
her to have more fun, even urged her to fly to California with me to see Bruce and Gail.

"You're not getting me up in a plane," she said.
"It might crash and I'd be killed."

"But auntie, I'd be in the plane, too," I said.

"Yes," was the reply, "but you know how to fly."

I never did quite figure that one out.

Little by little her behavior became irrational.
Always jealous of a neighbor, she took to screaming
obscenities at her. Convinced people were stealing
from her—another familiar pattern—she took to calling the police in the middle of the night to report im-
aginary thefts.

"What is missing?" the police would ask me.

"Only her marbles," I would sigh. "Couldn't you
make a note not to answer her calls? No, I suppose
you have to."

"Next time she has one of these spells, take her to
the hospital," her doctor told me. "Sign her in as my
patient and we'll try to treat her."

It was a warm day in February. I was picking her
up to take her out to our house for my father's birthday party. I had ice cream in the car. It was long
melted when I got home several hours later. But with
the persuasiveness of the policeman who had answered
another call, she was hospitalized.

I never met the psychiatrist assigned to her case, but his kindliness in our numerous phone conversations and his patience and sympathy earned my eternal gratitude.

I began the search for a nursing home and finally found one within her price range, $400 a month then. The first one didn't work out; after a month there, they said she was a problem and they would need twice as much to care for her. Back to the hospital and back to visiting homes. This time I found a place called Mountain View in Festus, Mo., thirty miles from our home. Nothing fancy but clean with capable kindly young women aides.

And Aunt Olie settled down nicely there, walking the long halls for exercise, visiting people she didn't know, going to the Dairy Queen for ice cream on my weekly visits.

There were grim sights there as in every nursing home. The woman in the next room who droned incessantly, "Pearl-Pearl-Pearl—come here this minute, Pearl." No one, not even her family knew who Pearl was—or had ever been.

But there were lighter moments too. One day a party was in progress and a volunteer pianist was playing "In the Good Old Summer Time," and I whirled Aunt Olie around the floor in a fast waltz.

Another time I decided I would go to O'Fallon, Ill., some distance across the river, and get Aunt Floss,

Aunt Olie's younger and only remaining sister, for a visit.

We had a complicated routine at that time. My father and his girlfriend, Harry Jane, would visit us for a weekend, then I would take them home. Since we had no trash pick-up out in the country, taking them back to her house usually involved also taking our trash to leave in her dumpster. On this occasion the trash was an accumulation of beer cans from a big party we'd had.

When I reached her house, rain began to fall, so I hurried the two of them in, then drove in, forgetting the trash was still in the trunk of my car.

But no matter, it was on to Illinois, and the drive back and down to Festus where the two sisters laughed and visited and then we drove to a nearby park for the picnic lunch I'd brought.

On the way down I noticed giant trash barrels. A perfect place for my sack of cans.

We had our lunch, sandwiches and salad and cake and coffee. The brief rain shower had been long ago and the sun shone brightly. When it was time to go, we started up the grassy hill to the car. Both Aunt Olie and Aunt Floss were wobbly so I linked arms, one on each side of me and propelled them up the hill. Suddenly a hilarious thought occurred to me.

"If any of the people in those houses up there happens to walk over here and investigate the trash can, you know what they'll think," I said.

"They'll think, 'No wonder those old gals couldn't make it up the hill. They must have put away a case of beer while they were sitting out there.' "

Aunt Olie lived at the home a little more than a year and then she, too, was gone.

The following spring we returned with another resident for Mountain View. This time it was Ray's mother-in-law, his first wife's mother, Alberta Shoemaker, called Grandmother Berta or B. by the family. Grandmother was a strong willed personality. Not only had she stated on one occasion that she intended being her own executor, but she had also stated that when she required care, she wanted a private nurse. A neighbor of considerable means had had that type of home care.

But times had changed. Even a part-time practical nurse was prohibitively expensive. It was daughter Harriet, the only one still at home with Grandmother who bore the burden. When Grandmother began hallucinating about "ten murders that took place in my room last night," we arranged for her to be admitted to the home.

She hated it. One day when Ray went to visit, she marched him down the hall, pointed at a sweet little old lady who was probably twenty years her junior, and said, "Look what I have to put up with. I'm surrounded by old people."

*Two beloved people in my life—my father and Harry Jane, shown in 1973.*

We had a birthday party for her August 3 and a week later she passed away.

Meanwhile, our remaining elders, my father and his girlfriend, Harry Jane, had managed to be fairly self- sufficient, staying at her house much of the time, still able to take the bus downtown to baseball games. Then during a prolonged hot spell, he became ill.

From the hospital, the doctor recommended nursing home care. Father wanted to go home and we never told him he would not be able to do so. Six weeks went by. On our last visit, he looked at Harry Jane with a twinkle in his eye and asked, "When are we going to get married?" That night, they called to tell me he had died.

As I've often expressed it, I inherited Harry Jane. She spent more and more time with us, and finally we were giving her full-time care in our home, taking her three meals a day to her bed. While she was able to get up to go to the bathroom we decided we could have her stay with us, although it meant hiring a house sitter when we went out of town, even overnight.

But then came the day she was unable to get to the

bathroom and fell. Over a period of weeks, she went to a hospital, was given therapy and training in using a walker. Back home, she fell again. Again we called in kind neighbors to help us get her on her feet. Finally the decision was made.

So, at this time, I visit Festus again each week. There have been changes. Mountain View is under different management, its name changed to Jefferson Oaks Nursing Center.

The rates are changed, too. Little by little they inched up from $400 to $600 to $800 to a present average of $1,400. Harry Jane does not have this much money. We worry as her life savings spirals downward.

It's a problem faced by many and there are many who feel "the government" should do something. But how can we pay for all the elderly when the elderly will soon outnumber the young? Nor does it seem fair to make those who have carefully saved and harbored their resources pay for those who lived it up.

There are better solutions for many—intermediate retirement homes which one enters before total care is needed, paying a more modest rate which does not escalate when total care is necessary. We considered such a plan at Friendship Village, but then decided to try independence a little longer.

We have both told our children not to agonize over the decision should nursing home care be advisable for us. Many a time I have told a guilt-ridden friend, ''You are taking what seems to be the best way. Do what you feel is right and don't apologize for your actions.'' We also tell our children not to waste money on fancy surroundings or feel they must visit us so often that their own daily life suffers.

We make weekly visits to Harry Jane because we are able to do so. She is still alert, much interested in the Cardinal baseball and Blues hockey games. We take her the sports pages and a bag of peppermints, and try to keep our visits cheerful. It's my theory that if you must perform a duty, you should do it with grace, not grudgingly. This may be what the Lord has in mind for you at this stage of your life. Be glad it is you doing the visiting rather than being visited.

Admittedly, it is the dark side of getting old. I hope to stay in my own home for many years. If not, I hope my family finds a home for me, explains that I cannot eat onions, that I like hot baths, a spot of sherry before dinner, and golden oldie music on the radio. I'd also suggest a supply of handbags. I've observed women in nursing homes frantically looking for a handbag. A woman is psychologically lost without one. With all that, I hope I will stay coherent and cheerful enough that people will want to come and see me.

# 28

## Back To Our Roots

I SEEMED TO BE programmed to change place of residence every fifteen years. After fifteen years of living in the country, I began to make noises about moving.

When I first mentioned it to Ray, he took a dim view of the idea.

"Where would we move?"

"I don't know. We'd find something."

"Better find another place before you sell this one," he said. "You don't want to jump out of the frying pan into the fire."

It was an expression he was to use a great many times over the next few years as the frying pan grew hotter.

I did have a vague idea of what I wanted and also what I didn't want. When well-meaning people would jump to the conclusion that, ''You probably want an apartment or a condo,'' or, ''You want to move back to civilization, closer to doctors and hospitals,'' I would recoil as if threatened by a rattlesnake.

The last thing in the world I wanted was to be denied the chance to garden, to walk in the out-of-doors and enjoy nature. I'd had enough apartment living in my youth. As for being close to doctors and hospitals and whatever ''civilization'' may be, I felt no need for that as yet. I knew from experience that a heart attack can take a life before the ambulance arrives.

No, what I thought I wanted was a three-bedroom, two-bath house on about an acre of ground. Style of architecture? I still liked a Cape Cod with dormer windows, and after fifteen years of walking the long halls in our sprawling ranch house, maybe upstairs bedrooms would be nice. Location? It could be in the suburbs, though a scenic site in the country might do.

At an antique show I fell into conversation with a fellow book lover. She mentioned that she was in the real estate business and I mentioned that I was ''thinking about selling my house.''

She asked questions and said, ''Why I have someone who's looking for a place just like that. Why not list it with me?''

Mindful of Ray's warning to find another house, I said I'd better look first. That week she called to show me the first of twenty-plus possibilities within a fifty-mile radius. Each time, Ray groaned anew. By this time he was saying we couldn't possibly move. We had too much accumulation. What about the attic, the basement, the Blue Barn full of antiques?

"The trouble with you is you haven't moved enough," I dismissed his protests blithely. "I'm an old pro at moving. There's nothing to it if you organize. Trust me."

He reminded me of this many times during our chaotic move. But that was years in the distance. I continued to look.

I looked at everything from a darling cottage in the suburbs ("No dining room but you could bump out a wall") to a former Nike missile site in Franklin County ("You could build what you want and the view is magnificent.")

Then one day in my weekly reading of the ads, I saw a listing: "Darling Cape Cod nestled in the trees." Without calling my agent, I located the house, drove by—and saw the home of my dreams. A Cape Cod, a classic in my favorite color, blue.

It was situated on the crest of a hill, overlooking a wooded acre in a subdivision of pretty homes. It was farther out in the country but a short distance from Highway 55.

My agent called the owner's agent. I went through the house and found it followed the blueprint I'd had in my mind and was decorated exactly as I would have done. Ray toured it, grudgingly admitted it was "all right," and we signed a contract to buy, contingent on selling my home. Then we listed it.

One of the happiest happenstances was that the house was a mere $89,000 and my agent thought her prospect would pay $109,000 for ours, so that was the figure at which we listed.

There is a real estate column I read regularly in which an expert answers questions on buying and selling. Regularly he advises readers of the pitfalls of trying to sell their own home and recommends an experienced agent. I would like to write a stinging rebuttal but it would take too much space. As you will see.

In our community, it is customary procedure to hold an open house for all agents of the listing company so they can become familiar with the property and presumably, become so enthusiastic that they'll bring prospects to see it. Since our agent already had a prospect in mind, this seemed unnecessary, but we went all out for an open house, even providing wine and cheese.

The agents had a marvelous time, standing around talking shop. Occasionally we would pluck at their sleeves and say things like, "Wouldn't you like to see the house?" Or, in Ray's case, "Hey, you've got to come down in the woods and see these trees. Why some of them go up fifty feet before they branch out."

A few of them toured the house, made comments like, "Oh, you don't have air conditioning?" Or, "A pool? Isn't that a lot of trouble?" No one went ten feet away from the house.

"They won't be back," Ray made the pronouncement. "Did you get a look at those fancy cars? They're not driving them down this country road."

Sadly, he proved to be right. Our own agent brought two or three prospects. One was an agent from another firm; his Oriental wife was enthusiastic about the grounds, but they had a contract on another house; maybe they could get out of it. From time to time I asked our agent about the man who was looking for something just like our house. She was vague about it.

Three months later, thoroughly discouraged, I wrote an ad and paid $47 to run it in the Sunday paper. Several people came out, among them an architect and his wife. My agent happily agreed to try to sell their house, a historic home in an older suburb. They made an offer on our house, $12,000 less than we were asking. Our agent suggested we accept so they signed a contract contingent on selling their house.

They also included a great many provisions in small print such as our paying for an inspection. I crossed those out.

"I know what's wrong with the house. They can pay to find out," I said.

"That's okay," my agent agreed. "They're very

motivated to sell. I think they'll be asking about the same thing you are.''

I was understandably stunned to read their ad and find they were asking $50,000 more. However, they obtained a buyer, someone with a newer house in one of what I thought of as ''those scalped earth subdivisions.'' I drove down to see it one day.

''It's never going to sell,'' I reported to Ray. By this time it was late October and I had held off planting the usual fall tulip bulbs and daffodils. ''I might as well do my planting.''

The little house did not sell and in the resultant domino effect, neither did any of the others including ours and my dream house. Its owner eventually decided to keep it herself.

We listed our house again that spring, this time with the agent who had sold my Webster Groves home years before. She, too, knew someone who wanted a house just like ours. Again we held an open house for agents—coffee and sweet rolls this time—and again Ray tried to lure them down into the woods to see the trees that ''go up fifty feet before they branch out.''

We had ten weekends of rain that spring and few lookers. The one I remember most vividly was the woman who said happily, ''We're not interested in buying, but I just love to look at other people's houses.''

My yearning for a Cape Cod with dormer windows

persisted. The following year one of our Saturday Night Crowd, Jan Long, moved to a darling one and again I renewed my search in the Sunday real estate pages and the multilist books.

We tried still another agency, a nationwide one. This time we got into the middle of a feud between the branch manager and the listing agent and in the resultant fray, we were a casualty. We did have the memory of a nice open house. We served iced tea this time because it was midsummer. Too hot to walk down into the woods, they all agreed. Eventually our listing expired.

A year later I was ready to try try again. By this time our personal situation had changed and so had our housing needs. Harry Jane was in a nursing home. We no longer had to find a house with a first floor bedroom and bath for her. Other facets of our life had changed as well.

When we first discussed moving we still had four of our five dogs. But then there were three, then two, then only Moose, the mother dog. My heart ached for Moose, failing in sight and hearing, so obviously lonely for the others. One day she found them, and we found her, lying alongside the dog graveyard we had on the edge of the woods, quietly breathing her last.

We had only one pet left, the cat who had been abandoned by someone and wandered up to our barn.

She was so thin and wide-eyed I'd named her Twiggy. Twiggy became a fat cat, an avid huntress of mice, moles, and other wildlife, but we felt that moving her would pose less of a problem than the dogs.

The swimming pool we had enjoyed so much had developed leaks and for a year it was inoperable. I was beginning to scale down my ideas of an acre garden to one that was small and manageable. One about the size of the yard of the flat I'd inherited from my aunt and uncle.

One of the tenants, Else, had lived there thirty years and we'd become great friends. Occasionally I'd say we might move there some day and she would say how much she'd like having us. The second flat had been rented half a dozen times, mostly to young couples or young singles. Perhaps next time we had a vacancy, I'd tell her, but in my mind this was far off.

Then Else became ill and died and it was her flat that was vacant.

"Maybe we ought to keep Else's flat open, list our house again and if we do sell, we'd have a place to go," I suggested. "It would be easier than trying to coordinate buying and selling at the same time."

Many other factors influenced our decision. Property prices were soaring in most places but not in our area. Beautiful as the natural setting was, it seemed to attract little but mobile home development. Ray kept insisting that in time the scenic acres would be appreciated and developed.

"I don't have that much time," I said. "I want out."

So again I tried my hand at ad writing.

"Tired of ticky ticky houses on scalped subdivision lots?" my ad began. It went on to describe our trees, view and the house that went with it.

One day later, we had two prospects. One was a young man who said he was interested in finding property with trees.

"Come down in the woods with me," Ray said eagerly. "Why we have trees that go up fifty feet before they branch out."

By July plans were fairly complete. Our lawyer supervised the entire procedure at a cost that was one-tenth the amount a real estate company would have collected. There were endless details, a house inspection, property survey, septic tank testing, water analysis. But by September our only problem was moving.

We did not move into Else's flat as it turned out. She had lived downstairs and we decided we'd prefer the upper floor, stairs and all. The upstairs tenant agreed to move downstairs. A single young man, Jim is an ideal person to share our home. He's rarely there, never in the way and best of all, he doesn't need any of the basement space for storage, which is a good thing because we needed it all. My packrat accumula-

*Aunt Olie and Uncle John lived at 4634A Wilcox. It is now our home.*
tion was appalling.

"Did you keep every high school paper Bruce ever wrote?" Ray asked in exasperation as boxes emerged from the attic. "Did Franklin Delano Roosevelt's mother keep this much of her son's memorabilia?"

"Of course she did," I said serenely. "They're all in a museum at Hyde Park."

"I hope your son's future fame justifies your saving all this," Ray replied.

Actually Bruce's high school papers were fascinating to read. I sat and read them for a long time instead of packing. Eventually I transported them to his house to let him make the agonizing decision of pitching them.

Disposing of my own papers took more time. I well remembered the pride with which I purchased a scrapbook and pasted my first newspaper byline story into it. Now, some fifty years later, I had seven big boxes of scrapbooks plus bags of loose clippings that had never gone into scrapbooks.

Somehow I heard that the University of Missouri at St. Louis—"Umsell," we call it for UMSL—had established an archives department and was interested in just such memorabilia. A nice young woman on the phone encouraged me to cart mine out. I took the precaution of having a few favorites photocopied, the story of Glenn Miller and one on Tallulah Bankhead, the one on Julie Nixon's wedding, lunch at the White House, a few period pieces of typical World War II interviews. These would go into the family trunk for posterity.

Before taking my collection to UMSL, I did some rough calculating. As best I could figure it out, I'd had more than five million words published in newspaper, magazine, and book form. Five million words! Good Lord! I should be rich and famous instead of well known and comfortable.

Two years later UMSL notified me that I now reposed, or my works did, in thirty-four drawers of microfilm. Did I want the originals back? No-no-no. Good. A journalism museum did.

Finally the day of moving arrived. It was September 23, 1987, and I recall it only in a series of disjointed flashbacks. Meeting the moving truck at the highway intersection, escorting the men to our house with some trepidation because the truck looked big and unwieldy to me.

My premonitions were right. They made it up our hill with difficulty but backing down went into a ditch. Poor Twiggy, who had been confined to a cage since

*Eventually we settled down and so did Twiggy.*

early morning, cried piteously as the day went on.

The thing I had dreaded most, moving the heavy antiques up the stairs proved to be a piece of cake. The experienced movers carried them as if they were as light as Twig's cage.

I carried the cage. When I released Twiggy and she realized she was among familiar scents and shapes, she settled down.

And eventually, so did we.

# 29

## Role Models For Aging

"THERE'S PEOPLE DYIN' today never died before."

A fellow copywriter in my Rice-Stix days used to make this sardonic comment whenever we heard of a death. We were all young in those days so the deaths seemed remote from our lives. Today it's a little different.

People of my generation tend to read the obituaries and funeral notice columns regularly. We joke that we look for our own names first to see if we should go ahead with our plans for the day. Quite often we find friends and old acquaintances in the list.

Everyone who has lost a loved one has had the experience of thinking, "Oh I must tell him—or her—this," only to realize that the person is gone from this earth. As the circle of friends narrows, it occurs with depressing frequency.

It's especially traumatic to hear of a death long after it's occurred.

After my marriage to Ray, I saw my one-time love, Charlie, only once. He came to hear me give a speech at SIU in Carbondale, Ill. He'd finished his studies there and was on the faculty, which was hilariously funny to my friends who'd known him. Our meeting was friendly, brief, and, I felt, conclusive.

Later I heard he'd married a faculty widow and still later I heard they were divorced. Occasionally I thought of him, not with nostalgia as much as curiosity. Sometimes I looked around at a dance or antique show, halfway expecting to see him.

"I'll bet that old so-and-so is in Australia," I'd think. "He always said he wanted to live there."

My partner, Joan Komlos, was taking her daughter, Joanni to visit colleges in the East. Among other places, they'd be in Boston several days.

"How about calling this lady if she's still in the phone book," I said, giving them the name of Charlie's mother. "She'd be pretty old now, almost ninety, so she may not be around any more. If you do talk to her, ask where her son's living now."

Joan called me when she returned.

"Well, your lady in Boston is still alive," she reported cheerfully. "Sounded real peppy on the phone. But he's dead.''

''Who's dead?'' I didn't comprehend at first.

''Her son. Your old boyfriend. Died of a heart attack, back in 1980. Early in March, I believe she said.'' I was stunned, absolutely stunned. In 1980! Why that meant he'd been gone five, almost six years. And I was still picturing him in Australia. It was hard to bring myself to realize it.

But little by little they've gone, some slowly, some quickly. And along the way, many old friends have furnished us with good role models for dying. And for living, too.

Right now, my oldest friend, Virginia Hay, lives in the state of Virginia. She called long distance to tell me with enthusiasm about the fun she'd had at her ninety-eighth birthday party. She added that she's taking writing lessons at William and Mary College.

''I'm not very good yet,'' she said, ''but I hope to improve in time.''

I've written of Hazel Knapp, who is nearly that old. Always a strong personality, she lived alone and managed her house and garden well into her nineties. At one time her house was crammed with antiques and memorabilia. But she did the smartest thing an aging person can do, and little by little disposed of her treasures. Her lovely and appreciative granddaughters received many of them. What they didn't want, she consigned to me to sell for her.

*My gardening role model is Hazel Knapp, center. At 90-plus she is still gardening. She is shown here with members of the Fenton Garden Club as they dedicated a garden in her honor.*

I'm sure she parted with some things reluctantly, but with good common sense and the awareness that times change and so must we.

One characteristic of Hazel's is that of many happy older people, the ability to keep a constant eye on the future, not the past. Recently she told me she had written Peter Raven, director of the Missouri Botanical Garden, to suggest that an international flower show be held there five years from now.

"Why don't you volunteer to be chairman?" I teased.

"No," she said seriously, "I don't believe I'd want to be chairman but I think a show would be a good idea."

Hazel was a moving spirit in the garden clubs and the establishment of the national headquarters in St. Louis. Gardeners seem to have a special talent for enjoying the golden years. Or maybe the healthy outdoor activity helps them live longer.

We've had a score of four-score-and-ten and older members of the St. Louis Horticultural Society to which I belong. Dorothy and Jack Sophir in their late eighties keep up a beautiful five-acre estate and enter every flower show even though Dorothy has won enough blue ribbons to make a tablecloth and a bedspread.

Dan O'Gorman attended meetings regularly into his nineties and took an active interest in the rose garden he'd planted at St. Agnes home where he lived.

Becky Gilliam, also in her nineties, gave up her garden to move to Friendship Village, but eagerly pointed out the advantage of its wooded acre where she could take her daily mile walk.

"It's well named, Friendship Village," she said, "because everyone there is so friendly."

People were friendly because Becky was friendly. She was appreciative, too, quick to thank you whenever you took her anywhere.

At one Friendship Village establishment in our metropolitan area, residents have a big garden area where anyone who wants to continue his hobby of roses or supersize tomatoes can do so. Still another Horticultural Society friend, John Brown, in Laclede Groves retirement home supervises a large-scale community garden for young and old.

Perhaps it's true that old gardeners never die; they simply spade away.

Not everyone our age is physically active, but some I've known have dealt with their impairments with outstanding courage. Marion Dickey has been blind in one eye for twenty-five years, but this has not prevented her from having a successful career as a stockbroker. Recently new vision problems arose.

As she related in a Christmas letter, her good eye developed a cataract, necessitating an operation. She postponed it until after she'd handled her clients' income taxes, then asked her daughter to come stay with her during recovery until a visiting nurse took over.

"I felt like a damn potted plant," she wrote. "I was put in one place and fed and watered."

Experiencing only slight improvement, she went back to her doctors.

"After four hours and $251 worth of tests," she reported, "I was told, 'We don't know why you can't see.' I asked a specialist about a problem I had with streetlights clustering. His answer was, 'I am a back-of-the-eye man. You will have to ask your doctor.' Reminded me of a joke I heard years ago. Two doctors met at a convention. One doctor asked the other, 'What is your specialty?' The other answered, 'The nose.' The first one then asked, 'Which nostril?' "

Marion did recover enough to read instructions on a TV dinner, set the oven, tell time, and read headlines.

"I had hoped for more," she admitted, "but have adjusted my life to my current vision level. I hired a 'seeing-eye person' who is my chauffeur/secretary. She takes me to the office and does my book work while I take care of clients. I have managed to win a few incentive awards like trips I can't take, but they're morale boosters.

"I have much to be thankful for. My friends have been wonderful. I have a job as long as I want it. My clients still love me. My vision is impaired but I have enough to enable me to take care of myself and I can afford to hire people to do for me what I cannot do for myself. So I am ending the year on an up-beat and looking forward to the next one."

There's always a bright side. Marion said she didn't mind not being able to get out into the holiday hubbub to shop. Instead she wrote:

"I'm giving my loved ones something I made myself —money."

June Rutter is another friend who has kept a happy, smiling demeanor despite the loss of sight. I attended a meeting which she conducted from a lengthy agenda she couldn't see but handled without a mistake. We've gone to dinner parties at her home and helped with the dishes while she directed from memory: "The big casserole goes on the second shelf behind the pink bowl."

Instead of sitting down and bemoaning her own handicap, June heads a committee which helps the handicapped in her suburb.

Ruth Dodge lost the use of her legs but not her sense of humor. When I visited her at a rehabilitation center, she drawled, "Well I always thought my mind would quit before my legs."

"I'm glad it didn't," I said. "It wouldn't be much fun, sitting here talking to your legs."

The trouble with old age is that there's no future to it. So say the cynical. This is true only if you look on the grave as the end.

"I wonder what the next phase will be like," Hal Qualls said thoughtfully, as we sat beside him in a hospital room.

At the time I interpreted this as meaning the next phase in his recovery. After his death a few weeks later I realized he had meant the phase after life.

For many, the thought of death is terrifying. I felt that way when I was in my teens. I would awaken in the middle of the night thinking, "Some day my life will end and then what?" and it seemed as if I were looking into a black abyss. The worst of it was realizing I had no control over that inevitability. Even as a teenager I wanted to be in control of my life.

Maturity comes when you face the fact that you will die and do not turn away from it.

My mother was in her early forties when I first recall her saying, "I'm not afraid of death. I think it will be interesting to see what's on the other side."

She made that remark to my grandmother, her mother-in-law and since there was little affection between them and Grandma was an "old lady" in her sixties, there may have been some malice there. But as far as I could tell, my mother continued to the end of her life this expectancy of something good "on the other side."

"I'll come back and tell you," she often said to me.

I have never been one to experience the supernatural but I believe she did make a brief return to reassure me.

It happened the summer after she died. Bruce was in Guatemala on a Spanish class trip. Because it was hot and the air conditioning from my father's room flowed into his, I was sleeping in his bed that July night. In the middle of the night, I felt the bed depress as if someone were sitting on the side and then I felt myself being hugged. It was not a frightening feeling at all.

"It must be mother," I found myself thinking. "She thinks Bruce is sleeping here."

But after I moved to the country, I had the same sensation, lying in bed one night. I felt the presence of someone lightly perched beside me who gave me a motherly good night squeeze.

Sound impossible? Of course. I can only say it happened and it was in no way scary or spooky but a calm expression of love beyond eternity.

Other people have had similar experiences. Ray tells of seeing his mother's smiling face after his wife died, again a motherly reassurance that he was not to worry. All was well.

Sometimes a message reaches us in strange ways. We attended a funeral service for Peggye Smith, a fellow antique dealer and friend. She'd chosen her favorite hymn, "Morning Has Broken," to be played. To my knowledge I'd never heard it before but I thought it was lovely.

A week later I attended another service for Lois Metzner, my Sunday School superintendent in Webster days. It was held in the church I'd attended many years. As I sat there I found myself thinking:

"I wonder if Lois and Peggye have met by now. They'd have a lot in common, both outgoing, fun people, lively and loving."

Casually I reached for the hymnal and opened it at random.

There was the hymn I'd never heard before, in my old church hymnal, reminding me if I had doubts that, "Morning Has Broken."

My closest friend, Julie, and I often talked of what death would be like. The talk had meaning because Julie knew her cancer was terminal.

"It's a terrible thing," she said of the disease she had battled for seventeen years in various forms. "It's like a criminal. You fight it on the street and then it sneaks down the alley and attacks you in another place."

She was not without fear. In a letter that last year, she wrote, "Clarissa, I'm dying by inches and I'm scared." But she went about calmly making the most of her last months.

She organized the household affairs which she had always handled, set up files and records for her husband and children, cleaned out the house systematically, had me help conduct a sale of all unnecessary possessions and make an inventory and appraisal of the things she deemed worth keeping.

"In some ways," she said, "This has been the best year of my life. I've had time to enjoy and appreciate things."

Together we read some of the things Dr. Elizabeth Kubler-Ross had written about dying. Especially interesting were documented accounts of persons who were adjudged physically "dead" but recovered to recount remarkably similar experiences of seeing loved ones long dead and feeling happiness on being surrounded by a bright shining light.

"I've read that many people are met by two or three loved ones to help them into their new life," I told Julie. "I wonder who will be there to meet me . . . my mother? Gary?"

"I'll be there," Julie said positively. "I'll be there to meet you."

A few weeks later Julie went to the hospital for the last time. Her daughter Julie had set the date for her wedding to be held in their home. Instead it was held in the hospital chapel, and Julie's son, Bill, and I guid-

*When the roll is called up yonder, she'll be there. And so shall I. Julie Lengfelder, March 28, 1914 – August 28, 1976.*

ed the stretcher into the elevator, down the halls and into the chapel, so Julie could see young Julie's marriage.

Following her wishes, we went from the hospital to a big reception where a longtime friend, Singleton Palmer, and his band played Dixieland music. Only a few of us knew that one of the songs he played was Julie's favorite: "Just a Closer Walk With Thee."

Her death came two weeks later. Sorrowful as I was, I realized that somehow her dying had removed my last fear of death. There is no black abyss. I am convinced of that. There is a brilliant light. There is a feeling of happiness. There is a strong possibility of reunion with the increasing number of those we loved who have left this life.

And Julie will be there.

# *30*

## *Don't Worry—Be Happy*

YEARS AGO, when I was the girl reporter, I interviewed that cinema sex symbol, Mae West. Her birthdate was a closely guarded secret, but I had figured out that she was pushing seventy, from one side or the other. Whatever her age, she looked great, especially her skin which was beautiful, smooth, and unlined. Possibly she'd had a face lift, but when I asked, "How do you do it?" she had another explanation.

"I don't worry," she said. "I started out not worrying about little things. Then I went on to not worrying about big things and now I just don't worry at all."

At the time I thought this was a monstrous

philosophy. Not worry about family, friends, the human race? How self-centered. Now that I'm about the age Mae West was then, I find myself worrying less and less about more and more.

One of the things I don't worry about is that my face is not smooth, unlined, and flawless. (She *must* have had a face lift.) Years of sun worship before we learned it was bad for our skin, coupled with lots of laughs, have etched deep lines and furrows. I'd be a prime candidate for a face lift but I don't want one. First of all, there's the expense, but also there's the possibility that I might not like the new face and then what could you do? You couldn't get your old one back.

Lines come naturally to a face that's been given a regular workout of expressiveness. At another point in my career, I moderated a television show once a week.

Called "Youth Speaks Up," it featured a panel of teenagers discussing such subjects as "Should There Be A Dress Code in High School?" and "Should We Admit Red China To The U.N.?" The program was taped on Friday nights and viewed on Saturday so I had the dubious delight of watching myself. The first show appalled me.

"Look at my mouth," I moaned. "It's all over my face. I look like that old elocution special, 'The Crooked Mouth Family.' "

"Mouths are funny," Gary agreed, "but yours isn't worse than others. Watch mouths on TV; the camera exaggerates every movement. If you notice, most of the pros are deadpan."

And so they are. The best ones rarely move a muscle. I practiced and eventually tamed my face, but I have a feeling that if you had that skin stretched taut, you'd have to be deadpan all the time to avoid cracking it.

Anyway I don't worry about the wrinkles. I'm grateful for nature's small kindnesses. My hair has not turned gray but retains its original shade, which they used to describe as "rich mouse" except for a single streak which the hairdresser styles into an inverse question mark over my widow's peak. I have to pluck the occasional stiff white maverick hair in my eyebrows and snip the hair under my chin but then I reason, all little old ladies have beards.

You could go crazy if you let yourself worry about every ache, pain, or sudden twinge. Every time I read of a prevalent illness, I develop all the symptoms. Since I've shrunk several inches, I'm sure I have osteoporosis. And it's too late for calcium.

As Eubie Blake said when he passed ninety, "If I'd known I was going to live this long, I'd have taken better care of myself."

I also like the advice on aging by Satchel Paige: "Don't look back. Something might be gaining on you.''

Getting old is a little like having an aging car. When your car is new, you take it for granted. If you hear a clanging noise, you assume it's the car idling next to you in traffic. When it puts on a few years, you begin to magnify every deviation in its engine's purr.

One of the Muny Opera comedians had a song, ''Some Little Bug Is Going To Find You Some Day.'' And so it will, perhaps, but no use going around looking for trouble.

''People used to ask you, 'What's your astrological sign?' '' Betty Munkres said. ''Now the opening question is, 'What's your cholesterol count?' ''

Today we all worry about eating the hearty breakfasts our grandparents ate without fear. Breakfast must be fiber now.

You can find something to worry about wherever you are. When I lived in the country, I'd be asked if I weren't afraid to be alone ''way out there.'' At times I was, especially after the drug culture got under way and noisy groups parked down at our dead-end driveway.

Now that I live in the city, people ask if I'm not afraid of urban crime. I remind them that we live in a safe, solid ethnic neighborhood, and don't mention that one of my neighbors was mugged and robbed on her way home from the supermarket.

I feel sorry for the young men we eye with suspicion. But then you can't blame the woman who's been mugged for being wary.

We do look back with a touch of nostalgia on those days when life in our city was safer. Ray recalls how his first wife took a night course and walked home from the bus past a long desolate uninhabited area without fear. And I remember riding crosstown on the bus and walking home alone when I was quite young.

Being aware of changing times doesn't mean you have to become paranoid. I have friends who carry their wallets in a shopping bag, their change purse around their neck and never carry their charge cards at all. Others have complicated systems of locks and bolts and bars and burglar alarms on their homes. It seems to me life's too short to be in a constant state of siege.

Of course, we oldsters all worry that we're losing our minds. Every time we find ourselves standing in front of the refrigerator or closet, thinking, "Now what was it I came here for?" we conclude, "Here it comes. Alzheimer's is setting in."

Ray and I still laugh about an exchange we had as we met in the hall one day.

"Did you find it?" he asked.

"What was I looking for?" I countered.

Actually the experts on aging assure us that most people do not suffer loss of memory as they age. It's just that we become more conscious of our inability to remember. It is comforting to be reassured that younger people have lapses, too.

"I suffer from C.R.S.," Joan Robinson said to me. "Can't Remember Stuff."

And Joan is a youngster in her forties.

One reason we have memory problems as we age is that we have more to remember. We lead busier, more complicated lives. There are all those little pieces of paper you need to keep for income tax. My husband opened a reminder from our tax accountant this year and we both fell apart as the computer readout unfolded to a continuous sheet of paper longer than he is tall, a six-foot-plus questionnaire.

At every turn you're asked to remember your social security number. Your checking account number must go on deposits and when you cash a check, you need your drivers license number.

There are all the new friends you make every time you take an AARP tour. There is the augmented family circle, the additional grandchildren, great-grandchildren, and the in-laws of the girl who's the second wife of your second husband's son. No wonder you find yourself referring to your husband as "Old what's-his-name."

Added to that, each procedure in life tends to become more complicated.

Time was when you procured a new license for your car by simply going to the license bureau, saying your license was about to expire and paying for the new one.

Now, in our state at least, you must first have a car inspected. Granted, I should have remembered to get it the day I was taking my car in for its 30,000-mile tune up, but I can claim shock when I received the bill.

I made another appointment, returned, and had the inspection done. We had just moved and I didn't know where the license bureau was located, but I found it in the blue pages hidden in between the white pages, and went directly there.

Triumphantly I placed the inspection papers on the counter, only to have the clerk say to me:

"Do you have your personal property tax receipt?"

"Oh, darn, I forgot. I know you're supposed to bring it."

I returned home, got the necessary papers, went to a license bureau office closer to home and had a time finding a place to park on their lot. Eventually mission accomplished.

I did have a problem remembering where I'd parked the car.

But, as I explained to Ray, "I'm not any more stupid than I was when I was young. 'As stupid as,' perhaps, but not more so."

And my memory isn't all that bad. I can remember the song that was being played when my first love leaned over and kissed me. It was "Please" from *The Big Broadcast of 1932* starring Bing Crosby. They don't write songs like that any more, or make movies like that anymore either.

Ah yes, I remember it well.

# 31

## What Am I Worth?

So IF I DON'T WORRY about death or health or crime in the streets or senility or vanishing vanity, what do I worry about? Well, I manage to find some things.

Every parent worries about children, even when they give as little cause for worry as mine has.

"Mom, how old does a mother have to be before she stops worrying about her children?" Bruce once asked me.

He was a college student then and he and Gail and I were in Tennessee attending the wedding of one of his friends, Bob Lucy.

"Well, Bruce," I replied. "Bob's father is sixty-five years old. But he just telephoned his eighty-six year old mother back in St. Louis to tell her he'd arrived safely. Does that answer your question?"

I worried hardly at all about my son while he was away at school but when he came home on vacation, I'd lie awake and wait for the sound of the wheels in the driveway.

When he went on his first navy deployment, I worried more about Gail, left alone, than I did about him on the high seas. His next deployment took him to the western Pacific at the time of the evacuation from Vietnam at the end of that action. Again I didn't worry as we watched the televised coverage of helicopters and refugees; I assumed a young ensign would have no part in this operation.

Later I was to learn he was right in the thick of it, had figured in the rescue of a pair of Marine pilots, and been put in charge of a ship taking refugees back to Subic Bay. I was glad I hadn't known about it at the time.

Some years later he was on another deployment and this time I knew his location and also the date his ship was to start home. When I tuned in an evening newscast and heard, "One U.S. aircraft carrier has had its leave canceled and another has delayed its homeward plans because of tensions. . ." I worried. I worried plenty. But a month later, the ship returned,

*Ranking number one in the joys of advancing years is being a grandparent Bruce and Gail are shown here with my newest, Kimberly Davidson.*

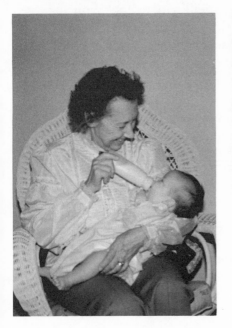

*It brings back long-forgotten skills, such as bottle-feeding Kimberly. She is shown above with her brothers, Brian, center, and Scott.*

*The left photo shows Brian Davidson doing something about the perceived surplus of Grandma Clarissa's cherry pies. At right are Ray's grandchildren, Jess, left, and Owen Lippert, shown with their mother, Margy, in 1981.*

*Two years later I took this picture of two disheveled guys after a romp with Owen and Jess—Grandpa Ray and his son Ted. Ted and his present wife, Pam, are shown at right.*

the flags waved, the bands played and we felt the special pride that families of men in service experience.

Grandchildren are a special reward of old age. When you hold the first one in your arms, you know the thrill that you thought would come only with your own firstborn. But there can be worries, too.

I have three grandchildren now, Brian, Scott, and Kimberly, each one different, each one a delight. Whether we're working jigsaw puzzles of playing bridge, we can relax with grandchildren in a way we never could with our own children. But when there's illness or an accident and we're many miles away, we worry. In one very worrisome situation, I would go out to a quiet corner of the garden, kneel, and pray with the psalmist, "Lord, lead me to the rock that is higher than I."

When Ray had his cancer operation, his grandson, Jess was four years old and grandson Owen was two. Ray's greatest fear was not of death itself, but that he would not get to see his grandsons grow up and they might not remember him at all.

We prayed that he would live long enough to take the boys fishing. Now every time he takes the teenagers fishing or watches them play soccer or baseball, we are thankful again for those answered prayers.

I pray a lot, so much so that I sometimes say, "Lord, if you're busy, just put me on 'hold.' "

When I'm not praying—or worrying—about our own family, I can worry about the state of the world. Not man's inhumanity to man or the prospect of nuclear war, which has eased somewhat, but about the physical state of the world and what we have done and continue to do to our environment.

I worry about the fresh fishing streams Ray remembers from his childhood, how they've been polluted and filled in from improper land usage. I worry about the proliferation of shopping centers and subdivisions where forests and wildlife once abounded.

I worry that our grandchildren who may live much longer because of medical miracles, so seldom have the pleasures of fresh food that was part of our childhood diet. In our little back yard we grow peaches and cherries so successfully that we freeze the surplus so I can make peach cobbler and the grandchildren's favorite cherry pie dessert year round. But unless you grow your own, it's become increasingly difficult to eat tasty strawberries or other fruit. Only the picked-green, shipped-in variety are available in stores.

I worry about a lot of things our children aren't getting in their diets, physical and mental.

It's a laugh to read a teacher's collection of bloopers in which a junior high student has written about the ''Sarah Dessert,'' meaning the Sahara Desert, and another has identified Homer's works as *The Iliad* and *The Oddity.* It's less funny when a junior high teacher tells me her students cannot locate Chicago on the map.

Yes, there's plenty to worry about but the paramount fear which chills most of us in our generation, who supplement our savings with social security, is the specter of inflation.

On the one hand, we laugh a little ruefully at what we've made on the sale of a house, what we spend at a dinner in a good restaurant, the price of a casual little skirt in one of the slick catalogs that are crammed in our mail box. There's a kind of perverse pride in it.

"If ever anyone told me years ago I'd be paying this much for such and such. . . ."

On the other hand is the thought in the back of our mind, "What if prices keep going up and up and up and I remain on this fixed income?"

The yuppie class of our society is often criticized for their materialism. Their values are in cars and homes and clothing and the right kind of white wine. We elders are a little envious because that period of our lives was best characterized by the old expression, "one jump ahead of the wolf."

But there's the danger that the golden-ager is also preoccupied with the material. Those of us who went through the depression never quite recovered from it. With Scarlett O'Hara we promised ourselves we'd never go hungry again. We're proud we've come so far, but there's always the possibility that it will disappear overnight, this cushy life to which we've become accustomed. It can't happen again—that's what the economic brains keep telling us. But could it?

We're also aware of how expensive is the cost of nursing home care. We hope we can avoid it, live out our lives with a degree of independence and dignity.

But we've seen others lose that independence and dignity.

We live with a cloud hanging over us. What if catastrophic illness befalls us? Some of our group sadly put off enjoying the good things of life, the trips, the little luxuries, because of a fear of the future. Even if they have a lot, they fear it may not be enough.

Twice a year I take my little black book and make a list titled "What I'm Worth," with the help of the stock market pages and some of those little pieces of paper I save for income tax. I usually emerge from these sessions feeling pretty good. Thinking back to those days of no food on the table and cardboard over the holes in the soles of my shoes, I say to myself, "Not bad. You've come a long way, baby."

But I follow this up with a quick reminder, "Of course the dollar's not worth what it used to be. And who knows what I'm likely to need in the future."

While we're all worrying justifiably over those facts of life, it might be a good idea to make up another list and ask ourselves, "What Am I Worth?"

What am I worth as a person to my family?

What am I worth as a wife to my husband. Or vice versa?

Am I someone to turn to in any situation, sorrow or gladness, pain or pleasure? Am I a comfortable companion, fun to be with, a source of strength when the going gets rough? Do I pull my own half of the load in the daily chores of life? Do I try to give more than I take?

What am I worth to my children and grandchildren?

Am I a port in the storm, an ace in the hole, someone they can count on if their whole world falls apart? A confidante, an adviser. Am I an example to them— on how to live and even how to die? Do I furnish them with a sense of family continuity and family pride and standards?

Am I fun to be around, someone whose visits are a joy to anticipate or a bore to dread? Am I open to new ideas, enthusiastic about their enthusiasms, or a wet blanket who sees no good in anything that's unfamiliar and new?

What am I worth to my neighbors, my friends, my community, my church? Do I do something for others? Do I try to reach out beyond my own limitations and now and then go beyond the call of duty?

What am I worth to my God? Do I try to share with others the joy I experience in His love? Do I, at least, remember to thank Him when I tally up all those tangibles and intangibles that go toward making up the sum total of what my life is worth?

If I'm worth more on the dollar ledger than I was at age twenty-one, how about the human side of the ledger?

Has all that experience, wisdom and maturity made me a worthier human being?

Just what am I worth anyway?

## 32
### *Summing It Up*

WHEN YOU THINK of the changes our generation has seen it really boggles the mind. One of those anonymous papers that makes the rounds addresses itself to "all those born before 1945," reminding us that, "We are survivors."

"We were before television, before penicillin, before polio shots, frozen foods, Xerox, plastic, contact lenses, frisbees and the pill," it reads. "We were before radar, credit cards, split atoms, laser beams and ballpoint pens, before pantyhose, dishwashers, garbage disposals, electric blankets, air conditioners, drip-dry clothes and before men walked on the moon. . . We even got married first and then lived together."

It lists other changes, technological and social. Some

have made life simpler. Others have made it much more complicated.

I try not to be like the old Maine farmer who, when asked, "I suppose you've seen a lot of changes?" replied, "Yep, and I've been agin' every one of them." Change is fine. All change isn't an improvement.

One change I've welcomed with enthusiasm. I shop almost entirely from my home. The combination of the many catalogs, the credit card and the 800 telephone numbers enables a woman to part with money it used to take hours of trudging through stores to spend. Women dedicated to "shop till you drop" might disagree. But the chance to order a dress from New York, pecans from Georgia, and Waterford crystal from Shannon, Ireland, has enlarged my horizons, not to mention my Visa bill.

I also appreciate the change to more casual dress. Where once we agonized over the right thing for an occasion, now you can get by with anything. It's even better when you're old. People think your kooky attire is a sign of the rich eccentric.

Some changes in lifestyle I appreciate. Being able to pump your own gasoline at a filling station is one. Not only does it save time and money, but it's great practice if ever you have to force feed a boa constrictor.

I haven't embraced all new things. Computers, for instance.

*The manuscript for this book was prepared on an ancient device called a "typewriter." In 1984 Scott Davidson failed in an attempt to talk his grandmother into using a computer.*

"I see you're still using a typewriter," my publisher said. I felt a little like an eighteenth-century poet with a quill pen.

I acknowledge the power of computers and the way they've reorganized our lives. They're like the radio of our generation, a toy for the technically oriented and a useful tool of everyday life for the rest of us. It does seem to me it takes longer to make a bank deposit or complete a store transaction than it used to.

Young family members tell me I should have a computer for my business. I could press a button and see my inventory at a glance. But I can open my record book or walk down to the basement storeroom and see my inventory at a glance. It's easier then peering up at a screen through my bifocals.

Friends who write with word processors tell me I don't know what I'm missing. You can remove one paragraph and redo it without rewriting a page. If I wanted to be mean I could say a lot of today's writing reads like a patch job. I have used a word processor at my son's house and even went so far as to FAX a column from Williamsburg when time was short. I still called up the editor when I got home to be sure it had arrived.

All this doesn't mean I'm an old fogey who wants to give up microwave, microfilm, and what sounds like microfish. The microwave oven is great for heating lunch. I have had restaurant food that was still icy in the middle.

I'm impressed that my entire output of published material is now compressed into thirty-four drawers of microfilm. Sure beats those crumbling yellowing pages.

Telephone answering machines serve a purpose, too, more so when their owners remember to listen to them. Some of the cutesy messages on them are pretty bad.

I am enthusiastic about VCRs. You can record a program you want to see on a night you're not going to be home, or preserve an event for posterity like President and Mrs. Bush dancing at their inaugural or the slalom at the Olympics.

They're great for grandmas, too. Instead of bringing out your brag book to bore your friends with snapshots, you sit them down in the living room, announce, "I have a fascinating new video," and before they know it, they're watching Brian, Scott, and Kimberly at Disney World.

Yes, I've become an avid user of the VCR, now that I've mastered the time setter and partly understand the instruction book, which must have been translated from the Japanese.

*A special joy to me are members of my extended family. In front, Ray's niece Babs Ferrenbach and her husband Lee, Jr. Their son, Lee III, is flanked by his daughters Suzy, left, and Judy. In the right photo are Lee III and his wife, Denny; Ted Lippert's stepdaughter, Jennifer; and Jess and Owen Lippert.*

I'm glad I don't have to be conversant with all the buzz words and phrases of our times. "Bonding" is one of the current expressions. To me, it sounds like facing the lapel of a suit or waterproofing the basement, but I believe it means getting close to someone. Parents are supposed to "bond" with their children, and our school librarian daughter speaks of students "bonding" with one another. I believe this means they're becoming friends, or, in some cases, fellow gang members.

"Networking" is another bit of educationese. I think this means talking or pulling strings to get something done. I could be wrong. "Cocooning," I understand. When daughter Harriet says she's "cocooning tonight," it means she's curled up, watching TV.

Everyone strives to have a "meaningful relationship" with someone of the opposite sex. I believe this means that after sleeping together you enjoy talking together, always a desirable state of affairs.

Sex is something that hasn't changed basically and it's something we oldsters know more about than we're given credit for. Like teenagers, more old folks are "sexually active" than is generally assumed.

"It's marvelous," an eighty-year-old man told me. "You can take a trip with a woman and no one raises an eyebrow because they're sure it's platonic. Ha, little do they know."

"When are you too old for sex?" I asked my mother once. She said, "I don't know, I'll let you know." She died when she was eighty-two and never did tell me, so I still don't know.

Some years ago I traveled round Missouri with Sally Danforth who was campaigning for her husband, Senator Jack Danforth. She was giving away copies of a book she'd written, at meetings and institutions along the way. We went through a nursing home in mid-Missouri and as she was handing out the books, our guide stopped her from giving one to a ninety-five year old man.

"He can't see to read," she explained.

"How sad. I guess he can't watch television either," said a member of our party. "No, and he's deaf so he can't even listen to radio."

We cluck-clucked our pity and someone wondered what one could do for amusement under such sad circumstances.

We rounded a corner, and a shapely, well endowed

attendant came out of a room. The elderly gent crept up in back of her, put his arms around her waist, cupped his hands under her breasts and squeezed.

"Now, John, you know I've told you not to do that," she scolded.

We exchanged glances. "Who needs radio or television?" one man said.

I would hate to be a young single woman or even a middle-aged widow or divorcee in today's singles scene. I just don't believe casual sex is in a woman's best interests. But if you are to take movies and television dramas as examples, and most people always have, it is quite acceptable to smile tentatively at an interesting stranger across a crowded room and end the evening heaving and thrashing about in his bed or yours. Seems to me a lot of romantic fun and suspense is lost along the way.

I'd find it difficult to feel romantic in a disco with lights flashing and electronic noises booming. Of all the things that were better in our youth, music and entertainment lead the list. Recently a columnist wrote she saw no reason for a divided television screen enabling you to watch two programs. It's hard enough, she observed, to find one program worth watching.

As for popular music, they just don't write them like Hoagy Carmichael's "Stardust." I have my car radio set permanently to a station (WEW) which plays the golden oldies, and on Saturday night radio, old friend Charlie Menees brings back the big bands.

"When I Grow Too Old To Dream" came up on a recent program, and I remembered Gary's little sister, Betty, and her partner, Lou, singing it and looking at us and giggling at big brother and his girlfriend holding hands.

When are you too old to dream? Never, really.

Some of your dreams you relinquish. I may never have my Cape Cod house, but Harriet bought one on her last move so I can enjoy it. And as I park my car in front of our square, solid brick two-family flat, I feel a familiar happiness at "being home."

Life does not center around a fireplace, a swimming pool or a faraway vista of woodland and meadow, but around the coziness of a back porch bathed in sunshine even in winter months. Here we eat our meals, tend the house plants and I do my typing and play my Dixieland records and look down at the pretty pocket-handkerchief size garden below.

No one can control the calamities and catastrophes that can come but we can control much of our happiness. I often reflect on Abraham Lincoln's statement that, "When I wake up each morning, I have two choices, to be happy or to be unhappy. I choose to be happy."

I also choose to remind myself of this as I take an afternoon nap in the second sunniest spot of our house, a sofa in what Aunt Olie called the sunroom, our TV room. Facing southwest as does our porch, it's another

*In ranking the joys of old age, grandchildren certainly come first. A close second is memories, such as the glorious night in 1951 when my mother came to the Gridiron Dinner as my guest.*

source of warmth and comfort on a winter day. At a craft fair at our church, I purchased a glass cross in blue and white and it hangs at that window. Like the mirrors at our big old house in Webster, the glass reflects and re-reflects, a shimmering sequence of crosses. I watch them and think how good God has been to me and how lucky I am, after a storm-tossed life to have found such a safe and comfortable haven.

My *Post-Dispatch* friend, Dorothy Brainerd, took advantage of one of those advertised suggestions to "plan your own funeral." She made it sound like a lark as she described picking out her coffin, lined in pink. The friend accompanying her said, "Oh, Dottie, that is absolutely *you*," and she said happily, "Yes, I can hardly wait to use it." The young salesman looked bewildered, but then he was young.

I haven't gone that far but I've left a few suggestions for my funeral, my favorite hymn, "How Great Thou Art," and my favorite Bible verses, Romans 8:38-39 and 28 which tell us so truly how things work together for good.

There's one message I'd like to leave for my family. It's a verse by Jan Struther, author of *Mrs. Miniver,* who wrote:

> Some day my life shall end and lest
> Some whim should prompt you to review it
> Let her who knows the subject best
> Tell you the quickest way to do it.
> Just say here lies one doubly blest.
> Say she was happy, say she knew it.

How lucky we are to have lived this long, in this wonderful country and in an era when there is literal

*My years at the* Post-Dispatch *provided some truly great memories, such as the time I interviewed "Mary," of the St. Louis Zoo, for a feature.*

*Brian, Scott, and Kimberly Davidson sent this ''Colossal Gram'' to their grandmother on the occasion of her seventieth birthday, in 1988.*

social security financially and a growing amount of consideration for oldsters.

''Growing old is not a penalty but a privilege,'' I read in a Portals of Prayer meditation booklet. The author pointed out the dividends of old age, the freedom from responsibility, the time to cultivate friendships and to witness to our Lord.

My friend Julie once speculated on what life would be like if we could play it like duplicate bridge, one hand two ways. After much discussion we agreed we'd have played our hands pretty much as we had. With maturity comes a realistic summing up.

''I've decided I'm as rich as I want to be and as famous as I want to be,'' I announced a few years ago. This wasn't a boastful statement since I'm not a lot of either. But I am satisfied with the status quo.

"I'm also as old as I want to be," I added, "but I'm afraid I can't do anything about that."

This was just before my seventieth birthday. Joan gave a party for me and some seventy-plus relatives and friends.

I had stipulated no presents, but friends came up with funny gifts like Marian and George Neumayer's "Seventy Super Saleswoman" T-shirt. And Pat Whealen found the perfect book. It is titled *At Seventy* and is a year's journal by May Sarton whom I interviewed when she was poet-in-residence at Lindenwood College in St. Charles, Missouri.

"What is it like to be seventy?" she was asked on her birthday, and answered, "I do not feel old at all, not as much a survivor as a person still on her way. I suppose real old age begins when one looks backward rather than forward."

Wise words. Encouraging, too, for we're still looking forward. So we're over the hill. True. But who knows what happy happenings may be over the next hill. . . or just around that bend in the road. . . .